The Context
of Youth Violence

Resilience, Risk, and Protection

Edited by
Jack M. Richman
Mark W. Fraser

Westport, Connecticut
London

Library of Congress Cataloging-in-Publication Data

The context of youth violence : resilience, risk, and protection / edited by Jack M. Richman and Mark W. Fraser.

    p. cm.

  Includes bibliographical references and index.

  ISBN 0–275–96724–7 (alk. paper)

    1. Youth and violence. 2. Resilience (Personality trait) in adolescence. 3. Children and violence. 4. Resilience (Personality trait) in children. I. Richman, Jack M. II. Fraser, Mark W.

  HQ799.2.V56C66   2001

  303.6'0835—dc21   00–032385

British Library Cataloguing in Publication Data is available.

Library of Congress Catalog Card Number: 00–032385
ISBN: 0–275–96724–7

First published in 2001

Praeger Publishers, 88 Post Road West, Westport, CT 06881
An imprint of Greenwood Publishing Group, Inc.
www.praeger.com

Printed in the United States of America

The paper used in this book complies with the
Permanent Paper Standard issued by the National
Information Standards Organization (Z39.48–1984).

10 9 8 7 6 5 4 3 2 1

Contents

Acknowledgments

The chapters in this volume are the result of a series of international conferences on Violence and Trauma in Childhood held in Chapel Hill, North Carolina, and Jerusalem, Israel. The planning of the conferences and the writing and re-writing of the chapters as they transformed from presented oral papers to written chapters was a challenging and time-consuming process. We thank the authors who contributed to this book. We thank also our friends and colleagues who generously shared with us their knowledge, experience, and expertise.

We are indebted to many people who helped to develop and support the conferences and, subsequently, this book. These people include Richard Edwards, dean of the School of Social Work at the University of North Carolina at Chapel Hill, and colleagues Gary Bowen, Joanne Caye, and Maeda Galinsky, also at the School of Social Work, whose interest and expertise in risk and resilience continually stimulated our thinking.

We give special thanks to Lenore Behar, chief of the Child & Family Service Section in the North Carolina Division of Mental Health, Developmental Disabilities, and Substance Abuse Services, and from the same office, Adele Spitz-Roth for their vision regarding mental health practice in the state. Their commitment to children and to improving mental health services for children has had a significant impact on the quality of life for many families.

We gratefully acknowledge Audrey Burkes, Elizabeth Benefield, Audrey Chase, Cindy Justice, Daniel Lebold, Alan Reep, and Kim Sprunk for their efforts to make the international conferences a success. In this same vein, we wish to thank Merritt Mulman and Hamutal Meiri of the North Carolina–Israel Partnership and Jack Habib of the J.D.C. Brookdale Institute in Jerusalem, Israel.

We are indebted to Shelly Wunder-Smith for her skill, energy, and patience in editing this manuscript.

We want to particularly express our appreciation to Lawrence Rosenfeld for his inspiration, creativity, editing expertise, and friendship as this process unfolded.

And, a special thanks to our families Mary, Alex, and Katy Fraser and Carol, Alice, and Erica Richman for the unending support and appreciation they provide and for their appearance of being interested in our work as we read sections of this book to them for comments and feedback.

Chapter 1

Resilience in Childhood: The Role of Risk and Protection

Jack M. Richman
Mark W. Fraser

In both the scientific and popular literatures, the related concepts of risk, protection, and resilience have emerged as useful constructs for conceptualizing the development of social and health problems, particularly the problems confronting children and their families (see, e.g., Fraser, 1997). When researchers and practitioners use these terms, they invoke a promising, new way to understand mental health disorders and social problems ranging from poor school achievement to youth violence. A "risk and resilience" orientation—as it is sometimes called—is based on the idea that adaptational behavior emerges from the interplay of (a) combinations of factors predictive of negative developmental outcomes (risk factors) and (b) combinations of counteracting factors that reduce or ameliorate risk. Usually referred to as protective factors (and sometimes referred to as assets or strengths), these counterbalancing factors provide a degree of protection in the presence of risk. Moreover, they lead—in some children—to successful coping and adaptation despite exposure to high levels of adversity. Successfully prevailing over adversity is called *resilience* (Masten, Best, & Garmezy, 1990; Rutter, 1987).

History is replete with stories of heroes and heroines who "beat the odds" and make extraordinary contributions to society. The theme of outwitting an apparently invincible foe or prevailing over utterly dire situations is often used to describe children—for example, Cinderella and the *Wizard of Oz*'s Dorothy—who, with exceptional skill, humor, and perseverance, overcome hostile families, living arrangements, or other dastardly circumstances. The theme is the lodestone of prime-time television, of movies, and even of video games. Inherently understandable, the concept of resilience has been extended and applied recently to family, group, school, neighborhood, and organizational contexts. For example, the term *educational resilience* is used to describe students who possess risk factors that are predictive of school failure, yet who perform successfully in school (Richman & Bowen, 1997; Wang, Haertel, & Walberg, 1994). Similarly, concepts of "family resilience" (McCubbin, Thompson, Thompson, & Futrell, 1998; Walsh, 1998), "couples resilience" (Conger, Rueter, & Elder, 1999), and "community resilience" (Sonn & Fisher, 1998) describe higher order systems that prevail through or over periods of travail.

Investigations into the mechanisms by which individuals and systems respond adaptively to stress, adversity, or trauma provide important new information for assessment and for the conceptualization of both individual service plans and the design of interventions, whether focused on remediation or prevention (Masten et al., 1999). In this book, we have invited leading scholars who have conducted much of this work to discuss their views of youth violence from the perspective of resilience, risk, and protection. Attending to the context in which youth violence arises, we have asked them to summarize their research and distill from it implications for practice with children and families. In this introductory chapter, we briefly describe the risk, protection, and resilience framework. Then we review the chapters in this volume, highlighting their contributions to the field.

RISK, PROTECTION, AND RESILIENCE

Definition of Risk

Risk is defined by the *presence of one or more factors or influences that increase the probability of a negative outcome for a child or youth*. Risk factors can have a genetic or biological etiology, an ecological basis, or a combined biosocial origin. In the field of substance abuse, Benard (1991) observed that one in four children of alcoholic parents would exhibit problem drinking. By virtue of "having an alcoholic parent," some children are thought to be at greater risk of alcohol and drug abuse (Anderson, 1995; Brook, Whiteman, Gordon, & Brook, 1990). This risk factor could have a biological and/or ecological foundation. We do not yet know why having an alcoholic parent elevates the odds of problem drinking, although one could speculate on the causal mechanism from a variety of theoretical perspectives. In this case, the risk factor of parental alcoholism is a marker for a negative outcome. Risks may be markers, correlates, predictors, and causes. While children with an alcoholic parent may be considered at higher risk than the population of children without an alcoholic parent, Benard notes that three out of four such youths "beat the odds" and do not exhibit problems with alcohol. In this sense, a risk is a probability associated with a negative influence. Risk factors vary in the degree to which they are correlated to poor developmental outcomes.

Risk factors may be individual traits and attributes or conditions in the environment. At the individual level, they include genetic or biological factors (such as attention deficit and hyperactivity disorder, or low birth weight) and social characteristics (such as having a risk-taking temperament). Ecological or contextual factors may be conceptualized also as risk factors. These include, for example, parental loss due to divorce, separation or death; or living in a neighborhood with high crime, social disorganization, and poverty. By definition, risk factors are thought to be predictive of negative outcomes, but they can also be conceptualized as maintaining or exacerbating a negative outcome. Understanding which risk factors or cumulation of factors predict negative outcomes is the focus of a new era of social science research on social and health problems.

Specific versus nonspecific risk factors. Risk factors have been conceptualized as *nonspecific* or *specific* (Fraser, Richman, & Galinsky, 1999). Nonspecific risk factors are not directly related to an increase in a particular outcome; rather they are linked to a variety of negative outcomes and conditions. For example, nonspecific risk factors—such as unskilled parenting, school failure, discrimination, and poverty—are known to be predictive of a variety of poor developmental outcomes for children (for reviews, see Coie et al., 1993; Kirby & Fraser, 1997). In contrast, specific risk factors are thought to be linked to specific negative outcomes. Benard (1991) argues that parental alcoholism is a specific risk factor for the alcohol involvement of children. Notwithstanding, parental alcoholism might be found to be a nonspecific risk if it were measured against a variety of other problems in childhood.

Cumulative risk. The research examining specific risk factors provides "insights into the sequelae of specific experiences, but their interpretation can be problematic because many adversities are interrelated and may have cumulative nonspecific effects" (Gest, Reed & Masten, 1999, p. 171). The fact that many risk factors have this nonspecific and cumulative property—that is, they affect many different social and health problems—has led some scholars to conclude that the number of risk factors may be more important than the specific nature of risk structures. This derives from research suggesting that social problems are multiply determined, that, for example, there may be many different ways that a child becomes violent. From this perspective, specific causal models will always fail to fit well because no single model captures the many different pathways that culminate in violence. This led Garmezy, Sameroff, and others in the field of resilience to argue that the specific nature of risk structures is outweighed in importance by the cumulative impact of the number of risks (see, e.g., Garmezy, 1994; Sameroff, Bartko, Baldwin, Baldwin, & Seifer, 1999; Sameroff, Seifer, Barocas, Zax, & Greenspan, 1987; Sameroff, Seifer, Zax, & Barocas, 1987).

Definition of Protection

Protective factors are those individual characteristics or environmental conditions that help children and youth resist or otherwise counteract the risks to which they are exposed. They delay, suppress, or neutralize negative outcomes (Benard, 1991; Kirby & Fraser, 1997; Rutter, 1987; Segal, 1986; Wang, Haertel, & Walberg, 1994). Discussed throughout this book, protective factors fall into three categories: individual factors, familial factors, and extra-familial factors. Individual factors include intelligence, coping capacities, and humor; protective factors in the family include high levels of family cohesion, family support, and the presence of family rituals or patterns. Extra-familial environmental protective factors include the availability of social support, community-level social cohesion, and neighborhood safety.

Compensatory and buffering effects. Regardless of whether they are individual, familial, or extra-familial, protective factors exert compensatory and/or buffering effects (Fraser, Richman, & Galinsky, 1999). A compensatory protective effect directly ameliorates a problem condition. That is, the protective factor proportionately lowers the odds of a negative outcome for each level of a risk condition. For example, intelligence is modestly and negatively correlated with delinquency (Farrington, 1996). It appears to exert a small "direct" or "main" effect on delinquency. In the emerging field of resilience, this would be called a compensatory effect.

In contrast to compensatory effects, a buffering effect is found when a protective factor interacts with risk. High intelligence, for example, may disproportionately protect children exposed to poverty. Suppose a researcher found, for example, that the effect of high intelligence is greater in the context of poverty. Intelligence then could be said to exert a buffering effect on poverty. Over and above its effect on children at all income levels, it reduces the likelihood of delinquency for low-income children who are fortunate enough to be gifted with greater intellectual capacity. In short, buffering effects are measured and tested by estimating interaction effects.

Protective factors provide important clues for designing more effective prevention programs. To realize the full potential of preventive practice, researchers and practitioners must increase their knowledge and understanding of the reasons why some children are not damaged by risks, hardships, and loss (Garmezy & Rutter, 1983). By understanding what protective factors, either personal or environmental resources, assist children in beating the odds, practitioners can design strategies that promote, develop, and enhance protection, while seeking at the same time to remediate risk.

Clearly, risk and protection are best considered in concert. However, some scholars and practitioners have advocated placing greater effort on protection. It is sometimes argued, for example, that services should focus on strengths or should fortify assets. The degree to which one must address risk and protection in the design of services or in the delivery of an individual plan of services for, say, a family with a juvenile offender is not clear (see Fraser, Richman, & Galinsky, 1999, for a discussion). One must ask these questions: Are the existing risk factors targetable and subject to manipulation in treatment? Are the apparent protective factors targetable and subject to manipulation in treatment? Do the risks endanger the child or the public? Would failing to remediate the risks raise an ethical issue? For clients who are already exhibiting some pathology or disorder, is it best to target intervention strategies that seek to reduce risk, or build protection, or some combination? As you will see, authors throughout the volume answer these questions differently.

Definition of Resilience

Resilience is at once the most enticing and most elusive concept discussed in this book. Most scholars agree that resilience is characterized by a successful response to adversity. However, while it is viewed as an individual's response, it is generally not considered to be a function solely of a trait possessed by the individual. Rather, resilience is thought to emerge in the dynamic interaction between individual characteristics and environmental resources. A child who maximally exploits resources—or simply benefits from them without considered strategy—and in so doing produces a successful outcome in the face of significant threat can be called *resilient* (Fraser, Richman, & Galinsky, 1999). Throughout the book, you will find this important theme: *Resilience is not necessarily based on individual characteristics; it occurs at the nexus of high risk and exceptional resources, whether these resources are personal or environmental in nature.*

Despite this general agreement, you will find throughout this volume competing views on the prevalence of resilience and the degree to which success must be observed before the label of resilient can be conferred. Rutter (2001, p. 13), for example, argues that

> the term *resilience* refers to the phenomenon of overcoming stress or adversity. Put in more operational terms, it [resilience] means that someone's life outcome has been relatively good, despite his or her experience with situations shown to carry a major risk for developing psychopathology. The focus is strictly on relative resistance to psychosocial risk experiences.

Rosenfeld, Lahad, and Cohen (2001, p. 142) use Apfel and Simon's (1996, p. 1) definition of resilience: "Resiliency is the child's capacity to bounce back from [or not succumb to] traumatic childhood events and develop into a sane, integrated, and socially responsible adult." And, according to Vance (2001, pp. 43–44): "Resiliency is defined by the ability of a person to rise above significant adversity and have a reasonably successful life course, avoiding serious psychiatric disorder, substance abuse, criminality, or social-relational problems."

In all three definitions, resilience requires exposure to significant risk, overcoming risk or adversity, and success that is beyond predicted expectations. Of course, problems arise when researchers and practitioners attempt to agree on what constitutes *significant* risk and *successful* outcomes that are *beyond predicted* expectations. For adaptations to be classified as resilient, should the outcomes be *highly* successful adaptations or can they be adaptations and outcomes that are at the level of social *competence* and *functionality*? For example, does a high school student who is identified as "at-risk" of school failure have to graduate at the top of his/her class to be considered "resilient"? Or is graduation from high school significant?

If we seek, as both a research and practice goal, to learn to design interventions that promote resilience in children and youth, it is crucial to know what resilience is and how to identify it with consistency. Masten et al. (1999) recently outlined three criteria for the study of resilience. Researchers and practitioners must indicate the

- developmental threat
- measures that will be used to determine successful adaptation
- protective factors hypothesized to modify or buffer risks.

If researchers and practitioners follow these guidelines, the result will be greater clarity in the ways risks are identified, successful adaptations measured, and protective mechanisms elucidated.

From a practice perspective, focusing on resilience begins with carefully identifying risk and protective factors because these can be the building blocks of intervention. Still more important may be developing a better understanding of the mechanisms that affect risk. Describing these processes will involve illuminating risk sequences that elevate dysfunction and the protective processes that disrupt risk sequences. In the way that social information processing (Crick & Dodge, 1994) and coercive parenting sequences (Dishion, Patterson, Stoolmiller, & Skinner, 1991) postulate risk mechanisms for the development of antisocial aggressive behavior in childhood, understanding the intersection of risk and protective processes is essential if programs to promote successful adaptation are to be designed. This constitutes a major challenge for research scholars interested in resilience in childhood.

STRUCTURE

This book was born out of a quest to understand the impact of violence and trauma on children, their families, and their communities. The perspective of risk, protection, and resilience provides a unifying structure from which to conceptualize the problem of youth violence and the design of practice with children. Each of the chapters in this volume examines the ways that an understanding of risk, protection, and resilience can inform practice. Each chapter also considers how practice is implemented within a risk and resilience conceptual framework.

From communications, education, human development, psychiatry, psychology, public health, and social work, experts from a variety of backgrounds contributed the chapters in this book. Within the resilience perspective, each author focuses on a somewhat different area of interest. In a major review of the status of research on risk, protection, and resilience, Michael Rutter focuses principally on psycho-social variables. In a comparably exhaustive review, J. Eric Vance focuses principally on biological risk and protective factors. Lawrence Rosenfeld, Mooli Lahad, and Alan Cohen and Deborah Prothrow-Stith apply the framework on the community level. Based on in-depth interviews with violent youthful offenders, James Garbarino examines the effect of toxic environments on individual factors. Drawing on their rich clinical research experiences, Scott Henggeler and Stephanie Hoyt take a multisystems, family-centered perspective. Across each perspective, chapter authors use a risk, protective, and resilience orientation to discuss the etiology and treatment of conduct problems in childhood. Several contributors—chapters written by Garbarino, Henggeler and Hoyt, and Prothrow-Stith—focus mainly on violent youth. Others, however, explore youth violence from a developmental perspective. From disparate backgrounds, the authors share common ground in their concern for social environments that produce violent behavior and their curiosity regarding children who appear to overcome toxic environments and succeed in life.

This book is divided into two sections: theory and practice. The first section consists of two chapters that present the model and discuss risk, protection, and resilience from a bio-psycho-social perspective. Rutter examines research on factors that produce or inhibit resilience. For example, he discusses the differences between "risk indicators" and "risk processes"—a useful clarification when attempting to describe the specific risk and protective factors that may affect child development. Further, his chapter considers eight characteristics of the resilience process, providing research evidence for each and distilling from each implications for prevention and practice. In the context of psychosocial research, Vance boldly extends the concepts of risk, protection, and resilience into biological research. He focuses on neurobiological and bio-psycho-social mechanisms related to conduct problems in children. From the work of Rutter and others, Vance outlines major social risk and protective factors and then delves into neurobiological research, identifying linkages between neurochemical and other biological research findings and psychosocial findings. For social scientists and practitioners, it is a provocative chapter.

With these two chapters serving as a theoretical base, the second section focuses on practice. Four chapters apply the framework of risk, protection, and resilience to different aspects of violence. Garbarino, for example, describes five "dark secrets" known by violent youths. In a compelling use of qualitative research, he describes the way socially toxic environments produce logical but deadly rules for social interaction among high-risk children. In as many words, he asks the question: How can a brutalized child unlearn brutality? Raising serious questions about the prevalence of resilience, he describes the dearth of resilience in children who grow up in environments exhibiting "community violence, family disruption, and personal experience of trauma." Are some environments so appallingly bereft of resources, of humanity, and of caring discourse that the concept of resilience is irrelevant? Through Garbarino, five children tell their stories.

Prothrow-Stith takes a public health perspective as she examines the issues of youth and community violence. She focuses on school violence; the interaction of race, poverty, and violence; and the impact of exposure to media violence, witnessing violence, and the availability of firearms on youth violence in America. Arguing for primary, secondary, and tertiary prevention, Prothrow-Stith outlines a broad spectrum of approaches that address youth violence. She concludes her chapter with a review of three promising violence prevention strategies.

Using the risk, protection, and resilience perspective, Rosenfeld, Lahad, and Cohen examine the impact of disasters on children and families. Often disasters, broadly defined, involve children and families responding and reacting to high degrees of violence and trauma in their lives. The violence perpetrated greatly alters their social context and physical environment. The authors discuss natural, technological and, complex (i.e., of human design) disasters and describe the consequences of trauma for children, including the responses children may exhibit following disasters. Their chapter traces child reactions to trauma invoked by hurricanes and earthquakes, airplane accidents, and war or terrorism. They specifically explore the Oklahoma City bombing, the Chernobyl nuclear accident, and political terrorism. The authors provide an extensive review of the research and intervention literature. Then they outline guidelines for practice dealing with violence and trauma. Finally, they present a community response prevention model—the BASIC Ph—that has been developed and piloted in Israel.

In the last chapter on practice applications, Henggeler and Hoyt review their pathfinding work on family interventions. They present Multisystemic Therapy (MST) as a family- and community-based model of intervention, and they summarize research showing it to be effective treatment for both violent and chronic juvenile offenders. MST focuses on the reduction of risk factors associated with problem behavior. In addition, it targets the enhancement of protective factors that have been predictive of violence reduction and resilience development. The chapter explains the family-based context in which MST services are delivered and outlines MST clinical treatment principles. Henggeler and Hoyt then provide a case study to illustrate the use of MST.

In their concluding chapter, Fraser and Richman (2001) discuss risk, protection, and resilience within the context of evidence-based practice (Gambrill, 1999). They summarize the literature regarding resilience and its prevalence, weaving in recent literature (including the chapters presented in this book). They synthesize promising findings emerging from research that uses the risk, protection, and resilience perspective.

Finally, they distill from the chapters promising principles for resilience-based practice.

Together, these chapters offer a framework for practice—including individual-, family-, and community-level interventions—that provides practitioners and researchers with a new way to conceptualize youth violence and other social problems. But perhaps as important, they outline a promising way to develop more focused practice strategies. Contributing to evidence-based practice and based on recent research, these strategies seek to concomitantly reduce risk and promote protection. They are the basis for growing optimism about the effectiveness of prevention and intervention programs for children.

REFERENCES

Anderson, S. C. (1995). Alcohol abuse. In R. L. Edwards (Ed.), *Encyclopedia of social work* (19th ed.) (pp. 203–215). Washington, D.C.: NASW Press.

Apfel, R. J., & Simon, B. (Eds.). (1996). *Minefields in their hearts: The mental health of children in war and communal violence.* New Haven, CT: Yale University Press.

Benard, B. (1991). *Fostering resiliency in kids: Protective factors in the family, school, and community.* Portland, OR: Western Center for Drug-Free Schools and Communities.

Brook, J. S., Whiteman, M., Gordon, A. S., & Brook, D. W. (1990). The role of older brothers in younger brothers' drug use viewed in the context of parent and peer influences. *Journal of Genetic Psychology, 151,* 59–75.

Coie, J. D., Watt, N. F., West, S. G., Hawkins, J. D., Asarnow, J. R., Markman, H. J., Ramey, S. L., Shure, M. B., & Long, B. (1993). The science of prevention: A conceptual framework and some directions for a National Research Program. *American Psychologist, 48*(10), 1013–1022.

Conger, R. D., Rueter, M. A., & Elder, G. H. (1999). Couple resilience to economic pressure. *Journal of Personality and Social Psychology, 76*(1), 54–71.

Crick, N. R., & Dodge, K. A. (1994). A review and reformulation of social information-processing mechanisms in children's social adjustment. *Psychological Bulletin, 115*(1), 74–101.

Dishion, T., Patterson, G., Stoolmiller, M., & Skinner, M. (1991). Family, school, and behavioral antecedents to early adolescent involvement with antisocial peers. *Developmental Psychology, 27,* 172–180.

Farrington, D. P. (1996). The explanation and prevention of youthful offending. In J. D. Hawkins (Ed.), *Delinquency and crime* (pp. 68–148), New York: Cambridge University Press.

Fraser, M. W. (Ed.). (1997). *Risk and resilience in childhood: An ecological perspective.* Washington, D.C.: NASW Press.

Fraser, M. W., & Richman, J. M. (2001). Resilience: Implications for evidence-based practice. In J. M. Richman & M. W. Fraser (Eds.), *The context of youth violence: Resilience, risk, and protection.* Westport, CT: Praeger.

Fraser, M. W., Richman, J. M., & Galinsky, M. J. (1999). Risk, protection, and resilience: Toward a conceptual framework for social work practice. *Social Work Research, 23*(3), 131–144.

Gambrill, E. (1999). Evidence-based clinical behavior analysis, evidence-based medicine and the Cochrane collaboration. *Journal of Behavior Therapy and Experimental Psychiatry, 30,* 1–14.

Garbarino, J. (2001). Making sense of senseless youth violence. In J. M. Richman & M. W. Fraser (Eds.), *The context of youth violence: Resilience, risk, and protection.* Westport, CT: Praeger.

Garmezy, N. (1994). Reflections and commentary on risk, resilience, and development. In R. J. Haggerty, L. R. Sherrod, N. Garmezy, & M. Rutter (Eds.), *Stress, risk, and resilience in children and adolescents: Processes, mechanisms, and interventions* (pp. 1–18). Cambridge: Cambridge University Press.

Garmezy, N., & Rutter, M. (1983). *Stress coping and development in children.* New York: McGraw-Hill.

Gest, S. D., Reed, M. J., & Masten, A. S. (1999). Measuring developmental changes in exposure to adversity: A life chart and rating scale approach. *Development and Psychopathology, 11*(1), 171–192.

Gibbs, L., & Gambrill, E. (1999). *Critical thinking for social workers: Exercises for the helping professions* (2nd ed.). Thousand Oaks, CA: Pine Forge Press.

Henggeler, S. W., & Hoyt, S. W. (2001). Multisystemic therapy with serious juvenile offenders and their families. In J. M. Richman & M. W. Fraser (Eds.), *The context of youth violence: Resilience, risk, and protection.* Westport, CT: Praeger.

Kirby, L. D., & Fraser, M. W. (1997). Risk and resilience in childhood. In M. W. Fraser (Ed.), *Risk and resilience in childhood: An ecological perspective* (pp. 10–33). Washington, D.C.: NASW Press.

Masten, A. S., Best, K. M., & Garmezy, N. (1990). Resilience and development: Contributions from the study of children who overcome adversity. *Development and Psychopathology, 2,* 425–444.

Masten, A. S., Hubbard, J. J., Gest, S. D., Tellegen, A., Garmezy, N., & Ramirez, M. (1999). Competence in the context of adversity: Pathways to resilience and maladaptation from childhood to late adolescence. *Development and Psychopathology, 11,* 143–169.

McCubbin, H. I., Thompson, E. A., Thompson, A. I., & Futrell, J. A. (Eds.). (1998). *Resilience in families series.* Thousand Oaks, CA: Sage.

Prothrow-Stith, D. (2001). Youth risk and resilience: Community approaches to violence prevention. In J. M. Richman & M. W. Fraser (Eds.), *The context of youth violence: Resilience, risk, and protection.* Westport, CT: Praeger.

Richman, J. M., & Bowen, G. L. (1997). School failure: An ecological-interactional-developmental perspective. In M. W. Fraser (Ed.), *Risk and resilience in childhood: An ecological perspective* (pp. 95–116). Washington, D.C.: NASW Press.

Rosenfeld, L. B., Lahad, M., & Cohen, A. (2001). Disaster, trauma, and children's resilience: A community response perspective. In J. M. Richman & M. W.

Fraser (Eds.), *The context of youth violence: Resilience, risk, and protection*. Westport, CT: Praeger.

Rutter, M. (2001). Psychosocial adversity: Risk, resilience, and recovery. In J. M. Richman & M. W. Fraser (Eds.), *The context of youth violence: Resilience, risk, and protection*. Westport, CT: Praeger.

Rutter, M. (1987). Psychosocial resilience and protective mechanisms. *American Journal of Orthopsychiatry, 57*, 316–331.

Sackett, D. L., Rosenberg, W. M. C., Gray, J. A. M., Haynes, R. B., & Richardson, W. S. (1996). Evidence-based medicine: What it is and what it isn't. *British Medical Journal, 312*, 71–72.

Sameroff, A., Bartko, W. T., Baldwin, A., Baldwin, C., & Seifer, R. (1999). Family and social influences on the development of child competence. In M. Lewis & C. Feiring (Eds.), *Families, risk, and competence*. Mahwah, NJ: Lawrence Erlbaum Associates.

Sameroff, A., Seifer, R., Barocas, R., Zax, M., & Greenspan, S. (1987). Intelligence quotient scores of 4-year-old children: Social-environmental risk factors. *Pediatrics, 79*, 343–350.

Sameroff, A., Seifer, R., Zax, M., & Barocas, R. (1987). Early indicators of development risk: The Rochester Longitudinal Study. *Schizophrenia Bulletin, 13*, 383–393.

Segal, J. (1986). *Winning life's toughest battles: Roots of human resilience*. New York: McGraw-Hill.

Sonn, C. C., & Fisher, A. T. (1998). Sense of community: Community resilient responses to oppression and change. *Journal of Community Psychology, 26*(5), 457–472.

Vance, J. E. (2001). Neurobiological mechanisms of psychosocial resiliency. In J. M. Richman & M. W. Fraser (Eds.), *The context of youth violence: Resilience, risk, and protection*. Westport, CT: Praeger.

Walsh, F. (1998). *Strengthening family resilience*. New York: Guilford Press.

Wang, M. C., Haertel, G. D., & Walberg, H. J. (1994). Educational resilience in inner cities. In M. C. Wang & E. W. Gordon (Eds.), *Educational resilience in inner-city America: Challenges and prospects* (pp. 45–72). Hillsdale, NJ: Lawrence Erlbaum Associates.

Werner, E. E. (1990). Protective factors and individual resilience. In S. M. Meisels & J. P. Shonkoff (Eds.), *Handbook of early childhood intervention* (pp. 97–116). New York: Cambridge University Press.

Chapter 2

Psychosocial Adversity: Risk, Resilience and Recovery

Michael Rutter

During the past twenty or thirty years, interest has grown in the concept of resilience (Rutter, in press). The term *resilience* refers to the phenomenon of overcoming stress or adversity. Put in more operational terms, it means that someone's life outcome has been relatively good, despite his or her experience with situations shown to carry a major risk for developing psychopathology. The focus is strictly on relative resistance to psychosocial risk experiences. The definition of resilience is necessarily and appropriately broad, as shown by numerous reviews of the topic (c.f., Anthony & Cohler, 1987; Egeland, Carlson, & Sroufe, 1993; Fonagy, Steele, Steele, Higgitt, & Target, 1994; Haggerty, Sherrod, Garmezy, & Rutter, 1994; Luthar, 1993; Rolf, Masten, Cicchetti, Nuechterlein, & Weintraub, 1990; Rutter, in press; Siefer, 1995), but also viewed as different from the acquisition of social competence (e.g., Masten et al., 1995) or self-efficacy (Bandura, 1995, 1997) or of positive mental health (e.g., Ryff & Singer, 1998). The phenomenon of resilience requires attention to a range of possible psychological outcomes and not to an unusually positive outcome or to supernormal functioning. Similarly, there is no necessary expectation that protection from stress and adversity should lie in positive experiences, nor indeed is there any assumption that the answer will lie in how the individual copes with a negative experience at the time. The starting point, then, is simply that in all studies of risk experiences, children's responses vary enormously.

METHODOLOGICAL CONSIDERATIONS

Several methodological issues must be addressed in any study of resilience (see Rutter, in press). Thus, children's resistance to stress and adversity cannot be investigated without first verifying that they have suffered experiences that carry a markedly increased risk for developing psychopathology. Within the conceptualization of resilience, three matters require particular attention. First, distinguishing between risk indicators and risk mechanisms is necessary. Many variables show a statistically significant association with psychopathology, not because they represent a risk process as such, but because they predispose individuals to other experiences that actually mediate the risk. For example, this association seems to be present with most of the risk associated with parental loss (see, e.g., Fergusson, Horwood, & Lynskey, 1992; Harris, Brown, & Bifulco, 1986; Rutter, 1971). Although the loss of a parent through divorce, separation, or death may carry some risk in its own right, most of the risk clearly derives from the family discord and conflict that precedes and follows family break-up and from the associated difficulties in parenting, rather than the broken home as such. Much the same applies with respect to family poverty (Brody et al., 1994; Conger & Elder, 1994; Conger, Ge, Elder, Lorenz, & Simons, 1994; Conger et al., 1992). Because poverty makes parenting well a more difficult task, it is associated with a psychopathological risk, but the proximal risk processes mainly involve impaired family functioning and family relationships rather than economic privation.

The second consideration is that some of the risks thought to represent environmental hazards of one kind or another actually involve genetic mediation (Plomin, 1994; Plomin, De Fries, McClearn, & Rutter, 1997), particularly as they apply to family risk factors. Parents both pass on their genes and shape their children's upbringing. Not surprisingly, the two tend to be intercorrelated. Parents who pass on increased genetic risks for their children also tend to provide suboptimal environments and rearing conditions. The consequence is that to some extent, family psychosocial risk situations that "look" environmental may involve some genetically mediated risk.

The third area to consider is that in some circumstances, the association between psychosocial risk factors and psychopathology may represent the child's influences on his or her environment, rather than the effects of the environment on the child (see Rutter et al., 1997a). Of course, children's effects on their environments do not rule out the possibility of influences of the environment's effect on children. Indeed, two-way interplay is likely to be usual. Nevertheless, it is necessary in the research design to ensure that a substantial environmentally mediated risk operates on the child.

As already noted, equal attention must be paid to assessing the outcome after the risk experiences. Resilience may be artefactual if too narrow a range of outcomes is considered, if there is reliance on just one data source, or if measurement is taken at only one point in time (see Fergusson, Horwood, Caspi, Moffitt, & Silva, 1996).

HETEROGENEITY OF OUTCOME

Even when all sources of artefact have been considered as much as possible, research findings consistently show a very large range of outcomes after the most severe forms of psychosocial adversities. For example, Figure 2.1 shows the cognitive level of six-year-old children who were adopted into families in the United Kingdom after spending at least two

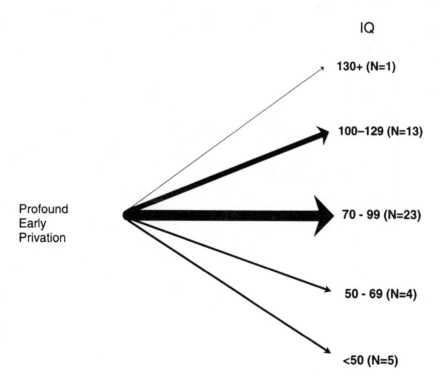

Figure 2.1   IQ Scores of Six-Year-Old Children Who Came from Romanian Orphanages to the United Kingdom.
Source: Data from O'Connor et al., 1998.

years in the appalling conditions of Romanian orphanages (see O'Connor et al., 1998; Rutter, Giller, & Hagell, in press). The largest proportion had a general cognitive index (on the McCarthy Scales) in the 70–99 range, but several children scored in the severely retarded range, and one child had a highly superior score (above 130). All the children suffered severe privation—both psychological and nutritional—with limited variation in the extent of their privation. Despite that, the range in the cognitive outcome at six years varied widely. Social, emotional, and behavioral measures had similar heterogeneous outcomes.

The other key feature of the findings in relation to this group of children who had suffered severe early privation concerned the extent of catch-up in cognitive development. Figure 2.2 shows the contrast between the developmental level at the time of arrival in the United Kingdom, at which time the mean was in the mildly retarded range, and the situation at four years, when the mean was in the middle of the normal range. After the radical change of environment from appallingly bad institutional conditions to above average rearing in their adoptive homes, the developmental quotient rose some forty points. For a variety of methodological reasons, this degree of catch-up should be seen only as an estimate, but without doubt, the cognitive gains after the change of environment were startling. Though not uniform throughout the group as a whole, the catch-up was very impressive. It would be difficult

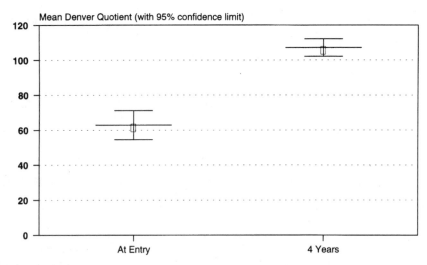

Figure 2.2   Denver Quotient of Romanian Adoptees at Entry to United Kingdom and at Four Years Later.
Source: Data from Rutter & E.R.A. Study Team, 1998.

to find a more striking example of what is meant by resilience. The findings from many other studies agree well with this general pattern (see Rutter, & the E.R.A. Study Team, in press).

MULTIPLE RISK AND PROTECTIVE FACTORS

The first clear, important result from research on the phenomenon of resilience is that multiple risk and protective factors are involved. Figure 2.3 presents the findings from the Christchurch longitudinal study (Fergusson & Lynskey, 1996). An adversity index based on thirty-nine measures of family life and composed of variables such as economic disadvantage, maladaptive parent–child interaction, marital conflict, and parental separation was devised. Outcome at fifteen to sixteen years was assessed on the basis of multiple measures of antisocial behavior and drug or alcohol misuse. Just over one-half of the sample had a family adversity score of 6 or less. In this very large subgroup, the rate of multiple problems was extremely low, just 0.2 percent. In sharp contrast, at the other end of the scale, more than one-fifth of those with scores of 19 or more showed multiple problems in the mid-teenage years—a 100-fold difference. In short, these family risk factors were associated with a greatly increased risk of multiple problems, but the risk was very small when any single risk factor was considered on its own. The findings are typical of the pattern found in numerous investigations.

This is a general pattern in the great majority of mental disorders and

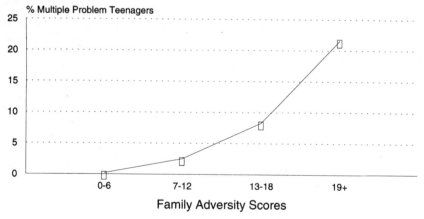

Figure 2.3   Number of Family Adversities and Rate of Multiple Problems at 15–16 years old.
Source: Data from Fergusson & Lynskey, 1996.

psychological traits. Exactly the same trend is found with genetic as well as environmental risk factors. That is to say, any single susceptibility gene has a very small effect, but the combination of multiple susceptibility genes may be quite powerful (Plomin, De Fries, McClearn, & Rutter, 1997; Rutter, Giller, & Hagell, in press). Often the cumulative effect of both environmental and risk factors involves synergistic interaction among risk factors. It is important to consider both risk and protective factors and the pattern of little effect from any one variable—but a much greater cumulative effect from the combination of variables—applies to protective factors just as it does to risk factors. This generalization also applies to genetics, as much as to psychosocial risks. Genetic influences may operate through either risk or protective mechanisms, and in practice, with most common disorders, it probably involves a complex mix of the two.

Sensitivity to Risk

Research results make clear that part of the variation in children's response to psychosocial stress and adversity is a function of their vulnerability to the risk factors. Figure 2.4 shows this function in relation to genetically influenced sensitivity to environmental risks. The data derived from Bohman's (1996) study of petty criminality in adult male adoptees in Sweden; biological risk was indexed by the occurrence of

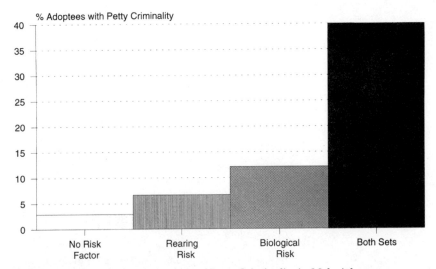

Figure 2.4   Cross-Fostering Analysis of Petty Criminality in Male Adoptees.
Source: Data from Bohman, 1996.

antisocial behavior or drug or alcohol problems in the biological parent. Rearing risk was determined on the basis of similar factors in the home of rearing by the adoptive parents, together with various associated family adversities. In the absence of either risk, the rate of the individuals showing petty criminality in adult life was extremely low—about 3 percent. The rate of petty criminality doubled (6 percent) in the presence of rearing risk, when it occurred in the absence of biological risk; it went up fourfold (12 percent) in the presence of biological risk but no rearing risk; and the rate of petty criminality was 40 percent when both rearing risk and biological risk co-occurred. The implication is that to a significant extent, the genetic factors were having their effect by influencing individual differences in susceptibility to environmental risk. Other studies have shown similar same results (see Rutter et al., in press).

Variations in sensitivity to environmental risks may also derive from children's prior experiences. Figure 2.5 presents data from Quinton & Rutter (1976) relating psychosocial disadvantage and multiple hospital admissions to the risk of emotional disturbance. Multiple hospital admissions were associated with a greatly increased risk of emotional disturbance in middle childhood, but the likelihood that such disturbance would develop was greater when the admissions took place in the context of marked longstanding psychosocial disadvantage. The experience of chronic psychosocial adversity may have sensitized children and made

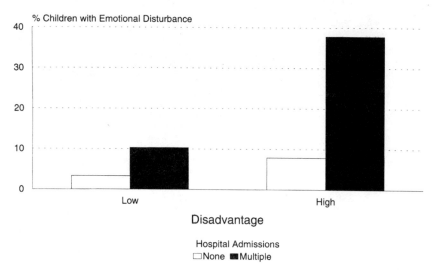

Figure 2.5   Psychosocial Disadvantage, Multiple Hospital Admissions and Emotional Disturbance.
Source: Data from Quinton & Rutter, 1976.

them more vulnerable to the risks associated with experience of acute stressors.

Individual differences in vulnerability to family adversity have also been investigated in relation to a range of characteristics in the child. The key question is whether the individual features that carry an increased risk for later psychopathology operate through a direct effect that is independent of life circumstances or experiences or whether the risk mediation is indirect, with the individual features serving to make children more susceptible to adverse experiences. The evidence from a wide range of studies (see Rutter, in press) indicates that there are *both* direct and indirect effects. Figure 2.6 provides some findings initiated by Boyce and his colleagues (Tschann, Kaiser, Chesney, Alkon, & Boyce, 1996) from the study of preschool children attending child care centers. Family conflict was assessed using the Moos & Moos Family Environment Scale; temperament was measured using Keogh's Teacher Temperament Questionnaire based on the Thomas and Chess approach; and externalizing behavior problems were measured using the Child Behavior Checklist. Regardless of the level of family conflict, children with a difficult temperament were much more likely to show disruptive behavior. In addition, there was an interaction by which a difficult temperament made children more likely to show disruptive behavior in the presence of family conflict, family conflict having no measurable effect in children

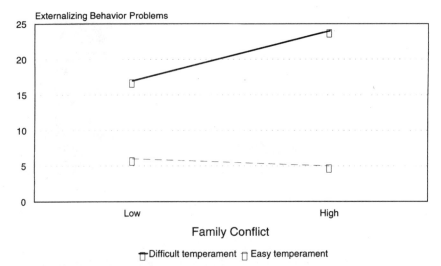

Figure 2.6 Temperament, Family Conflict, and Externalizing Behavior Problems. *Source:* Data from Tschann et al., 1996.

of easy temperament. The findings are limited because the temperamental measure and the measure of externalizing behavior both derive from the same informant (the teacher) and from the fact that the data were cross-sectional and applied to children in relatively advantaged circumstances. Nevertheless, the suggestion is that temperamental differences may play a role in variations in children's sensitivity to psychosocial risk.

Children's cognitive level has been studied in comparable fashion with similar results (Moffitt, 1990a, 1990b; Rutter et al., in press). In general, children with a lower intellectual level show an increased risk for antisocial behavior. This elevated risk is evident throughout the IQ range and not just at the lower extreme. In part, the effects appear to operate directly insofar as they apply across a wide range of environmental circumstances. However, the Dunedin longitudinal study data suggest that a lower IQ score serves as a risk factor partly because it makes children more vulnerable to family adversity (Moffitt, 1990a, 1990b). Children who had a combination of a lower IQ score and family adversity had a much higher aggression score than any other group of children.

For many years, there has been particular interest in the possibility of "steeling effects," by which the experience of overcoming adversity may serve to strengthen people's resistance to later environmental hazards (Rutter, 1981b, 1987). The notion has plausibility for several reasons. Animal studies have shown the experience of stressors in early life has effects on the neuroendocrine system that may be associated with a reduced vulnerability to later stresses (Hennessey & Levine, 1979; Hunt, 1979). In addition, both human (Rose, 1980; Ursin, Baade, & Levins, 1978) and animal studies (Levine, 1982) show that the experience of stress leads to physiological changes reflecting adaptation. It is also clear that people's attitudes about themselves and their confidence in their ability to deal effectively with life challenges is likely to be influenced by how they have coped with stress and challenge in the past. Rutter (1995) has drawn the parallel with resistance to infection. Immunity to infections does not result from unusually healthy living. To the contrary, it comes about through the experience of successfully overcoming mild infections—either through immunization or through infections that arise through the ordinary course of life. This perspective is likely to apply in the field of psychosocial experiences. Nevertheless, although certain pointers indicate that this is the case, there is a paucity of systematic evidence. The suggestion is implicit, for example, in Elder's findings (Elder, 1974; Elder, Liker, & Jaworski, 1984) that older children who took on increased family responsibilities during the Great Depres-

sion were able to cope with these increased demands and were strengthened by them. By contrast, younger children, given comparable responsibilities, were able to cope less well and were often damaged by the
experience. More recently Phelps, Belsky, and Crnic (1998) sought to
test the hypothesis by means of a study of parenting of preschoolers aged
eleven to twenty-seven months. The Adult Attachment Interview was
used to assess the security or insecurity of the mothers' current attachment relationships and also the extent to which they themselves suffered
from a difficult upbringing. The interview compared mothers with
"earned security" (meaning that they obtained adult security despite a
difficult childhood) with those showing "continuous security" (i.e., security in adult relationships preceded by positive experiences of childhood) and those with current "insecurity" in their relationships. Current
stress was measured on the basis of daily challenges. The findings are
summarized in Figure 2.7.

The level of positive parenting was similar under both low and high
stress conditions for those with "continuous security" and with "earned
security." In addition, the groups did not differ in their parenting when
current stress was low. However, although the level of positive parenting
for the "earned security" group was equally good under conditions of
low and high stress, this was not the case for the mothers showing insecurity in their current relationships. The level of positive parenting was

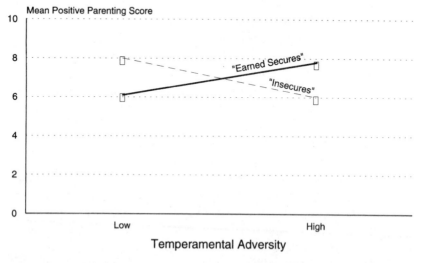

Figure 2.7   Effects of Earned Security on Positive Parenting Under Conditions of
Low and High Stress.
Source: Data from Phelps et al., 1998.

significantly lower in the insecure group when stress was high. As the authors point out, the study had many limitations: The data on childhood experiences relied on retrospective recall; both the independent and dependent variables came from the same informant; the range of experiences was relatively small; and there was no formal statistical test of the significance of the observed interaction effect. Nevertheless, the study is useful in its attempt to begin to test a hypothesis that has important implications for understanding resilience and for approaches to prevention.

REDUCTION OF EFFECT OF ADVERSITY
ON THE INDIVIDUAL

Until relatively recently, most studies of psychosocial risks focused on familywide influences. Thus, most studies focused on comparisons of children growing up in families with and without some risk experience such as family discord or conflict. Research findings confirmed that these familywide risk experiences did indeed involve a substantially increased risk that the child would develop some later psychopathology (particularly antisocial behavior). Behavioral genetic studies then posed a challenge to this set of findings that on the whole, the effects of experiences that impinged on just one child in the family tended to be greater than those that affected all children (Plomin & Daniels, 1987). In other words, on the whole, environmental effects make children in the same family different from one another rather than similar. Subsequent research has shown that shared environmental effects are probably more important than the initial behavioral genetic research suggested (see Rutter et al., in press). Nevertheless, evidence suggests that familywide influences impinge on children in quite different ways (Dunn & Plomin, 1990). Thus, it seems that hostility, criticism, and negative feelings directly focused on an individual child, as with scapegoating, is a more potent risk factor than is general family discord (see, e.g., Reiss et al., 1995).

Evidence has also accumulated that children's own characteristics play a major role in determining whether they are the selective target of negative feelings in the family (see Ge et al., 1996; O'Connor, Deater-Deckard, Fulker, Rutter, & Plomin, in press; Rutter et al., 1997a). Figure 2.8 illustrates the point with respect to the temperamental qualities of children being reared in high-risk families (Rutter, 1978). Children with temperamental adversity, meaning difficult temperamental characteristics, were twice as likely as those with easy temperaments to be subjected

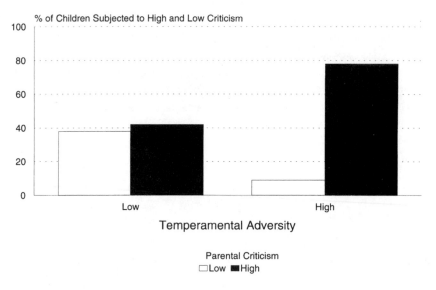

Figure 2.8   Temperamental Adversity and Parental Criticism.
Source: Data from Rutter, 1978.

to criticism. Conversely, nearly two-thirds of the children without temperamental adversity experienced only mild criticism from their parents, whereas only about one-fifth of those with difficult temperamental
features experienced only mild parental criticism.

The extent to which psychosocial risks within the family impinge on
a particular child makes a big difference to that child's chance of developing psychopathology. Figure 2.9 presents findings from a longitudinal
study of boys in a socially disadvantaged area of inner London
(Maughan, Pickles, & Quinton, 1995). Parental marital discord was associated with an increased likelihood that the boys would show conduct
disturbance. The risks associated with parental harshness in the way that
parents dealt with that particular child, however, proved to be a more
important risk factor. Thus, as shown in Figure 2.9, even in the absence
of parental marital discord, parental harshness was associated with a very
high proportion of boys developing conduct disturbance.

The implication of these and other findings is that children's interactions with other people help determine how other people behave
toward them. These interpersonal processes can either increase or
decrease the effect of the psychosocial risks. In addition, children—by
their own abilities to distance themselves from risks existing in their
home—can influence the extent to which they are exposed to these psychosocial risks based on whether their emotional ties and their leisure
activities are largely within or outside the home environment. Thus,

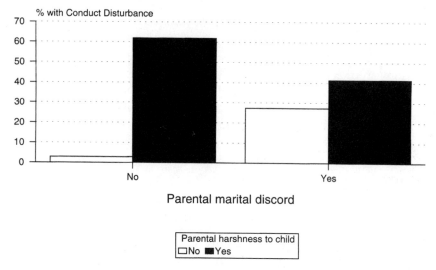

% with Conduct Disturbance

Parental marital discord

Parental harshness to child
☐No ■Yes

Figure 2.9 Parental Harshness and Marital Discord in Relation to Conduct Disorder in Boys.
Source: Data from Maughan et al., 1995.

Werner and Smith (1982) noted that individuals from high-risk backgrounds often felt the need to detach themselves from their parents. It seemed that when children's own families provided pervasively negative experiences, it was helpful for the children to develop social ties outside the family and to seek pleasures and rewards from extra-familial activities.

Somewhat similarly, Lösel and Bliesener (1994), studying resilient and deviant children who had been placed in residential institutions, found that resilient youngsters from highly troubled backgrounds tended to identify more strongly with their residential home and school than with the families from which they had been removed, partly because of the psychosocial risks in that environment.

This discussion might seem to suggest that all psychosocial risks for children stem from experiences within the family. That is not the case, however. An increasing body of evidence indicates that the quality of the peer group is also influential (see Rutter et al., in press). Particularly during adolescence, many of children's formative social experiences arise within the peer group. Membership in a delinquent peer group not only makes it more likely that children will continue with their antisocial activities, but also it increases the likelihood that they will marry or cohabit with, and have children by, a partner from a similar high-risk background who also exhibits antisocial behavior (see Pawlby, Mills, & Quinton, 1997a; Pawlby, Mills, Taylor, & Quinton, 1997b; Quinton, Pickles, Maughan, & Rutter, 1993). Given this situation, the degree to which parents exercise effective and appropriate monitoring and supervision of their children's leisure activities makes a difference to the children's exposure to high-risk environments outside the home (Small, 1995). Many studies have suggested that appropriate supervision by parents, teachers, and neighbors may help children avoid deviant group activities (see Rutter et al., in press). Of course, it is not just a matter of "policing" adolescents to prevent them from being part of groups engaged in antisocial behavior. Equally important is making sure there are equally attractive alternative activities both in and outside the family that do not carry the same risks.

REDUCTION OF NEGATIVE CHAIN REACTIONS

For many years, one of the key controversies with respect to psychosocial adversities concerned the extent to which effects are long-lasting. Bowlby's (1951) review of maternal deprivation initially made strong claims about the permanence and irreversibility of effects. Empirical evidence soon showed that children frequently changed as they grew up. The idea that personality was fixed during the preschool years was mistaken. The pendulum then swung and arguments were made suggesting that there were no long-term effects (see Kagan, 1984). Clarke and Clarke (1976) took a somewhat intermediate position suggesting a "wedge hypothesis," whereby effects markedly attenuated over time with the main environmental influences being those operating at the time, rather than in the past. Rutter (1981a) somewhat similarly concluded that the evidence pointed to few long-term effects independent of later experiences. It is now apparent that, in certain key respects, these conclusions addressed the wrong question. Empirical findings have increasingly shown that later experiences are not independent of what has occurred before (Rutter & Rutter, 1993). Indeed, it is the existence of long-term indirect negative chain effects that leads to the persistence of the ill effects of early stress and adversity (Rutter, 1989). "Bad" experiences are not randomly distributed in the population. There are, in fact, huge individual differences in people's exposure to environmental risks (Rutter, Champion, Quinton, Maughan, & Pickles, 1995). The extent of environmental risk exposure is determined in part by societal circumstances but also is influenced significantly by how people themselves behave. By their actions, people do much to shape and select their experiences. In this way, vicious cycles build.

Figure 2.10 illustrates this process, using data from Champion, Goodall, & Rutter's (1995) eighteen-year follow-up of inner-London children

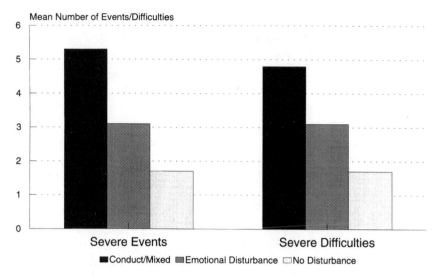

Figure 2.10 Severe Events and Difficulties in Early Adult Life and Type of Disturbance at 10 years, in Females.
Source: Data from Champion et al., 1995.

first assessed at the age of ten. Their findings suggest that children who showed conduct problems on a teacher questionnaire at age ten were more than twice as likely than children without emotional or behavioral disturbances to experience severe acute negative life events and severe negative long-term experiences nearly two decades later. Emotional disturbance in childhood was also associated with an increase in the risk of negative life experiences in adult life, but the effects were not as marked. From Robins's (1966) classic follow-up study onward, it is apparent that individuals who show antisocial behavior are—in adult life—much more likely to fall out with their friends, to have repeated marital breakdowns, to lose jobs through arguments and unreliability, and to lack social support. Psychosocial risk experiences play a substantial role in the development of conduct problems in childhood (see Rutter et al., in press). The extent of the ill-effects into adult life is much influenced by these negative chain reactions by which people's behavior increases the likelihood that they will have further adverse experiences. Caspi and Moffitt (1993) have discussed these accentuation effects in terms of the concept of "cumulative continuity."

Particularly during the 1970s and 1980s, there were many efforts to determine the nature of effective coping mechanisms by which individuals deal with the stress and adversity to which they are exposed (see Rutter, 1981b). Research findings indicated that there were many different sorts of coping strategies and that, on the whole, individuals who coped well did so because they had a repertoire of possible ways of dealing with things rather than because they had one particularly effective coping tactic. Nevertheless, even though effective coping strategies may not be universal, certain responses tend to be maladaptive in their consequences. Thus, using drugs or alcohol to relieve stress, dropping out of school, becoming pregnant, or entering into a teenage marriage as a way of escaping family conflict all involve a much increased likelihood that adverse sequelae will persist. The chance of a resilient outcome is enhanced if young people—either through their own actions—or through support and guidance from others, avoid these maladaptive coping strategies. One of the features that brings about vicious cycles of negative experiences is the belief of many young people exposed to chronic adversity that they are at the mercy of fate and can do little to influence their lives (Quinton & Rutter, 1988). Conversely, negative chain reactions are much less likely if young people show what Clausen (1991) called *planful competence.* Similarly, Quinton and Rutter's studies of institution-reared children (Quinton & Rutter, 1988; Quinton et al., 1993; Rutter & Quinton, 1984; Rutter, Quinton, & Hill, 1990) showed that a tendency to act in planful ways in relation to key life decisions constituted an important protective factor with substantial beneficial effects in relation to social functioning in adult life.

INCREASING POSITIVE CHAIN REACTIONS

Because most research has tended to focus on maladaptive outcomes, less is known about the features and mechanisms associated with positive chain reactions, although clearly these do exist. Thus, Quinton and Rutter's (1988) study of institution-reared children showed that positive school experiences made it more likely that young people would develop a tendency to plan in relation to life decisions concerning both marriage and careers. Precisely how this occurs is not known, but presumably success in one arena enhances self-esteem and self-efficacy, making it more likely for individuals to feel more confident that they could handle new challenges and act accordingly. Individual qualities also play a role in these positive chain reactions. Positive temperamental features are likely to elicit warm responses from other people, a mechanism emphasized by both Werner and Smith (1982) and Masten (1982). It is a common experience in clinical settings to find that some children with even marked psychopathology nevertheless tend to elicit positive responses from those about them. Although regrettably understudied up to now, it seems probable that some responses to stress and adversity are much more likely than others to elicit supportive responses from other people and, by so doing, predispose these children to positive chain reactions that foster resilience.

OPENING UP OPPORTUNITIES

Given the important influence of negative chain reactions predisposing children to the continuation of adverse experiences and their sequelae, it is evident that to break the vicious cycle, new experiences that provide a break from the past and open up new opportunities are likely to be significant. Research findings have confirmed that this is indeed the case. For example, Elder (1986) in his re-analysis of the California longitudinal studies, found that U.S. Army experiences often provided a way out of psychosocial adversity and disadvantage for youths who entered the armed forces immediately after leaving high school. Being in the army was not inherently good in its effects; indeed, effects tended to be negative for young people from a privileged background who joined the army at a later age after marrying and establishing their careers. Going into the armed forces for them was disruptive. Rather, what was protective was the opportunity provided by the army for disadvantaged youths to continue their education in an adult environment, postponing marriage until after they had established careers, and gaining a more positive self-image by their successes in this environment. Closely comparable findings were evident in Sampson and Laub's (1996) re-analysis of the Gluecks's archival data set. Turning point effects of the army experience for young people from a disadvantaged background were evident even after taking into account a wide range of risk features, as well as antisocial behavior in childhood. The key mediating influence for the benefits was provided by the on-the-job training and educational opportunities provided by the G.I. bill. In addition, it may be that the army experiences broadened horizons and created opportunities for the disadvantaged youths. Overseas service may have also helped to negate past social disadvantage and criminal stigmatization (Sampson & Laub, 1996).

Figure 2.11 deals with the turning point effect of a harmonious marriage to a nondeviant partner using data from Quinton et al.'s (1993) longitudinal studies. The graph gives the findings for a subsample, all of whom showed antisocial behavior in childhood (Rutter et al., 1997b). This group was then subdivided according to whether or not they had support from a nondeviant partner in adult life. Those who lacked such marital support had a strong tendency to continue their antisocial

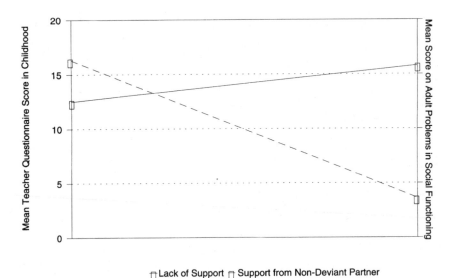

Figure 2.11   Turning Point Effect of Partner in Females with Antisocial Behavior in Childhood.
Source: Data from Rutter et al., 1997b.

behavior and had multiple social problems involving relationships with other people, employment, and other aspects of everyday life. By sharp contrast, those who had marital support showed a marked, and statistically significant, tendency to desist from crime and to show much better social functioning. Laub, Nagin, and Sampson (in press) found similar results in their re-analysis of the Gluecks's data set. It was suggested that the protective effect might be mediated by the informal controls implicit in adult social bonds. In addition, however, harmonious marriage may have changed people's images, attitudes, and expectations. It is likely, too, that involvement in family activities may have reduced the opportunities for crime.

NEUTRALIZING EXPERIENCES

For the most part, positive experiences alone do not exert much of a protective effect. However, evidence suggests that there may be some benefits if the positive experiences are of a kind that directly counter or compensate for a particular risk factor. In the field of adult depressive disorder, this process has been discussed in relation to so-called neutralizing or fresh-start life events (Brown, Adler, & Bifulco, 1988; Brown, Lemyre, & Bifulco, 1992; Craig, Drake, Mills, & Boardman, 1994; Tennant, Bebbington, & Hurry, 1981) that help to counteract or counter-balance the negative effect of an earlier threatening acute event or long-term difficulty.

Figure 2.12 shows findings from Jenkins and Smith's (1990) study of factors protecting children living in disharmonious homes. In keeping with the findings from other studies, a poor relationship between the parents was associated with a higher level of child psychopathology than that found in children from harmonious, cohesive families. This nega-tive effect of marital discord was mitigated to a very considerable extent, however, when the child had a warm, close relationship with one of the parents. On the whole, it seems that for there to be protection, the neu-tralizing experience must closely parallel the relationships where there is discord and conflict. Thus, for example, a good relationship with peers has only a very minor benefit in negating the effects of family discord (see also Gore & Aseltine, 1995). However, the importance of context does seem to depend a good deal on the nature of the risk mechanisms involved.

For example, Quinton and Rutter (1988) found that positive experi-ences at school were associated with a much increased likelihood of pos-itive social functioning in adult life for children who were being reared in residential group foster care. The particular form of the positive school experiences did not seem to matter very much. In one group, it

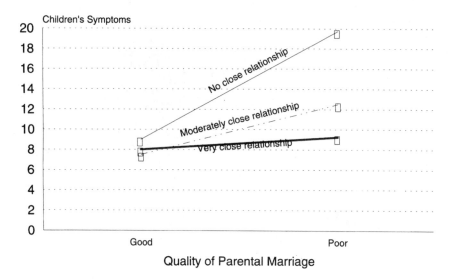

Figure 2.12   Child Psychopathology, a Close Relationship with an Adult, and Mar-riage Quality.
Source: Data from Jenkins & Smith, 1990.

infrequently took the form of academic success. More often, it involved positive experiences in relation to sports, music, positions of responsibility, or social activities. Circumstantial evidence suggested that the benefits came from the sense of self-esteem and self-efficacy that were thereby engendered. Young people who had positive school experiences were, for example, more likely to show planning in relation to their key life decisions. As Figure 2.13 shows, this beneficial effect of positive experiences at school was marked in the institution-reared girls, but no such effect was found in the general population comparison group. Although the data do not show unequivocally why this was so, it seems highly likely that the lack of effect in the community sample reflected the fact that the girls there had many other sources of satisfaction and of self-esteem and self-efficacy. Given multiple positive experiences at home, one or two more at school made very little difference. By contrast, such sources of positive self-concept were much more limited in the institution-reared group, and positive school experiences did seem to make an important difference.

Despite consistent pointers to the likely benefits associated with neutralizing positive experiences and of experiences that provide opportunities for satisfaction not available elsewhere, the topic has been subjected to remarkably little systematic study. Accordingly, little is known

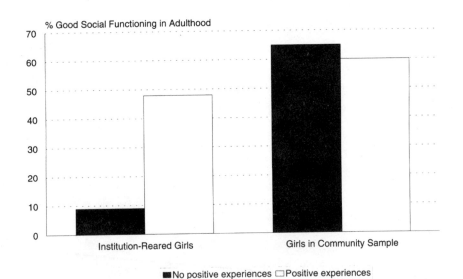

Figure 2.13 Positive School Experiences and Social Functioning in Adulthood. *Source:* Data from Quinton & Rutter, 1988.

about the strength or pervasiveness of effects. The topic warrants further investigation.

COGNITIVE PROCESSING OF EXPERIENCES

It has been known for a long time that children actively process their experiences, adding meaning to what has happened to them. The recognition of the importance of this cognitive processing led to studies showing the significance of negative attributions in the persistence of depressive disorders (Teasdale & Barnard, 1993) and of a tendency to assume that other people's actions are hostile in the maintenance of antisocial behavior (Dodge & Schwartz, 1997). A recognition of the importance of cognitive processing has also played a key role in the development of various cognitive–behavioral therapy and of interventions designed to enhance social problem solving (Kendall & Lochman, 1994; Pellegrini, 1994).

Because people differ in how they think about their bad experiences, it seems reasonable to suppose that individual differences in style of cognitive processing could be important in whether resilience develops. Such a concept played a central role in the development of Mary Main's Adult Attachment Interview (see Main, Kaplan & Cassidy, 1985; Van Ijzendoorn, 1995), in which the main focus is on how people think about bad relationships they may have had with their parents when young. The notion underlying the interview is that, for psychologically healthy adult development and relationships, people must accept the importance of such relationships, to accept the reality of the bad experiences that they have had, and to find a way of incorporating the reality of these experiences into their own self-concept, but doing so in a way that builds on the positive while not denying the negative. The data are far too sparse to constitute an adequate test of this hypothesis, but there are some findings that are at least consistent with the hypothesis (see Fonagy et al., 1994; Patrick, Hobson, Castle, Howard, & Maughan, 1994; Phelps et al., 1998). Again, this is a topic that requires further study.

CONCLUSION

Resilience does not constitute an individual trait or characteristic. Moreover, children may show resilience to some stresses and adversities but not to others; similarly, they may exhibit resistance to some sorts of psychopathological sequelae but yet not others. The concept is an important one because, if properly dealt with, it can provide a better understanding of risk and protective mechanisms, an understanding that should help in planning effective modes of protection and intervention for mental disorders. However, resilience involves many processes that bring together quite diverse mechanisms operating before, during, and after the encounter with the stress experience or adversity that is being considered.

This chapter draws attention to eight features involved in resilience processes, each of which has an implication for prevention. The overall *level of risk* is crucial, with the damage coming from the accumulation of many risk experiences. Any single experience, however negative, has only a small effect. The implication is that reducing the overall level of risk may be very helpful, even if considerable risks remain. Individual differences in *sensitivity to risk* are also crucial. These differences reflect both genetic influences and the effects of prior experiences, including the benefits from overcoming adversity or dealing effectively with challenges in the past. Individual features associated with sensitivity to risk include both temperamental characteristics and cognitive level. The ill effects of psychosocial adversities are much influenced by the extent to which the adverse experience directly impinges on the child. Accordingly, *a reduction of negative effect* becomes a critical issue in prevention. Parental supervision and monitoring of children's activities is important in limiting exposure to risks in the peer group and community. Steps to avoid or reduce the scapegoating or targeting of individual children when parents are under stress are also vital. When the atmosphere and experiences at home are very bad much of the time, children may choose to distance themselves from the family, and it may be helpful for them to do so.

Although no single effective coping strategy exists, young people need help avoiding tactics that bring with them marked risks of a different kind. Thus, reliance on drugs and alcohol may bring its own problems, as may dropping out of school or becoming a teenage parent to escape from a stressful parental family. Preventive actions must focus on steps to *reduce negative chain reactions.* Protection may also lie in *fostering positive chain reactions.* Research findings have been important, too, in showing the substantial benefits that may come from turning point experiences in early adult life that provide a discontinuity with the past and *open up new opportunities.* Educational provision and a harmonious marriage can both serve this role. Prevention must be involved with what can be done in adult life to counteract the ill effects of earlier adversities to make it less likely that psychopathology will persist from childhood into adulthood. On the whole, simply providing positive experiences is of limited benefit, but *neutralizing experiences* that negate or counteract the ill effects of negative ones may be beneficial. Finally, attention must be paid to the way people *process their experiences,* adding meaning to them and incorporating such experiences into their concept of themselves and of their lives. Although evidence on this point is quite limited, it seems that how this cognitive processing is done may make resilience more or less likely.

The lessons for early prevention include the following implications:

- Long-term gains usually will require continuing intervention.
- Multimodal intervention is desirable.
- Intervention should be focused and targeted on relevant risk and protective processes.
- Practitioner should attempt to foster positive coping behavior and to minimize maladaptive responses.
- Interventions are likely to be most effective when families can see the need for them.

The lessons for later intervention include the following:

- the need to focus on both family interaction and individual social problem solving and cognitive processing.
- the need to capitalize on the potential benefits of a positive peer group and the dangers of a negative one.
- the need to provide opportunities for responsibility and decision making.
- the need to be aware of the "knock-on" consequences (positive or negative) of experiences as the result of direct or indirect chain effects that they tend to set in motion.

Reviews of systematic evaluations now suggest that cautious optimism is justified with respect to the value of interventions designed to prevent or ameliorate antisocial behavior (Rutter et al., in press) as well as other forms of psychopathology and social problems (Graham, 1994).

REFERENCES

Anthony, E. J., & Cohler, B. J. (Eds.). (1987). *The invulnerable child.* New York: Guilford Press.

Bandura, A. (Ed.). (1995). *Self-efficacy in changing societies.* Cambridge: Cambridge University Press.

Bandura, A. (1997). *Self-efficacy: The exercise of control.* New York: Freeman.

Bohman, M. (1996). Predisposition to criminality: Swedish adoption studies in retrospect. In G. R. Bock & J. A. Goode (Eds.), *Genetics of criminal and anti-social behaviour. Ciba Foundation Symposium 194* (pp. 99–114). Chichester, United Kingdom: John Wiley & Sons.

Bowlby, J. (1951). *Maternal care and mental health.* Geneva: World Health Organization.

Brody, G. H., Stoneman, Z., Flor, D., McCrary, C., Hastings, L., & Conyers, O. (1994). Financial resources, parent psychological functioning, parent co-caregiving and early adolescent competence in rural two-parent African-American families. *Child Development, 65,* 590–605.

Brown, G. W., Adler, Z., & Bifulco, A. (1988). Life events, difficulties and recovery from chronic depression. *British Journal of Psychiatry, 152,* 487–498.

Brown, G. W., Lemyre, L., & Bifulco, A. (1992). Social factors and recovery from anxiety and depressive disorders: A test of the specificity hypothesis. *British Journal of Psychiatry, 161,* 44–54.

Caspi, A., & Moffitt, T. E. (1993). When do individual differences matter? A paradoxical theory of personality coherence. *Psychological Inquiry, 4,* 247–271.

Champion, L. A., Goodall, G. M., & Rutter, M. (1995). Behavioural problems in childhood and stressors in early adult life: A 20-year follow-up of London school children. *Psychological Medicine, 25,* 231–246.

Clarke, A. M., & Clarke, A. D. B. (1976). *Early experience: Myth and evidence.* London: Open Books.

Clausen, J. S. (1991). Adolescent competence and the shaping of the life course. *American Journal of Sociology, 96*(4), 805–842.

Conger, R. D., & Elder, G. (1994). *Families in troubled times: Adapting to change in rural America.* Hillsdale, NJ: Aldine.

Conger, R. D., Conger, K. J., Elder, G. H., Jr., Lorenz, F. O., Simons, R. L., & Whitbeck, L. B. (1992). A family process model of economic hardship and adjustment of early adolescent boys. *Child Development, 63*(3), 526–541.

Conger, R. D., Ge, X., Elder, G. H., Jr., Lorenz, F. O., & Simons, R. L. (1994). Economic stress, coercive family process, and developmental problems of adolescents. *Child Development, 65*(2 Spec. No.), 541–561.

Craig, T. K., Drake, H., Mills, K., & Boardman, A. P. (1994). The South London Somatisation Study: Influence of stressful life events and secondary gain. *British Journal of Psychiatry, 165,* 248–258.

Dodge, K. A., & Schwartz, D. (1997). Social information processing mechanisms in aggressive behavior. In D. Stoff, J. Breiling, & J. D. Maser (Eds.), *Handbook of antisocial behavior* (pp. 171–180). New York: Wiley.

Dunn, J., & Plomin, R. (1990). *Separate lives: Why siblings are so different.* New York: Basic Books.

Egeland, B., Carlson, E., & Sroufe, L. A. (1993). Resilience as process. *Development and Psychopathology, 5*(4), 517–528.

Elder, G. H. (1974). *Children of the Great Depression*. Chicago: University of Chicago Press.

Elder, G. H., Jr. (1986). Military times and turning points in men's lives. *Developmental Psychology, 22*(2), 233–245.

Elder, G. H., Liker, J. K., & Jaworski, B. J. (1984). Hardship in lives: Historical influences from the 1930s to old age in postwar America. In K. McCluskey & H. Reese (Eds.), *Life-span developmental psychology: Historical and cohort effects*. New York: Academic Press.

Fergusson, D. M., & Lynskey, M. T. (1996). Adolescent resiliency to family adversity. *Journal of Child Psychology and Psychiatry, 37*(3), 281–292.

Fergusson, D. M., Horwood, L. J., & Lynskey, M. T. (1992). Family change, parental discord, and early offending. *Journal of Child Psychology and Psychiatry, 33*(6), 1059–1075.

Fergusson, D. M., Horwood, L. J., Caspi, A., Moffitt, T. E., & Silva, P. A. (1996). The (artefactual) remission of reading disability: Psychometric lessons in the study of stability and change in behavioral development. *Developmental Psychology, 32*(1), 132–140.

Fonagy, P., Steele, M., Steele, H., Higgitt, A., & Target, M. (1994). The Emanuel Miller memorial lecture 1992. The theory and practice of resilience. *Journal of Child Psychology and Psychiatry, 35*(2), 231–257.

Ge, X., Conger, R. D., Cadoret, R. J., Neiderhiser, J. M., Yates, W., Troughton, E., & Stewart, M. A. (1996). The developmental interface between nature and nurture: A mutual influence model of child antisocial behavior and parenting. *Developmental Psychology, 32*(4), 574–589.

Gore, S., & Aseltine, R. J., Jr. (1995). Protective processes in adolescence: Matching stressors with social resources. *American Journal of Community Psychology, 23*(3), 301–327.

Graham, P. (1994). Prevention. In M. Rutter, E. Taylor, & L. Hersov (Eds.), *Child and adolescent psychiatry: Modern approaches* (pp. 815–828). Oxford: Blackwell Scientific Publications.

Haggerty, R. J., Sherrod, L. R., Garmezy, N., & Rutter, M. (Eds.). (1994). *Stress, risk, and resilience in children and adolescents: Processes, mechanisms, and interventions*. New York: Cambridge University Press.

Harris, T., Brown, G. W., & Bifulco, A. (1986). Loss of parent in childhood and adult psychiatric disorder: The role of lack of adequate parental care. *Psychological Medicine, 16*(3), 641–659.

Hennessey, J. W., & Levine, S. (1979). Stress, arousal and the pituitary-adrenal system: A psychoendocrine hypothesis. In J. M. Sprague & A. N. Epstein (Eds.), *Progress in psychobiology and physiological psychology* (pp. 133–178). New York: Academic Press.

Hunt, J. McV. (1979). Psychological development: Early experience. *Annual Review of Psychology, 30*, 103–143.

Jenkins, J. N., & Smith, M. A. (1990). Factors protecting children living in disharmonious homes: Maternal reports. *Journal of the American Academy of Child and Adolescent Psychiatry, 29*(1), 60–69.

Kagan, J. (1984). *The nature of the child.* New York: Basic Books.

Kendall, P. C., & Lochman, J. (1994). Cognitive-behavioural therapies. In M. Rutter, E. Taylor, & L. Hersov (Eds.), *Child and adolescent psychiatry: Modern approaches* (pp. 844–857). Oxford: Blackwell Scientific Publications.

Laub, J. H., Nagin, D. S., & Sampson, R. J. (1998). Trajectories of change in criminal offending: Good marriages and the desistance process. *American Sociological Review, 63:* 225–238.

Levine, S. (1982). Comparative and psychobiological perspectives on development. In W. A. Collins (Ed.), *Minnesota symposia on child psychology: Vol. 15. The concept of development* (pp. 29–53). Hillsdale, NJ: Lawrence Erlbaum.

Lösel, F., & Bliesener, T. (1994). Some high-risk adolescents do not develop conduct problems: A study of protective factors. *International Journal of Behavioral Development, 17*(4), 753–777.

Luthar, S. S. (1993) Annotation: Methodological and conceptual issues in research on childhood resilience. *Journal of Child Psychology and Psychiatry, 34*, 441–453.

Main, M., Kaplan, N., & Cassidy, J. (1985). Security in infancy, childhood and adulthood. In I. Bretherton & E. Waters (Eds.), *Growing points of attachment theory and research. Monographs of the Society for Research in Child Development, 50* (Serial No. 209, Nos. 1–2, pp. 66–106). Chicago: University of Chicago Press.

Masten, A. S. (1982). Humor and creative thinking in stress-resistant children. Unpublished doctoral dissertation. University of Minnesota, Minneapolis, Minnesota.

Masten, A. S., Coatsworth, J. D., Neeman, J., Gest, S. D., Tellegen, A., & Garmezy, N. (1995). The structure and coherence of competence from childhood to adolescence. *Child Development, 66*(6), 1635–1659.

Maughan, B., Pickles, A., & Quinton, D. (1995). Parental hostility, childhood behavior and adult social functioning. In J. McCord (Ed.), *Coercion and punishment in long-term perspectives* (pp. 34–58). New York: Cambridge University Press.

Moffitt, T. E. (1990a). Juvenile delinquency and attention deficit disorder: Developmental trajectories from age 3 to 15. *Child Development, 61*(3), 893–910.

Moffitt, T. E. (1990b). The neuropsychology of juvenile delinquency: A critical review. In M. Tonry & N. Morris (Eds.), *Crime and justice: Volume 12* (pp. 99–169). Chicago: University of Chicago Press.

O'Connor, T. G., Deater-Deckard, K., Fulker, D., Rutter, M., & Plomin, R. (1998). Genotype-environment correlations in late childhood and early adolescence: Antisocial behavioral problems and coercive parenting. *Developmental Psychology, 34:* 970–981.

O'Connor, T. G., Rutter, M., Kreppner, J., Beckett, C., Keaveney, L., & the English and Romanian Adoptees (E.R.A.) Study Team. (1998). The effects of global early privation on cognitive competence: A longitudinal follow-up. Unpublished manuscript.

Patrick, M., Hobson, P., Castle, D., Howard, R., & Maughan, B. (1994). Personality disorder and the mental representation of early social experience. *Development and Psychopathology, 6*(2), 375–388.

Pawlby, S. J., Mills, A., & Quinton, D. (1997a). Vulnerable adolescent girls: Opposite sex relationships. *Journal of Child Psychology and Psychiatry, 38*(8), 909–920.

Pawlby, S. J., Mills, A., Taylor, A., & Quinton, D. (1997b). Adolescent friendships mediating childhood adversity and adult outcome. *Journal of Adolescence, 20*(6), 633–644.

Pellegrini, D. (1994). Training in interpersonal cognitive problem-solving. In M. Rutter, E. Taylor, & L. Hersov (Eds.), *Child and adolescent psychiatry: Modern approaches* (pp. 829–843). Oxford: Blackwell Scientific Publications.

Phelps, J. L., Belsky, J., & Crnic, K. (1998). Earned security, daily stress, and parenting: A comparison of five alternative models. *Development and Psychopathology, 10*(1), 21–38.

Plomin, R. (1994). *Genetics and experience: The interplay between nature and nurture.* Thousand Oaks, CA: Sage Publications.

Plomin, R., & Daniels, D. (1987). Why are children in the same family so different from each other? *Behavioral and Brain Sciences, 10*(1), 1–15.

Plomin, R., De Fries, J. C., McClearn, G. E., & Rutter, M. (1997). *Behavioral genetics* (3rd ed.). New York: W. H. Freeman.

Quinton, D., & Rutter, M. (1976). Early hospital admissions and later disturbances of behaviour: An attempted replication of Douglas' findings. *Development Medicine and Child Neurology, 18*(4), 447–459.

Quinton, D., & Rutter, M. (1988). *Parenting breakdown: The making and breaking of inter-generational links.* Aldershot, United Kingdom: Avebury.

Quinton, D., Pickles, A., Maughan, B., & Rutter, M. (1993). Partners, peers and pathways: Assortative pairing and continuities in conduct disorder. *Development and Psychopathology, 5*(4), 763–783.

Reiss, D., Hetherington, E. M., Plomin, R., Howe, G. W., Simmens, S. J., Henderson, S. H., O'Connor, T. J., Bussell, D. A., Anderson, E. R., & Law, T. (1995). Genetic questions for environmental studies: Differential parenting and psychopathology in adolescence. *Archives of General Psychiatry, 52*(11), 925–936.

Robins, L. N. (1966). *Deviant children grown up: A sociological and psychiatric study of sociopathic personality.* Baltimore, MD: Williams & Wilkins.

Rolf, J., Masten, A., Cicchetti, D., Nuechterlein, K., & Weintraub, S. (1990). *Risk and protective factors in the development of psychopathology.* New York: Cambridge University Press.

Rose, R. M. (1980). Endocrine responses to stressful psychological events. *Psychiatric Clinics of North America, 3*(2), 251–276.

Rutter, M. (1971). Parent–child separation: Psychological effects on the children. *Journal of Child Psychology and Psychiatry, 12*(4), 233–260.

Rutter, M. (1978). Family, area, and school influences in the genesis of conduct disorders. In L. A. Hersov, M. Berger, & D. Shaffer (Eds.), *Aggression and anti-social behaviour in childhood and adolescence* (pp. 95-113). Oxford: Pergamon Press.

Rutter, M. (1981a). *Maternal deprivation reassessed* (2nd ed.). Harmondsworth, Middlesex, United Kingdom: Penguin.

Rutter, M. (1981b). Stress, coping and development: Some issues and some questions. *Journal of Child Psychology and Psychiatry, 22*(4), 323-356.

Rutter, M. (1987). Psychosocial resilience and protective mechanisms. *American Journal of Orthopsychiatry, 57*(3), 316-331.

Rutter, M. (1989). Pathways from childhood to adult life. *Journal of Child Psychology and Psychiatry, 30*(1), 23-51.

Rutter, M. (1995). Psychosocial adversity: Risk, resilience and recovery. *Southern African Journal of Child and Adolescent Psychiatry, 7,* 75-88.

Rutter, M. (in press). An update on resilience: Conceptual considerations and empirical findings. In S. J. Meisels & J. T. Shonkoff (Eds.), *Handbook of early childhood intervention.* New York: Cambridge University Press.

Rutter, M., & Quinton, D. (1984). Parental psychiatric disorder: Effects on children. *Psychological Medicine, 14*(4), 853-880.

Rutter, M., & the English and Romanian Adoptees (E.R.A.) Study Team. (1998). Developmental catch-up, and deficit, following adoption after severe global early privation. *Journal of Child Psychology and Psychiatry, 39:* 465-476.

Rutter, M., & Rutter, M. (1993). *Developing minds: Challenge and continuity across the lifespan.* New York: Basic Books.

Rutter, M., Champion, L., Quinton, D., Maughan, B., & Pickles, A. (1995). Understanding individual differences in environmental risk exposure. In P. Moen, G. H. Elder, Jr., & K. Lüscher (Eds.), *Examining lives in context: Perspectives on the ecology of human development* (pp. 61-93). Washington, D.C.: American Psychological Association.

Rutter, M., Dunn, J., Plomin, P., Simonoff, E., Pickles, A., Maughan, B., Ormel, J., Meyer, J., & Eaves, L. (1997a). Integrating nature and nurture: Implications of person-environment correlations and interactions for developmental psychopathology. *Development and Psychopathology, 9*(2), 335-364.

Rutter, M., Giller, H., & Hagell, A. (in press). *Antisocial behavior by young people.* New York: Cambridge University Press.

Rutter, M., Maughan, B., Meyer, J., Pickles, A., Silberg, J., Simonoff, E., & Taylor, E. (1997b). Heterogeneity of antisocial behavior: Causes, continuities and consequences. In R. Dienstbier (Series. Ed.) & D. W. Osgood (Vol. Ed.), *Nebraska symposium on motivation: Vol. 44. Motivation and delinquency* (pp. 44-118). Lincoln, NE: University of Nebraska Press.

Rutter, M., Quinton, D., & Hill, J. (1990). Adult outcomes of institution-reared children: Males and females compared. In L. N. Robins & M. Rutter (Eds.), *Straight and devious pathways from childhood to adulthood* (pp. 135-157). Cambridge: Cambridge University Press.

Ryff, C. C., & Singer, G. (1998). The contours of positive human health. *Psychological Inquiry, 9*(1), 1–28.

Sampson, R. J., & Laub, J. H. (1996). Socioeconomic achievement in the life course of disadvantaged men: Military service as a turning point, circa 1940–1965. *American Sociological Review, 61*(3), 347–367.

Siefer, R. (1995). Perils and pitfalls of high-risk research. *Developmental Psychology, 31*(3), 420–424.

Small, S. A. (1995). Enhancing contexts of adolescent development: The role of community-based action research. In L. J. Crockett & A. C. Crouter (Eds.), *Pathways through adolescence: Individual development in relation to social contexts* (pp. 211–234). Mahwah, NJ: Lawrence Erlbaum.

Teasdale, J. D., & Barnard, P. J. (1993). *Affect, cognition, and change: Re-modelling depressive thought.* Hove, United Kingdom: Lawrence Erlbaum.

Tennant, C., Bebbington, P., & Hurry, J. (1981). The short-term outcome of neurotic disorders in the community: The relation of remission to clinical factors to "neutralizing" life events. *British Journal of Psychiatry, 139,* 213–220.

Tschann, J. M., Kaiser, P., Chesney, M. A., Alkon, A., & Boyce, W. T. (1996). Resilience and vulnerability among preschool children: Family functioning, temperament, and behavior problems. *Journal of the American Academy of Child and Adolescent Psychiatry, 35*(2), 184–192.

Ursin, H., Baade, E., & Levins, S. (1978). *Psychobiology of stress: A study of coping men.* New York: Academic Press.

Van Ijzendoorn, M. H. (1995). Adult attachment representations, parental responsiveness, and infant attachment: A meta-analysis on the predictive validity of the adult attachment interview. *Psychological Bulletin, 117*(3), 387–403.

Werner, E. E., & Smith, R. S. (1982). *Vulnerable but invincible: A longitudinal study of resilient children and youth.* New York: McGraw Hill.

Chapter 3

Neurobiological Mechanisms of Psychosocial Resiliency

J. Eric Vance

The life stories of the resilient youngsters now grown into adulthood teach us that competence, confidence, and caring can flourish, even under adverse circumstances, if children encounter persons who provide them with the secure basis for the development of trust, autonomy, and initiative.
—*Emmy Werner and Ruth Smith (1992)*

INTRODUCTION

Ironically, the dawning of resiliency theory grew out of the study of putative risk factors for developing psychiatric disorder. As they studied the children of parents afflicted with schizophrenia, Anthony (1974) and others began to note the phenomenon of the "invulnerable child," who seemed impervious to the effects of such hardship. Since then, a number of prospective, longitudinal studies have added empirical validation to the concept of resiliency among certain high-risk individuals (Elder, 1974; Garmezy, 1983; Rutter, 1979; Sameroff & Seifer,1983; Werner & Smith, 1982). Studies of resilient children have converged in their findings, suggesting that a number of psychosocial "protective factors" are common to those children who grow up successfully, despite their exposure to multiple serious psychosocial risk factors. In short, resiliency is defined by the ability of a person to rise above significant adversity and have a reasonably successful life course, avoiding serious psychiatric disorder, substance abuse, criminality, or social-relational problems.

The triumph of resilient individuals over a variety of psychosocial risk conditions (Anthony & Cohler, 1987) leads to the question of what the underlying mechanisms of psychosocial resilience might be. Prospective, longitudinal studies of resilient individuals indicate that they share unique temperament and personality characteristics, early care-giving environments, and later social–relational experiences that seem to confer protection in the face of risk. Specifically, these protective factors include positive temperamental characteristics of the young child, exceptional social skills, various competencies and abilities, confident perceptions and outlooks, positive aspects of the parents and child-rearing environment, warmth and caring in the parent–child relationship, and the existence of a variety of social supports for the child during the course of development (see Table 3.1). Even in the setting of serious psychosocial challenge with multiple risk factors (see Table 3.2), resilient children have consistently better life outcomes than other high-risk individuals who are not endowed with protective factors.

The underlying mechanisms for the stress-buffering effect of these various psychosocial protective factors are not well understood. These factors, ranging from inherent qualities of temperament to experiences of life and social relationships, certainly arise by a variety of underlying mechanisms. Because resiliency implies an exceptional ability of the individual to adapt to stressful life conditions, one would expect to find characteristic capacities in the biological, psychological, and social stress–coping mechanisms of resilient youth.

In the psychological realm, the use of adaptive or "mature" psychological coping mechanisms (altruism, humor, suppression, anticipation, sublimation) has long been recognized to predict superior psychosocial adjustment in resilient adults (Vaillant, 1977), and the seeds of these adaptive psychological defenses can be found in the protective factors of resilient children. Likewise, in the social realm, research strongly suggests that the existence of social support has a powerful protective effect on a variety of health outcomes (House, Landis, & Umberson, 1988), and resilient youths are well known to surround themselves with rich social support networks. Although these psychosocial characteristics of resilient individuals have been well studied, the neurobiological underpinnings of resiliency have not. This chapter reviews some of the emerging research on the neurobiological mechanisms of stress coping, temperament, and social behavior in an attempt to suggest putative neurobiological mechanisms for psychosocial resilience.

Table 3.1
Psychosocial Protective Factors

Temperamental characteristics of the child
- Easy temperament type (Rutter, 1985b; Smith & Prior, 1995; Tschann, Kaiser, Chesney, Alkon, & Boyce, 1996; Werner & Smith, 1982)
- Independent, outgoing toddler (Anthony & Cohler, 1987; Tschann et al., 1996; Werner & Smith, 1982)

Social Skills of the Child
- Seen as likeable (Garmezy, Masten, & Tellegen, 1984; Wyman et al., 1992)
- Gets along with peers (Garmezy et al., 1984; Offord et al., 1992; Werner & Smith, 1982)
- Gets along with adults (Garmezy et al., 1984; Werner & Smith, 1982; Wyman et al., 1992)
- Has a good sense of humor (Masten, 1986)
- Demonstrates empathy and nurturance (Luthar & Zigler, 1991; Parker, Cowen, Work, & Wyman, 1990; Werner & Smith, 1992)

Child Competencies
- Above average intelligence (Rutter, Tizard, & Whitmore, 1970/1981; Werner & Smith, 1982)
- Good problem-solving abilities (Felsman & Vaillant, 1987; Parker et al., 1990; Werner & Smith, 1982)
- Good reading abilities (Werner & Smith, 1982, 1992)
- Good school student (Felsman & Vaillant, 1987; Werner & Smith, 1982)
- Extracurricular or vocational involvement (Felsman & Vaillant, 1987; Werner & Smith, 1992)

Protective Perceptions
- Child-perceived competency (Seifer, Sameroff, Baldwin, & Baldwin, 1992; Werner & Smith, 1992; Wyman et al., 1992)
- Internal locus of control (Bandura, 1977; Luthar & Zigler, 1991; Parker et al., 1990; Werner & Smith, 1992)
- Realistic hopes and expectations for the future (Werner & Smith, 1992; Wyman et al., 1992)
- Independent mindedness (Furstenburg, Brooks-Gunn, & Morgan, 1987; Werner & Smith, 1992)

Aspects of the Home Environment
- First-born child (Werner & Smith, 1982)
- Parent with high school education or better (Werner & Smith, 1982, 1992)
- Parent consistently employed (Werner & Smith, 1982)
- Alternate caretakers available to the family (Seifer et al., 1992; Werner & Smith, 1982; Wyman, Cowen, Work, & Parker, 1991)
- Regular church involvement (Werner & Smith, 1982)
- Rules, routines, curfews, and rituals (Felsman & Vaillant, 1987; Werner & Smith, 1982; Wyman et al., 1992)
- Discipline with discussion and fair punishment (Seifer et al., 1992; Wyman et al., 1991; 1992)

continued

Table 3.1 (*continued*)

Parent–Child Relationship
- Secure mother–infant attachment (Nachmias et al., 1996; Werner & Smith, 1982, 1992)
- Child perception that parent cares (Werner & Smith, 1982; Wyman et al., 1992)
- Warm and positive relationship with a parent (Anthony & Cohler, 1987; Rutter, Cox, Tupling, Berger, & Yule, 1975; Seifer et al., 1992; Werner & Smith, 1982; Wyman et al., 1991, 1992)

Social Support Network
- Adult mentor outside of the home (Freedman, 1989; Tierney et al., 1995; Werner & Smith, 1982, 1992)
- Peer support (Seifer et al., 1992; Werner & Smith, 1982)
- Church group (Anthony, 1974; Ayala-Canales, 1984; Werner & Smith, 1992)
- Inner spiritual faith (Moskovitz, 1983; Werner & Smith, 1992)

Individual Variation

The study of vulnerability and resiliency is the study of individual variation in response to stress. Individual variation along almost any biopsychosocial dimension results from the complex interplay of genetic and experiential forces. Research has finally moved beyond debates of "nature versus nurture" to efforts to understand the underlying mechanisms of how nature effects nurture and nurture shapes nature. One example of the complex developmental interplay between person and environment is the seemingly insoluble "chicken-or-egg" development of social support networks. Although social support networks are clearly a characteristic of the environment, careful twin studies have suggested that there is a significant heritable component to social support, possibly mediated by heritable aspects of personality, such as sociability (Kendler, 1997). As more is learned about the complex interactions of genetic and environmental influences on human development, what is needed now is an understanding of the mechanisms by which experience translates into biology and how such biology then effects the environment that surrounds it.

Rutter and others have carefully reviewed how aspects of the person and environment interact to modulate the effects of risk factors in psychopathogenesis (Rutter et al., 1997). In fact, most research efforts have attempted to define the deleterious neurobiological effects of environmental stress and the mechanisms of psychopathogenesis, that is, how risk factors (such as trauma) effect physiological substrates (Friedman,

Table 3.2
Major Psychosocial Risk Factors

Early Developmental Risk Factors
- Complications of pregnancy, birth, or prematurity (Paneth, 1995; Werner & Smith, 1982)
- Fetal substance exposure (Lester & Tronick, 1994; Lewis, 1992; Sampson, Streissguth, Barr, & Bookstein, 1989)
- "Difficult" temperament (Kingston & Prior, 1995; Rutter, 1978; Thomas et al., 1982; Tschann et al., 1996)
- Shy or anxious temperament (Biederman et al., 1993; Kagan et al., 1988; Lonigan et al., 1994)
- Siblings born within 2 years (Werner & Smith, 1982, 1992)

Family Stress Factors
- Poverty (Elder, 1974; Halpern, 1993; Rutter, 1979; Werner & Smith, 1982)
- Divorce, separation, or single-parent home (Wallerstein, 1985; Werner & Smith, 1982)
- Four or more siblings (Rutter, 1979; Werner & Smith, 1982)
- Frequent family moves (Masten et al., 1988)

Parental Disorders
- Parental substance abuse (Loeber & Stouthamer-Loeber, 1986; O'Connor, Sigman, & Brill, 1987; Werner & Smith, 1992)
- Parental emotional or mental disorder (Anthony, 1974; Rutter, 1979; Werner & Smith, 1982)
- Parental criminality (Hutchings & Mednick, 1974; Loeber & Stouthamer-Loeber, 1986; Rutter, 1979)

Parent–Child Relationship
- Insecure or poor mother–infant attachment (Werner & Smith, 1982)
- Long absences of main caregiver in infancy (Werner & Smith, 1982)
- Mostly conflicted parent–child relationship (Werner & Smith, 1982, 1992)

Trauma and Neglect
- Witness to violence and conflict (Cummings, Pelligrini, Notarius, & Cummings, 1989; Offord et al., 1992; Rutter, 1979)
- Physical abuse and harsh punishment (Livingston, Lawson, & Jones, 1993; Pelcovitz et al., 1994; Werner & Smith, 1982)
- Sexual abuse (Kendall-Tackett, Williams, & Finkelhor, 1993; Livingston et al., 1993; Oates, O'Toole, Lynch, Stern, & Cooney, 1994)
- Substantiated child neglect (Loeber & Stouthamer-Loeber, 1986; Widom, 1989)
- Removal from home by public agency (Rutter, 1979; Werner & Smith, 1982)

Childhood Disorder
- Chronic medical problems (Werner & Smith, 1982)
- Neurodevelopmental delays and disorders (Lewis, 1992; Werner & Smith, 1982)
- Mental retardation or IQ < 70 (Farrington, 1989; Werner & Smith, 1982)

continued

Table 3.2 (*continued*)

- Mental or emotional disorder (Werner & Smith, 1982)
- Drug or alcohol use (Huizinga, Loeber, & Thornberry, 1993)
- Delinquency (Huizinga et al., 1993; Werner & Smith, 1982, 1992)
- Pattern of aggressive behavior (Kingston & Prior, 1995; Lewis, 1992; Loeber, 1982)

Social Drift
- School failure or drop-out (Farrington, 1991; Werner & Smith, 1992)
- Delinquent peer group (Huizinga et al., 1993)
- Teen pregnancy (Furstenberg et al., 1987; Osofsky, Hann, & Peebles, 1993; Werner & Smith, 1982)

Charney, & Deutch, 1995). Far less research has been done to understand the mechanisms underlying the salubrious effects of psychosocial protective factors on the neurobiological substrates of the individual organism, leading to stress coping and resiliency.

A number of likely candidates might serve as neurobiological substrates underlying resilient functioning in a given individual, including the neurophysiological systems involved in stress reactions, those involved in regulating emotional responses, those related to personality traits, those modulating social interactions, and those responsible for higher cognitive functioning. Recent work in neurobiology has revealed that individual variation exists in neuroendocrine stress responsiveness as well as in the functioning of the autonomic nervous system functions to regulate emotion (Porges, Doussard-Roosevelt, & Maiti, 1994; Susman et al., 1997). Additionally, certain personality dimensions (harm-avoidance, novelty-seeking, reward-dependence, sensation-seeking, social-dependency), formerly understood only in psychological terms, have begun to reveal underlying neurochemical bases (Cloninger, 1987; Uvnas-Moberg, Arn, Jonsson, Ek & Nilsonne, 1993; Zuckerman, 1991). Other recent work has an increased understanding of the neuroendocrine mechanisms involved in social and affiliative behaviors, heretofore understood only in the theoretical frameworks of infant–mother attachment, object relations, or the romantic language of love (Carter, 1998; Insel 1997). Furthermore, a growing body of knowledge suggests that certain aspects of developmental experience, including positive social relationships and certain sensory experiences, are transduced via neurobiological mechanisms into stable patterns of psychophysiological and cognitive functioning (reviewed in Nash, 1997), which seem to promote resiliency. These are some of the neurobiological substrates that will likely prove crucial in determining whether an individual might rise above or succumb to psychosocial adversity.

Other Developmental Considerations

To fully understand the mechanisms by which resilience might arise from complex neurobiological systems, it is important to appreciate some basic principles of neurodevelopment. The interaction of the environment with the biological endowment of the individual has been alluded to. A primary way in which environmental stimuli are transduced into stable biological systems in the brain is by a process known as *long-term potentiation* (Brown, Chapman, Kairiss, & Keenan, 1988). Long-term potentiation involves a mechanism by which repeated exposure to a given pattern of neural stimulation (exogenous or endogenous) strengthens a specific neural pathway and lowers the threshold for future neural transmission along the specified neural circuit. In this way, learning occurs by repetition, memories are formed, and physiological feedback loops are established. Conversely, lack of inputs to a developing neural circuit results in atrophy, weakening, and sometimes eventual neuronal cell death. Herein lies the mechanism by which enriched environmental stimuli enhances neurodevelopment—or causes it to suffer by deprivation.

Furthermore, excessive stress on the developing organism can have neurotoxic effects. For example, high levels of cortisol (the body's main stress hormone) results in cell death within the hippocampus portion of the brain, an area vital to the formation of long-term memory and emotional regulation (McEwen et al., 1992). In contrast, experiencing moderate amounts of stress, known as "stress inoculation," seems to be crucial for the developing brain to create the capacity to adaptively respond to normal stressors (Eysenck, 1983). This process is akin to long-term potentiation of a neuroendocrine circuit responsible for stress coping in the healthy individual.

These neurodevelopmental mechanisms provide a way of understanding how psychosocial risk and protective factors might be transduced into enduring patterns of neurobiological response. For example, extremely stressful risk factors may be associated with excessive levels of circulating cortisol, toxic to the developing brain, whereas other risks may be associated with the deprivation from some crucial experience, failing to potentiate a vital neural pathway. Likewise, certain protective factors may serve to either attenuate the effects of stress on the brain or potentiate a neural circuit that fosters adaptive behavior.

STRESS COPING AND THE HPA AXIS

The quality of psychosocial resiliency in high-risk individuals may be defined as the exceptional ability to produce an adaptive response to stress. One of the chief neurophysiological systems responsible for adaptation to stress in humans is the hypothalamic–pituitary–adrenal (HPA) axis, which results in the secretion of cortisol, the body's glucocorticosteroid stress hormone. Stressors provoking the eventual secretion of cortisol include a variety of challenges to the organism, including noxious or novel stimuli, illness, threat, mother–infant separation, and social isolation (Levine & Wiener, 1989). Conversely, social contact, predictability, and the perception of control have been shown to attenuate stress-induced activation of the HPA axis (Gunnar, 1987; Hofer, 1984). In this framework, stress may be defined less by the magnitude or intensity of adversity than by the perception of control over it.

The concept of stress has been widely studied, and although disagreement exists on the definition of stress, it can be operationally defined here as any significant perturbation of, or challenge to, the homeostatic state of a biopsychosocial system. All of the major psychosocial risk factors (see Table 3.2) can be understood as conditions or events that cause major disruptions to such homeostatic systems, with biological, psychological, or social implications. A variety of studies indicate that stressors result in a predictable chain of neuroendocrine events, beginning with incoming (afferent), noxious sensory inputs to amygdala, which project to the paraventricular nucleus of the hypothalamus, causing release of corticotropin-releasing factor (CRF) to the pituitary, where it stimulates the release of adrenocorticotropic hormone (ACTH) into the bloodstream, quickly leading to the secretion of cortisol from the adrenal glands (Grossman et al., 1982). Cortisol metabolically mobilizes the organism for a challenge by increasing available energy stores to fuel the body's stress response. As such, serum cortisol level has been viewed as a key indicator of a stress reaction.

A number of the major psychosocial risk factors have been associated with serious abnormalities in the function of the HPA axis. For example, infants born with the shy or behaviorally inhibited temperament type show excessive secretion of cortisol in response to novel or frightening stimuli (Kagan, Resnick, & Snidman, 1988). Mother–infant separations in mammals, including humans, have been shown to result in predictable elevations in serum cortisol, which may be long lasting in severe cases (Levine, Lyons, & Schatzberg, 1997). Evidence exists that suggests chronically stressed infants, such as institutionalized, socially deprived orphans, develop abnormalities in the normal diurnal secretion of cortisol, as well as tonically higher levels of cortisol throughout the day. These HPA axis abnormalities were associated with significant motor and cognitive developmental delays in comparison to control infants (Carlson & Earls, 1997). Multiply-traumatized adults, such as repeatedly raped women, have been shown to develop decreased responsivity of the HPA axis in situations of stress (Resnick, Yehuda, Atman, & Foy, 1995). A variety of medical and psychiatric illnesses result in hyper-responsiveness of the HPA axis, with resultant hypercortisolemia (Gold, Goodwin, & Chrousos, 1988; Susman et al., 1997). Although normal cortisol secretion is a critical physiological response to stress, chronic stressors, resulting in chronic elevations of cortisol, can cause immunosuppression and damage to the hippocampus, a limbic brain structure crucial to the storage of long-term memories (McEwen et al., 1992).

Self-Regulation of the HPA Axis by Resilient Individuals

If psychosocial resiliency is seen as exceptional stress coping, resilient individuals would be expected to have the ability to attenuate stress or maintain adaptive HPA functioning in the face of stress. Some of the most powerful attenuators of stress-related HPA activation are the perception of control or predictability (Gunnar, 1987). Animal models have clearly demonstrated that excessive reactivity in the HPA axis can be diminished in stressful situations by giving the animal control over the administration of the stressful stimulus (Levine & Wiener, 1989). This finding is in marked contrast to the severe HPA dysregulation that occurs in experimental or unfortunate real-life paradigms of "learned helplessness" and unrelenting trauma (Seligman, 1975). The perception of control over the stressor, resulting from the ability to attenuate the cortisol response, may explain the protective effects of possessing a sense of internal locus of control among resilient individuals.

Resilient youths with an internal locus of control may be more likely to psychologically prepare for and actively deal with stressors, thereby moderating the neuroendocrine stress response. In studies of adolescents, behaviorally disordered teens show an excessive cortisol elevation in response to a stressor, whereas the high-functioning youths develop a high anticipatory cortisol level prior to the stressor but very little further reactivity in response to the stressor itself (Susman et al., 1997). This finding may indicate a capacity for resilient youths to realistically anticipate a stressor, mount a physiologically appropriate anticipatory cortisol response, and subsequently blunt further reactivity during the stressor.

These neuroendocrine findings seem to reflect the psychological abilities of resilient youths, who are characterized by an internal locus of control, the use of planning strategies, and realistic expectations for the future. This style of coping contrasts with the plight of those who have succumbed to serious trauma, and develop a sense of "futurelessness," with an inability to anticipate and actively deal with life stresses (van der Kolk, 1989). Somehow, resilient individuals may "reach down" and exert acute control over the HPA axis by accurately anticipating and actively dealing with the stressful events of life.

Thus, it has been suggested that adaptive (or resilient) functioning of the HPA system should be not only characterized by normative levels of serum cortisol but also by appropriate *reactivity* of the system to stressors (Gunnar, 1987). An exceptionally competent HPA axis would be expected to anticipate and rise to the occasion of stress promptly, but not excessively, and bring cortisol levels back down to a physiologically healthy level with the passage of the stressor. Studies of preschool children have shown that children characterized as outgoing, likeable, and socially competent had a pattern of high cortisol reactivity early in the school year, which progressed to low or normal reactivity as the social group stabilized during the course of the year (Gunnar, Tout, de Haan, Pierce, & Stansbury, 1997). This finding contrasted with those children classified as affectively negative—solitary—who maintained high HPA reactivity throughout the year, or those with impulsivity and attention problems, who had tonically elevated levels of cortisol. Here again is evidence that children with certain protective factors, in this case likeability and social competence, may benefit in part from competent HPA axis functioning.

Mother–Infant Attachment and the HPA Axis

Having a secure pattern of mother–infant attachment is an early developmental experience that has been shown to exert protective effects on psychosocial function well into adulthood (Werner & Smith, 1992). A number of neuroendocrine and physiological changes occur in the context of attachment interactions between the mother and infant. For example, as mother–infant interaction occurs in the context of the attachment bond, brief separations of the dyad are inevitable and have been shown to predictably result in elevations of the infant's serum cortisol. The return of the mother, and tactile interaction in particular, causes the return of the infant's serum cortisol to normal. In this repeating cycle, the mother serves as a sort of neuroendocrine regulator for the infant (Hofer, 1984). The dependable availability of a sensitive mother to resolve the separation distress of the infant repeatedly stimulates the neuroendocrine pathways of the HPA axis, and cortisol rises and falls accordingly. This may be one example of long-term potentiation of a neural pathway in the context of a secure pattern of attachment behavior. Such repeated physiological "exercise" of the stress-coping axis of the infant may serve as "stress inoculation" (Eysenck, 1983) in the context of a secure attachment relationship.

One could speculate that this process of neuroendocrine development is the precursor to later adaptive HPA function among resilient individuals. As an infant cries, and his or her needs are met by the predictable behavioral responses of a sensitive mother in the context of a secure attachment, we are likely witnessing the earliest developmental examples of the infant's exertion of control over the environment. If these successful patterns of interaction repeat over the course of development, secure attachment may allow the evolution of a perception of an internal locus of control, with the consequent stress-buffering effect on the HPA axis.

Whether or not the process of secure attachment behavior induces stress resistance, the existence of a secure pattern of attachment may buffer against psychosocial risks beginning very early in life (Bowlby, 1988). Consistent with this hypothesis, some research evidence suggests that the presence of a secure pattern of mother–infant attachment buffers against cortisol-mediated stress responses. For example, in the proximity of a secure attachment relationship, the predictably excessive cortisol reactivity of shy or behaviorally inhibited children to nonnoxious, novel stimuli is significantly attenuated (Nachmias, Gunnar, Mangelsdorf, Parritz, & Buss, 1996). The stress-buffering effects of social relationships is well established in the studies of the effects of social support networks on medical health outcomes (House et al., 1988). Although these outcome studies have not directly examined the association of social support to HPA axis functioning, the central role of cortisol in mediating some damaging effects of serious medical illness may partially explain how social relationships seem to exert a protective effect. As secure patterns of mother–infant attachment lead to the development of positive relationships of social support in resilient individuals, it may be that these supportive relationships continue to serve as a buffer against risk, in part by attenuating cortisol secretion under stress.

Protective Environments and the HPA Axis

Beyond the effect of internal locus of control and secure attachment on HPA axis function, predictability in the environment is also known to modulate the secretion of cortisol (Gunnar, Marvinney, Isensee, & Fisch, 1989; Levine, 1985). Cortisol is secreted in a predictable diurnal rhythm, which is highly responsive to sleep–wake cycles and other environmental cues, called *zeitgebers,* or time keepers (Moore-Ede, Sulzman, & Fuller, 1982). Such diurnal rhythms, and the resultant rhythmic neurohormonal secretions, regulate the internal milieu of the body. In a predictable and regulated family environment, often seen in the homes of resilient youths, diurnal variations of neuroendocrine function would become well established, perhaps leaving children less vulnerable to stress. It may be that families that have predictable rules, routines, and consistent discipline, where a parent rises each day to go to work, are unwittingly entraining the HPA axis and buffering against excessive stress responses.

Inborn Resiliency in the HPA Axis

In addition to the shaping influences of the environment and social relationships on development, certain individuals may be genetically or congenitally endowed with superior HPA axis functioning. For example, many resilient youths are born as infants with so-called easy temperament, which is characterized by having strong endogenous rhythmicity, regularity in sleep–wake and feeding cycles, and predominantly positive emotionality. Even from birth some newborns, classified as "extremely healthy," have characteristic differences in cortisol response to stressors than do other newborns with temperamental difficulties (Gunnar, 1992). Specifically, these presumably resilient infants rapidly adjust to repeated stressors, return to baseline cortisol levels faster after a stressor, and tolerate physical handling comfortably, despite cortisol elevations. Most likely that optimal HPA axis functioning and resiliency can be arrived at, or thwarted by, both congenital characteristics and neurobiological shaping at the hands of the environment.

AUTONOMIC AGILITY AND THE RESILIENT CHILD

The autonomic nervous system (ANS) regulates many of the body's automatic and instinctive physiological systems, ranging from cardiovascular homeostasis and gastrointestinal digestion to protective responses such as "fight or flight" reactions. The ANS is composed of two subsystems that largely oppose and counteract each other: the sympathetic nervous system (SNS) and the parasympathetic system (PNS). Much work has been done to elucidate the functions and malfunctions of the SNS in response to stress or danger. In normal situations of threat, the SNS responds by increasing cardiovascular capacity, increasing blood flow to somatic musculature, heightening mental and emotional arousal, and mobilizing metabolic resources for "fight or flight." Considerably less attention has been paid to emerging evidence that the PNS may play a central role in mediating key aspects of adaptive functioning. Traditionally, the PNS has been viewed as the "vegetative" component of the autonomic nervous system, predominantly consisting of the ramifying vagus nerve, responsible for functions of digestion and slowing the heart rate. The PNS has been understood to oppose the excitatory effects of the SNS. In fact, recent work has suggested that the vagus, in concert with other cranial nerve components of the PNS, has a much broader function in emotional regulation and social engagement and may serve as an "antistress" system, with important implications for psychosocial resiliency (Porges, 1997; Uvnas-Moberg, 1997).

Functional Neuroanatomy of the PNS

Based on careful neuroanatomic and functional studies of the vagus nerve, in addition to phylogenetic analysis of vagal function in other nonhuman species, a "polyvagal" theory has been developed to account for the integrated function of the PNS in humans and other mammals (Porges, 1997). This theory provides evidence that the PNS is not only involved in vegetative functions such as digestion and heart regulation, but also plays a substantial role in emotional regulation. The vagus nerve, which accounts for most of the overall PNS function, originates from two separate sets of nerve cells (nuclei) in the brain stem. One of these nuclei, the dorsal motor nucleus (DMX), is a phylogenetically ancient structure that stimulates the digestive tract and exerts low tonic influences to slow the heart and constrict the bronchi of the lungs. The other source nucleus of the vagal nerve, the nucleus ambiguus (NA), is a more recent mammalian adaptation that integrates incoming neural stimuli from the cranial nerves of facial expression and oral function, while providing neural stimulation to the heart, bronchi, larynx, pharynx, and esophagus. This configuration of neural circuits provides the capacity to integrate the complex emotional expressions of the face with important physiological responses of the organism.

The NA, as part of the ventral vagal complex (VVC), arises developmentally from the same embryonic branchial arches that give rise to the cranial nerves responsible for facial expression, sucking, swallowing, vocalization, and attending to auditory stimuli in the frequency range of the human voice (via orienting responses and middle ear muscle functioning). Functionally, a primary role of the VVC is to maintain a strong suppressive influence on the cardiovascular fight-or-flight response, acting as a "vagal brake" on the excitatory discharge from the sympathetic nervous system (Porges, Doussard-Roosevelt, Portales, & Greenspan, 1996). Additionally, the VVC coordinates both the sensory and motor function of many of the cranial nerves of facial and vocal expressiveness, creating a role for the PNS in the modulation of social engagement. Both the ability to dampen the SNS response to stressors and the role in processing and executing social and emotional interaction provide ways in which the PNS may serve as a neurophysiological substrate for psychosocial resiliency.

Techniques for the measurement of vagal tone and reactivity (which is a reflection of overall PNS function), by derivation from variations in cardiac respiratory sinus dysrythmia, has allowed researchers to study the relation between PNS function and emotional regulation (Porges, 1986). Vagal tone increases during the course of early development but eventually maintains some stability within an individual as a "trait." However, it also rises and falls under a variety of stimulus conditions, reflecting "state changes," measured as vagal reactivity or responsivity. The polyvagal theory of emotional regulation allows that individuals with high vagal tone, and the ability to exquisitely regulate vagal tone, will possess a neurobiological protective factor contributing to exceptional stress coping and emotional regulation. Conversely, the inability to apply timely or adequate vagal tone to suppress the potentially damaging effects of SNS-mediated stress responses would be expected to increase susceptibility to stressors (Porges, 1992).

Autonomic Dysregulation and Psychosocial Risk

The functioning of the autonomic nervous system shows characteristic interindividual variability, which is first seen in the congenital temperament types of young children. Infants with certain high-risk temperament types, such as shy or behaviorally inhibited children, are known to have an exceptionally reactive sympathetic nervous system and HPA axis (Kagan, Resnick, & Snidman, 1987). These reactive neurophysiological systems are thought to be partially responsible for excesses in emotional reactivity and stress responsiveness, respectively. Likewise, infants with so-called difficult temperament (negative emotionality, high motor activity, stress reactivity, dysrhythmia) are thought to have in-born abnormalities of the autonomic nervous system (Thomas, Chess, & Korn, 1982). Consistent with these findings, abnormalities of the vagal tone component of PNS function have been noted in infants with features of difficult temperament (Porges et al., 1994; Stifter, Fox, & Porges, 1989). Vagal tone abnormalities have also been found in a variety of other high-risk conditions, including hyperactive–inattentive children, medically compromised premature infants, and adult neurosurgical patients who suffer excessive morbidity. (Donchin, Constantini, Szold, Byrne, & Porges, 1992; Porges et al., 1994).

Evidence indicates that some deficits in socioemotional communication are associated with problems in vagal regulation. For example, infants with a predominance of negative or unreactive facial expressiveness have been shown to have lower vagal tone than those with more positive affective expressions (Stifter et al., 1989). Infants born to depressed mothers show less orientation to social stimuli and fewer facial expressions, along with lower vagal tone, in comparison to infants of nondepressed mothers (Field, Pickens, Fox, Nawrocki, & Gonzalez, 1995; Lundy, Field, & Pickens, 1996). Shy or behaviorally inhibited children have been found to have abnormalities of neural outflow from the NA to the vocal cords, causing increased muscle tension under stressful conditions, suggesting compromise of parasympathetic regulatory function through the VVC (Kagan et al., 1987; Porter, Porges, & Marshall, 1988). Conceivably, certain aspects of major psychiatric syndromes, including schizophrenia and childhood autism, that are characterized by constricted or inappropriate affect, poor social engagement, and abnormalities in vocalization may in part reflect problems in vagal regulation.

Beyond congenital temperament, autonomic abnormalities can also be induced by powerful postnatal experiential influences, such as child abuse, which results in autonomic nervous system dysregulation and concomitant emotional and affective and behavioral abnormalities (Perry, 1994). Adult victims of chronic stress or serious trauma have been shown to develop increased heart rates, elevated blood pressure, increased galvanic skin responses, and exaggerated startle response, which might arise either from excessive SNS activity or down-regulation of the PNS (Krystal, Kosten, Perry, Southwick, & Mason, 1989). Also, both shy and difficult temperament types are at increased risk of psychopathogenesis from the effects of trauma, which may be mediated by autonomic vulnerability in these children (Lonigan, Shannon, Taylor, Finch, & Sallee, 1994). Clearly, autonomic function has developmental influences that are both congenital (either genetic endowment or shaped within the prenatal environment) and shaped postnatally, as experience unfolds against the backdrop of underlying neurophysiological make-up.

Protective Effects of Strong and Flexible Parasympathetic Functioning

A number of findings on the individual variability in PNS functioning comprise a possible neurobiological mechanism for some aspects of psychosocial resiliency. For example, the protective factors of inborn "easy" temperament and confident gregariousness in resilient infants and toddlers seem to be associated with high and reactive vagal tone (Porges et al., 1996). In resilient individuals, these qualities of positive early temperament seem to progress to later social competence, evidenced by likeability, the ability to get along well with others, a sense of humor, and keen empathic abilities. Because the vagal brain stem nuclei and closely related parasympathetic components of the cranial nerves are integral in modulating facial and vocal expressiveness, these social skills may be underpinned by exceptional PNS functioning of resilient individuals.

In contrast to the problems created by ANS dysregulation, high vagal tone and capacity for vagal reactivity have been associated with adaptive or resilient functioning. Relatively high vagal tone has been shown to predict better medical outcomes among infants in neonatal intensive care and among adults in post-neurosurgical care (Donchin et al., 1992; Doussard-Roosevelt, Porges, Scanlon, Alemi, & Scanlon, 1997). In research with infants, high vagal tone has been associated with enhanced visual recognition memory, greater ability to sustain attention, more rapid habituation to novel visual stimuli, more advanced neurological development, and positive emotionality as measured by facial expression and vocalizations (Bazhenova & Porges, 1997; Field et al., 1995; Huffman, Bryan, Pedersen, & Porges, 1988; Linnemeyer & Porges, 1986). Together, these findings may suggest that maintaining high resting vagal tone may contribute to the developmental processes, neurocognitive development, rapid habituation, and positive emotionality, some of which are features of "easy" temperament.

As with the HPA axis, studies of the ANS suggest that not only the tonic levels of the system are important, but also the reactivity of the system seems to be crucial to adaptive functioning. For example, infant studies have shown that the ability to apply the "vagal brake" serves as a protective factor against the development of behavior problems early in life (Porges et al., 1996). The vagal brake is the ability to withdraw vagal tone in situations demanding attentiveness. This ability has also been noted in studies of adult subjects classified as "ego-resilient," defined psychologically by an ability to adapt flexibly to environmental demands and use effective problem-solving skills as needed (Block & Block, 1980). Specifically, such ego-resilient individuals showed an anticipatory withdrawal of vagal tone before and during a major cognitive stressor yet quickly returned to a higher level of resting vagal tone than "low ego-resiliency" subjects after the challenge (Spangler, 1997). Similarly, support exists demonstrating that adolescent delinquents, who later desist from adult criminality, have higher autonomic reactivity than their recidivistic counterparts, as measured by heart rate and galvanic skin responses to orienting auditory stimuli (Brennan et al.,1997; Raine, Phil, Venables, & Williams, 1995). Although these results have often been interpreted to mean that desistors had higher SNS reactivity, such relative autonomic reactivity may reflect an exceptional ability for these resilient individuals to quickly remove suppressive tonic vagal influences (apply the vagal brake) in the presence of orienting stimuli. This capacity for parasympathetic "agility" may explain the observed autonomic reactivity, possibly allowing desistors to be more emotionally responsive and perhaps more empathic, lowering their potential for antisocial behaviors. Other supportive findings show that youths with persistent antisocial behavior have been shown to have diminished cardiac vagal modulation (Mezzacappa, et al., 1997).

"Emotional intelligence" has been described as the capacity to get along well in social situations, accurately read the emotions of oneself and others, control one's emotions, and thereby achieve success in interpersonal and vocational settings (Goleman, 1995). These features of personality correspond closely to the social skills that have been repeatedly identified in resilient individuals: ability to get along with others, likeability, empathic ability, and sense of humor. Exceptional emotional intelligence may rely in part on an exceptional ability of key components of the PNS to read and respond to emotional states and effectively produce well-controlled psychophysiological responses in interpersonal situations while inhibiting SNS arousal.

It is not known how plastic or changeable vagal functioning is, although vagal tone is enhanced in a variety of positive social interactions, including massage and gentle tactile stroking, reunion of infants and mothers after separation, and during sexual activity (reviewed by Uvnas-Moberg, 1997). In contrast, a variety of drugs, such as tricyclic antidepressants and alcohol, cause systematic depression of vagal tone (Donchin, Feld, & Porges, 1985). In any case, it seems likely that strength and flexibility of the PNS well serves the resilient child. The good fortune of an easy temperament in infancy enables positive emotional engagement and the effortless formation of important early social attachments. As the easy temperament evolves into the social skills of an engaging personality, a flexible PNS may call forth charm or a poker face as needed, while it helps dampen the disorganizing effects of sympathetic storms, assisting the cortex in allowing for competent emotional functioning, even in adversity.

NEUROBIOLOGICAL ASPECTS OF ATTACHMENT, RELATIONSHIPS, AND SOCIAL SUPPORT

Oxytocin and the Effect of Relationships

A variety of neurobiological systems are involved in the development of social relationships, starting in infancy with the emergence of stereotypical mother–infant attachment behaviors. Early attachment progresses to acquiring social skills in childhood and finally to building social support networks later in life. These complex human social behaviors, which have great relevance to the emergence of either stress vulnerability or psychosocial resilience, are undoubtedly multiply determined by a variety of interacting functions of the nervous system. The effect of the mother–infant attachment phenomena and social support systems on the HPA axis, as well as the importance of the autonomic nervous system in contributing to temperament type and social skills, has been reviewed. Certainly cerebral cortical functions contribute to the development of healthy relationships, and these will be discussed subsequently. In addition, strong evidence in a variety of mammal species, and suggestive evidence in humans, indicates that certain brain neuropeptides, especially oxytocin (OT), are crucially involved in affiliative social behaviors.

Oxytocin is a neuropeptide that has long been known to promote milk expression in response to nipple stimulation during breastfeeding, as well as to strengthen uterine contraction at the time of childbirth. These functions are mediated by its release to the periphery through the posterior pituitary gland. Within the brain, the hypothalamus projects OT to areas of the limbic system, including the amygdala and hippocampus, and to the autonomic structures of the brain stem, including the vagal nuclei, where it is thought to stimulate vagal outflow. As a result, OT release in the brain and periphery has profound psychophysiological effects that include lowered sympathoadrenal tone, elevated vagal tone, relaxation, and behavioral calm.

OT appears necessary for the initiation of maternal behaviors in several mammal species (Keverne & Kendrick, 1992; Pedersen & Prange, 1979). Synthesized and stored in massive amounts in the maternal hypothalamus during the prenatal period, it is released with the cervical stimulation of childbirth. The effect of exposure of the infant to circulating OT is thought to account for the impressive social learning abilities of the infant, who almost immediately begins to selectively attend to the smells, vocalizations, and visual cues of his or her mother (Corter & Fleming, 1995; DeCasper & Spence, 1986; Nelson & Panksepp, 1996).

Breastfeeding, through nipple stimulation, repeatedly releases OT in the mother, likely serving to strengthen the attachment to the nursing infant. Breastfeeding also has been shown to have antistress and anxiolytic effects on the nursing mother (Lightman, 1996). Thus, the interaction of sensory and hormonal influences is rapidly integrated in the brains of both the mother and infant to initiate the process of maternal behavior and attachment. Plasma levels of OT in newly postpartum women have been positively correlated with personality features of attachment, calm, and social dependency (Uvnas-Moberg et al., 1993).

Beyond the profound effects of OT in mother–infant bonding, evidence suggests that it may have an important role in mediating a wide variety of social and affiliative behaviors (reviewed by Carter, 1992; Insel, 1997). For example, OT is known to promote monogamous pair-bonding in certain mammalian species (Carter, DeVries, & Getz, 1995). It is also secreted in a pulsatile manner during sexual orgasm in male and female humans and has a variety of functions to both promote and terminate sexual activity in other mammalian species (Carter, 1992). A variety of nonsexual social sensory stimuli, which commonly occur in the context of close relationships, such as light touch and giving or receiving massage, release OT peripherally and may release central OT (Uvnas-Moberg, 1997). It is no surprise, therefore, that massage has been shown to reduce anxiety and lower cortisol levels in humans and that the relative frequency of positive physical touch during childhood correlates with adolescent mental health (Field et al., 1992; Gonzalez et al., 1994; Pearce, Martin, & Wood, 1995). The release of OT in those who nurture others, as has been demonstrated in mothers, and in those who administer massage may help to explain the psychosocial protective effects of empathic and nurturant personality characteristics. It may be that OT release in those who commonly use altruism as a "mature" psychological defense contributes to their associated positive mental health (Vaillant, 1971).

Support exists for the suspicion that repeated positive social interactions, with central OT release, may serve to induce long-term potentiation of vagally mediated antistress mechanisms (Uvnas-Moberg, 1997), providing a potential neurobiological pathway by which nurturant relationships may foster resiliency via vagal mechanisms. For example, OT receptors have been identified in a number of peripheral immune cells and tissues and provide a possible explanation of some of the beneficial effects of social support on recovery from medical illnesses. Afferent vagal pathways, which are stimulated by circulating OT, often transduce peripheral immune regulatory signals, such as interleukin activation, into brain and behavioral responses, providing another potential mechanism by which social interactions might induce vagal afferent pathways to modulate immune functioning (Bluthe, Dantzer, & Kelley, 1997).

Even as secure and positive social relationships seem to attenuate stress, in some cases, stressful conditions may actually enhance the process of social bond formation. Mounting evidence indicates that stressful conditions and high HPA activity may actually facilitate the actions of OT in promoting monogamous bonding in prairie voles (DeVries, DeVries, Taymans, & Carter, 1996). In humans, studies have shown that the extremely high levels of cortisol seen in both mothers and infants at the time of birth, in conjunction with high levels of OT, enhance olfactory and auditory learning in both the mother and infant, thereby facilitating the formation of the attachment relationship (Corter & Fleming, 1995; DeCasper & Spence, 1986; Nelson & Panksepp, 1996). High levels of cortisol (or stress) in new mothers has also been shown to increase maternal affective responsiveness to crying infants (Fleming, Stallings, Steiner, Corter, & Worthman, 1997), one component of competent maternal attachment behavior. The presence of many OT receptors in the hippocampus, a site for long-term emotional memory storage, may explain why OT-mediated social bonds are highly specific relationships to particular individuals over a long time (i.e., mother-infant attachments, monogamous bonds). Infants, like resilient survivors of childhood trauma, do not seem to bond haphazardly but instead benefit from enduring relationships with very specific, caring individuals (Zimrin, 1986).

Other examples of "stress bonding," such as the close relationships formed between men in combat (Milgram, 1986), may be explained by the finding that significant stressors or prolonged exposure to glucocorticoids increase OT receptor numbers and sensitivity in areas of the hippocampus that may in turn facilitate bond formation, while partially attenuating the stress response (Liberzon & Young, 1997). Excessive HPA reactivity is associated with behavioral disorders in some teenagers, but ironically, pregnant teenagers with a highly reactive HPA axis seem to enjoy some protection against poor psychosocial adjustment during and shortly after the pregnancy (Dorn, Susman, & Petersen, 1993). In the hormonal context of pregnancy, the ability to generate high cortisol levels for brief periods of time may facilitate both the bond formation with the unborn infant and the formation of helpful and supportive social relationships during and after the pregnancy. Together, these findings suggest that stressed organisms may increase their sensitivity to OT, which in turn may function to increase affiliative social bond formation, thus serving as a buffer on the stressed system. The exceptional ability of resilient children to tolerate inordinate stress appears to be explained in part by their frequent use of close social attachments as a shield against adversity.

Finally, it is tempting to wonder whether oxytocin, or its vagally mediated effects, explain the powerful protective effect of several factors that consist simply of certain perceptions. For example, the simple perception of feeling cared for by one's parent serves as a psychosocial protective factor, independent of the objective quality of the relationship. Just as the perception of internal locus of control modulates the HPA axis, the perception of being loved may result in the stimulation of OT mechanisms, with consequent stress-buffering effects. Even the positive bio-psycho-social effects of inner religious faith and attendance at religious services (Koehnig, 1997; Wallis, 1996), which are shown to exert positive effects on both medical and emotional health, might conceivably be mediated by OT release in response to the belief that one prays to a divine entity that truly cares. Attendance at religious services recently has been shown to be associated with improved biological parameters of immune function in elderly human beings, affecting interleukin levels, which are known to modulate social behaviors via vagal-mediated mechanisms in mice (Bluthe et al., 1997; Koehnig et al., 1997). Further, certain types of meditation—which might be equated with prayer—act to lower baseline cortisol levels and enhance HPA responsivity, thus creating the characteristics of a maximally resilient HPA axis (MacLean et al., 1997). Abstractions such as faith, hope, and prayer, which serve resilient youths, may soon be demonstrated to have a discrete neurobiological mechanism by which their positive effects are mediated.

COMPETENCE, CONFIDENCE, AND TESTOSTERONE

A number of the known psychosocial protective factors are related to the acquisition of certain childhood competencies, such as being a competent student, being involved in extracurricular activities, or even having the perception of competence. These various experiences of success, particularly during the school years, have been shown to propel some high-risk children onto a more positive life course (Rutter, 1985a). In fact, immersing oneself in the role of a student, or some extracurricular pursuit, and the accompanying perception of competency, corresponds to the use of sublimation, as one of the highest order, or mature, psychological defenses against stress (Vaillant, 1971). In essence, these activities rely not so much on excellence as they do on participation and the benefits derived therein. However, social ascendancy through achievement, and perhaps merely the perception of competency, may carry with them special neurobiological advantages.

In this light, some recent findings on testosterone should be mentioned because they relate to putative neuroendocrine mechanisms of resiliency. First, neuroendocrine studies of nonhuman, primate social dominance hierarchies have revealed elevated levels of testosterone among dominant individuals, as expected, but also among certain submissive individuals. These high testosterone but lower-ranking individuals succeed by avoiding the power struggles of the dominance hierarchy and instead obtain mating opportunities by forming close social affiliations or "friendships" with female companions, with whom they eventually mate (Sapolsky, 1991). These same studies have also shown that high levels of psychosocial stress with cortisol elevation are generally associated with suppression of testosterone levels. However, dominant males and the aforementioned "socially competent" submissive individuals, seem to be able to sustain testosterone levels despite stress and cortisol elevations. These findings in primates suggest that testosterone levels correspond roughly to social and reproductive success and that levels may change in response to social context. Furthermore, although stress and cortisol generally suppress testosterone, social success seems to be able to sustain testosterone levels in the face of stress.

In humans, testosterone has been found to show short-term increases and decreases in response to social victories and defeats, respectively (McCaul, Gladue, & Joppa, 1992). This same study revealed a strong association of elevated testosterone to a sense of pleasure and positive mood, an affective state that would be expected to facilitate prosocial behaviors. In a recent study of young adolescent males, higher levels of testosterone were found to correlate not so much with persistent aggression, as is often assumed, but instead with social dominance, as assessed by peers (Schaal, Tremblay, Soussignan, & Susman, 1996). In this context, boys thought to be socially dominant by peer nomination (these boys might also be thought of as likeable or popular) have higher levels of testosterone and benefit from the psychosocial protective effects of likeability and the social support of peers, which may well be mediated in part by their positive affective states. In contrast, boys who are persistently aggressive, unpopular, and often failing in school are more likely to have high levels of cortisol and suppressed levels of testosterone. The profoundly damaging psychosocial effects of peer rejection are well documented (Coie, Dodge, & Kuperschmidt, 1990). Hence, the effects of testosterone elevations in response to "social victories" during childhood (such as the acquisition of certain competencies, and leading to likeability and peer support) may also decrease the effect of social stress by creating relative resistance to the suppressive effects of cortisol and some degree of psychosocial buffering. In short, success as a student or in other extracurricular endeavors may build the perception of competence, bolster confidence, and boost testosterone.

Testosterone's significance for girls—if any—is not known. Although absolute plasma levels of testosterone are lower for females than for males, performance on certain visual–spatial cognitive tasks was still strongly related to absolute levels of testosterone, even in females (Gouchie & Kimura, 1991). Conceivably, the dynamics of testosterone level in females, although lower in absolute terms, may also have a beneficial effect in realms of competence and confidence, much as it does in males.

CEREBRAL CORTEX AND COGNITIVE PROCESSING IN RESILIENCY

The human brain is notable in the animal kingdom for the relative enormity of the cerebral cortex. Many aspects of higher intellectual functioning are attributable to the ability of cortical networks of neurons to interact and formulate adaptive responses to environmental challenges. The exceptional adaptive capacities of resilient individuals are probably in part the result of a variety of exceptional cortical capacities. Protective factors such as high intelligence quotient, good problem-solving and planning skills, good reading abilities, sense of humor, perception of internal locus of control, realistic hopes and expectations for the future, and the use of religious faith and prayer are all mental processes that require the complex associational functions of the cerebral cortex and other interpretive structures of the brain.

Recent formulations of the functional organization of human cognition indicate that the brain consists of interactive neural "modules" that perform distinct cognitive tasks, such as forming visual images, attending to the environment, planning motor movements, or comprehending language (Gazzaniga, 1989). Clearly, no single module can be thought of as the seat of intelligence; rather the integrated interactions between modules generates intellect. Individuals may vary greatly with respect to the functional abilities of the various neurocognitive modules, reflecting the existence of "multiple intelligences" (Gardner, 1983). Perhaps some of the unique capacities of resilient individuals, such as the use of humor, creativity, and problem-solving skills, may arise from the unconstrained and liberal associative interactions of seemingly unrelated cortical modules (Masten, 1986).

Interestingly, several of the known psychosocial protective factors relate to particular patterns of anticipation and perceptual interpretation. These factors include realistic hopes and expectations for one's future, the use of planning, the perception of internal locus of control, and the perception of being cared for, whether by one's social supports or by faith in a divine power. These capacities are higher cognitive processes that require careful modulation of perceptual interpretations and particular assumptions about cause and effect. Neuropsychological observations on split-brain patients suggest that humans are endowed with a particularly important neurocognitive module that has been called "the interpreter," which allows the integration and interpretation of cause and effect among a variety of sensory inputs to the brain (Gazzaniga, 1988). Studies of resilient individuals suggest that their interpreter function is biased toward specific patterns of interpretation that can be seen as "protective perceptions." For example, in the psychological testing of people resistant to the development of learned helplessness under stress, it emerges that such individuals tend to internalize credit for positive life events while they externalize blame for the negative (Seligman, 1991).

The interpretation and anticipation of life experiences are perhaps the most complex performances of the human brain. In addition to involving the associational areas of the cerebral cortex, a great deal of interpretation and reaction to both aversive and rewarding experiences is carried on in the limbic system, specifically the amygdala and hippocampus (reviewed by LeDoux, 1995). With concurrent input from the cortex, processing within various nuclei of the amygdala seems to be responsible for interpreting incoming sensory experiences as stressful and projecting a variety of efferents to activate the SNS and the HPA, while suppressing the PNS. In contrast, when positive or rewarding stimuli are processed within the amygdala and hippocampus, certain coping responses or social approach rather than flight behaviors are produced (Gaffan, 1992; Jacobson & Sapolsky, 1991).

Regarding the genesis of such resilient cerebral cortical functioning, the neurodevelopmental literature is replete with evidence of the salubrious effects of early exposure to diverse sensorimotor experiences, as well as the damaging effects of deprivation. The limits of neurocognitive recovery in the face of early deprivation or damage are currently being studied, and remarkable plasticity has been observed in some studies. For example, a great deal of language function has been shown to develop (albeit delayed), even in children who suffered massive infarcts of the crucial left hemisphere language regions in infancy (Bates et al., 1997). The investigators noted that a variety of language functions can be co-opted or compensated for by unexpected brain regions, suggesting a remarkable degree of plasticity. The power of experiences and interventions in late life, such as near-death experiences, religious conversion, and even psychotherapy to change an individual's adaptive functioning suggests brain plasticity exists to some degree through the life span (Frank & Frank, 1991; Raft & Andresen, 1986). The current understanding of the neurobiology of learning suggests that repeatedly experiencing highly rewarding or positive emotional stimuli, or practicing effective coping behaviors, will result in long-term synaptic potentiation of these neural circuits, thus lowering the threshold for similar events in the future of the organism (Brown et al., 1988). Arguably, the prodigious size of the human cortex, with its capacity for creating new neural associations, learning, and adaptive responses throughout the life cycle, has facilitated evolutionary success.

CONCLUSION

Resiliency theory has emerged in recent years as a powerful explanation of the observation that certain individuals somehow escape the effect of severe and multiple psychosocial risk factors. To predict psychosocial outcomes among high-risk individuals, it has become crucial not only to account for the negative effect of risk factors, but also for the buffering effects of existing protective factors. As a result, the paradigm of resiliency theory has profound implications for outcomes research, as well as prevention and intervention strategies, in children's social and health services. For example, in research designs, failing to account for the existence of various protective factors in a study population could easily lead to misinterpretation of the effect of interventions, because both risk factors *and* the level of relative resiliency are known to affect outcomes. In terms of clinical assessment, and prevention or intervention strategies, programs that identify and build on existing protective factors may best serve high-risk populations. Failure to aggressively promote protective factors may account for the apparent failure of many traditional intervention strategies in high-risk populations.

Some research challenges the utility of the concept of resilience when it refers to an absolute invulnerability of certain individuals to the ill effects of stress. Among a large group of impoverished, urban, high-risk youths, one study failed to find any youth who totally escaped problems in functioning (Tolan, 1996). Others have pointed out that certain putative psychosocial protective factors may, in certain settings, actually act as risk factors for increased problems (Luthar & Zigler, 1991). However, it is important to recognize that resilience, as defined by exceptional coping with adversity, must be a relative construct, because no bio-psycho-social system is absolutely invulnerable to extreme perturbation. Long-term follow-up studies of adults who were classified as resilient high-risk youths have found that they often suffer from mild or moderate psychosomatic and internalized psychosocial ailments, even as they continue to function well in their adult lives (Werner, 1989). The concept of psychosocial resilience is strengthened by the acknowledgement that it is a relative phenomenon and it arises through the ongoing developmental interaction of a variety of protective factors with the neurobiological systems of an individual. Likewise, as with any neurobiological feature of an individual, we may discover that certain individuals are congenitally or genetically endowed with exceptional functioning in specific neurobiological systems, which in turn contribute to an easier acquisition of relative psychosocial resiliency through the course of development.

Ironically, members of the mental "health" profession have traditionally concerned themselves with the study of discrete disorders and the process of psychopathogenesis. As a result, a great deal of research has closely examined the neurobiological effect of stress and the effects of risk factors in generating bio-psycho-social disorders. This focus on mechanisms of psychopathogenesis has resulted in the relative neglect of clarifying the neurobiological mechanisms responsible for the generation of healthy psychophysiological functioning. Much remains to be learned about the neurobiological mechanisms of psychosocial protective factors and how they may serve to reverse or diminish the ravages of various disorders. An overview of what has been discovered suggests that a benefit could be obtained by focusing attention and efforts more strongly on the neurobiological mechanisms by which psychosocial resilience is fostered.

It has been well established, for example, that relatively minor maternal stressors, such as random auditory stimuli, during pregnancy can result in disorders of behavioral stress responsiveness in primate offspring, in comparison to nonstressed control animals (Clarke & Schneider, 1993). It is possible that such an effect arises because of transplacental effects of the maternal HPA axis or sympathetic nervous system on the developing autonomic system and stress axis of the fetus. What has not been well examined is whether the effect of certain ambient psychosocial protective factors for a pregnant mother might neurobiologically induce behavioral *resilience* in the offspring. Could a pregnant mother's immersion in a safe and predictable environment, with regular circadian "zeitgebers" and a strong social support network, facilitate entrainment of a resilient HPA axis in the fetus? Could a close, loving relationship, with plenty of warm touch from a mate, produce oxytocin release in the expectant mother, kindling her own maternal behaviors, promoting bonding to both the unborn infant and available social supports, and enhancing vagal tone with transplacental effects on the developing autonomic nervous system of the infant? Clearly more research is needed to determine whether certain such positive social and environmental experiences might activate neurobiological pathways that in turn contribute to the development of more resilient offspring.

Beyond the intrauterine environment, the neuroendocrine effects of mother–infant attachment have begun to be discovered. With congenitally shy and inhibited children, a secure mother–infant attachment can attenuate an excessive cortisol response to stress (Nachmias et al., 1996). Also, breastfeeding and the warm touch of maternal love release oxytocin in both the mother and infant, facilitating social bonding and at the same time enhance vagal tone. It is not unreasonable to assume that these repetitive influences on the vagus and PNS might produce plastic changes in brain functioning, which extend to the neurobiological components responsible for emotional regulation, within the limbic system and parasympathetic cranial nerve nuclei in the brain stem. These nervous system connections, which are just beginning to be elucidated, provide a possible developmental pathway by which warm social relationships may ultimately promote positive temperamental attributes and competent social skills. Such neurobiological mechanisms may help to explain the profound protective effect of a positive mother–infant relationship, which has been observed to temper the negative effect of risk factors such as shy temperament or early adverse experiences. Finally, conceivably the action of secure attachment serves the developing infant as a first cognitive model of a responsive social milieu, leading eventually to a sense of internal locus of control, with resultant benefits on HPA axis functioning.

The neurobiological effect of a caring relationship may explain why high-risk youths seem to benefit more from the more intimate atmosphere of therapeutic foster homes than they do from stays in more behaviorally oriented group homes (Chamberlain, 1990). Not surprisingly, treatment foster care seems to work by establishing long-term caring relationships with the child, and when compared with group homes, greater gains are seen in psychological and behavioral adjustment and the acquisition of social skills (Reddy & Pfeiffer, 1997). Likewise, entering into a caring relationship with a Big Brother/Big Sister mentor has been shown to have broad therapeutic effects on high-risk children, reducing entry into substance abuse, improving school attendance, decreasing aggression and delinquent behaviors, and improving the quality of their family relationships (Tierney, Grossman, & Resch, 1995). The broad range of effects from the provision of this single protective factor suggests far-reaching bio-psycho-social alterations that might serve to ameliorate some of the deleterious neurobiological effects of a high-risk childhood.

Beyond the effect of caring relationships, high-risk children benefit from the effects of a safe and structured living environment. Neurobiological evidence suggests that environments with predictability, routines, and caring relationships might facilitate the development of well-regulated neuroendocrine systems, prepared to buffer against stressors (Hofer, 1984). Children immersed in such environments are likely to emerge from home with strong periodicity in HPA axis functioning, as well as reactivity and responsivity that has been entrained by responsive social environments. The development of a sense of internal locus of control in this manner might foster the confidence to work at developing skills and competencies, which could translate into "social victories," giving rise to testosterone surges, with further increments in mood state (McCaul, Gladue, & Joppa, 1992). The mood-altering and stress-buffering effects of love, social support, predictability, and competence are likely to arise from a variety of neurobiological substrates and may well be at least as therapeutic as many of the pharmacological or psychotherapeutic interventions currently used to treat high-risk youths.

Whether interventions that somehow instill or impose psychosocial protective factors can turn the tide of discrete psychiatric disorders remains a question. However, if resiliency theory is integrated with recent findings in neuroscience, a significant backdrop for the treatment for high-risk individuals or those with discrete disorders may be to somehow immerse them in protective factors and sustain this while their neurobiological systems are entrained to more adaptive patterns of behavioral and emotional responses. It has been shown by rigorous outcome studies that various extremely high-risk and conduct-disordered youths, treated by the technique of "multi-systemic therapy," which actively promotes the development of child and family protective factors, consistently outperform those treated in conventional mental health or juvenile justice modalities (Henggler et al., 1986).

The neurobiological evidence reviewed here suggests that resilient neurophysiological functioning is characterized by the ability of the individual to maintain tonically low levels of arousal, with the ability to mount proactive, anticipatory responses to a stressor, sustain the response in the midst of the stressor, and quickly return to a healthy pre-stress baseline in the aftermath. Can such a pattern be shaped by psychosocial interventions? Studies of the effect of interventions such as transcendental meditation suggest that plastic changes can occur, even in adult neurophysiological systems, including the HPA axis and cardiovascular function (MacLean et al., 1997; Schneider et al., 1995). Given the remarkable plasticity of the nervous system, and the evolutionary advantages of resiliency in the face of adversity, it seems likely that protective factors may continue to enhance functioning well into old age. For example, support strongly demonstrates that frequent religious involvement and other forms of social support enhance immune functioning and improve health outcomes, even in elderly people (House et al., 1988; Koehnig, 1997).

One of the challenges facing those who work with high-risk children is to elucidate the "active ingredients" contained in the various known protective factors, such that they might design efficient techniques for delivering them to those at risk. As advancements in neuroscience continue to uncover the mechanisms by which experience and neurobiological endowment are translated, one into the other, old arguments of nature versus nurture become less relevant. What becomes more relevant is the discovery of specific interventions that may potentially affect neurobiological substrates underlying resilient functioning. The critical elements of a loving relationship, for example, as manifested by predictable responsiveness, tactile interaction, and the perception of being cared for, seem to exert profound effects on central neuropeptides, the parasympathetic nervous system, and the HPA axis. These neurobiological effects of close relationships may be sufficient to account for the observed psychosocial protective effects of social support. What is needed now is a change in mental health care, away from a narrow focus on simply treating discrete psychopathological disorders toward also promoting specific protective factors that will allow for improved psychosocial outcomes, even in the face of disorder.

Finally, it is hard to overstate the prescience with which Erik Erikson formulated his stages of healthy psychological development, requiring trust, autonomy, initiative, industry, identity, intimacy, generativity, and integrity (Erikson, 1950). The experiential contributors to these standards of psychosocial health are found in the protective factors that have echoed through the resiliency literature. Vaillant (1977) later validated the common psychological defenses used against anxiety and stress by resilient adults: altruism, humor, sublimation, anticipation, and suppression. The early seeds of these qualities are also easily discovered in the life stories of resilient youths. We stand now on the brink of understanding some of the neurobiological underpinnings of these characteristics of resilient individuals.

REFERENCES

Anthony, E. J. (1974). The syndrome of the psychologically invulnerable child. In E. J. Anthony & C. Koupernik (Eds.), *The child and his family: Vol. 3. Children at psychiatric risk* (pp. 529–544). New York: Wiley.

Anthony, E. J., & Cohler, B. J. (1987). Children at high risk for psychosis growing up successfully. In E. J. Anthony & B. J. Cohler (Eds.), *The invulnerable child* (pp. 147–184). New York: Guilford Press.

Ayala-Canales, C. E. (1984). *The impact of El Salvador's civil war on orphan and refugee children.* Unpublished masters thesis, University of California, Davis.

Bandura, A. (1977). Self-efficacy: Toward a unifying theory of behavioral change. *Psychological Review, 84,* 191–215.

Bates, E., Thal, D., Trauner, D., Fenson, J., Aram, D., Eisele, J., & Nass, R. (1997). From first words to grammar in children with focal brain injury. *Developmental Neuropsychology, 13*(3), 275–343.

Bazhenova, O. V., & Porges, S. W. (1997). Vagal reactivity and affective adjustment in infants: Convergent response systems. In S. C. Carter, I. I. Lederhendler, & B. Kirkpatrick (Eds.), *The integrative neurobiology of affiliation* (pp. 469–471). New York: New York Academy of Sciences.

Biederman, J., Rosenbaum, J. F., Bolduc-Murphy, E. A., Faraone, S.V., Chaloff, J., Hirshfeld, D. R., Kagan, J. (1993). A 3-year follow-up of children with and without behavioral inhibition. *Journal of the American Academy of Child & Adolescent Psychiatry, 32,* 814–821.

Block, J., & Block, J. (1980). The role of ego-control and ego-resiliency in the organization of behavior. In W. Collins (Ed.), *Minnesota symposium on child psychology: Vol. 15* (pp. 39–102). Hillsdale, NJ: Lawrence Erlbaum.

Bluthe, R., Dantzer, R., & Kelley, K. W. (1997). Central mediation of the effects of interleukin-1 on social exploration and body weight in mice. *Psychoneuroendocrinology, 22*(1), 1–11.

Bowlby, J. (1988). *A secure base: Parent-child attachment and healthy human development.* New York: Basic Books.

Brennan, P. A., Raine, A., Schulsinger, F., Kirkegaard-Sorensen, L., Knop, J., Hutchings, B., Rosenberg, R., Mednick, S. A. (1997). Psychophysiological protective factors for male subjects at high risk for criminal behavior. *American Journal of Psychiatry, 154*(6), 853–855.

Brown, T. H., Chapman, P. F., Kairiss, E. W., & Keenan, C. L. (1988). Long-term synaptic potentiation. *Science, 242*(4879), 724–728.

Carlson, M., & Earls, F. (1997). Psychological and neuroendocrinological sequelae of early social deprivation in institutionalized children in Romania. In S. C. Carter, I. I. Ledehendler, & B. Kirkpatrick (Eds.), *The integrative neurobiology of affiliation* (pp. 419–428). New York: New York Academy of Sciences.

Carter, C. S. (1992). Oxytocin and sexual behavior. *Neuroscience and Biobehavioral Reviews, 16,* 131–144.

Carter, C. S. (1998). Neuroendocrine perspectives on social attachment and love. *Psychoneuroendocrinology, 23*(8), 779–818.

Carter, C. S., DeVries, A. C., & Getz, L.L. (1995). Physiological substrates of mammalian monogamy: The prairie vole model. *Neuroscience and Biobehavioral Reviews, 19*(2), 303–314.

Chamberlain, P. (1990). Comparative evaluation of specialized foster care for seriously delinquent youths: A first step. *Community Alternatives, 2*(2), 21–36.

Clarke, A. S., & Schneider, M. L. (1993). Prenatal stress has long-term effects on behavioral responses to stress in juvenile rhesus monkeys. *Developmental Psychobiology, 26*(5), 293–304.

Cloninger, C. R. (1987). A systematic method for clinical description and classification of personality variants. *Archives of General Psychiatry, 44*(6), 573–588.

Coie, J. D., Dodge, K. A., & Kuperschmidt, J. B. (1990). Peer group behavior and social status. In S. R. Asher & J. D. Coie (Eds.), *Peer rejection in childhood* (pp. 17–59). Cambridge: Cambridge University Press.

Corter, C. M., & Fleming, A. S. (1995). Psychobiology of maternal behavior in human beings. In M. H. Bornstein (Ed.), *Handbook of parenting: Vol 2. Biology and ecology of parenting* (pp. 87–116). Hillsdale, NJ: Lawrence Erlbaum.

Cummings, J. S., Pelligrini, D. S., Notarius, C. I., & Cummings, E. M. (1989). Children's response to angry adult behavior as a function of marital distress and history of interparent hostility. *Child Development, 60*(5), 1035–1043.

DeCasper, A. J., & Spence, M. J. (1986). Prenatal maternal speech influences newborn's perception of speech sounds. *Infant Behavior & Development, 9*(2), 133–140.

DeVries, A. C., DeVries, M. B., Taymans, S. E., & Carter, C. S. (1996). The effects of stress on social preferences are sexually dimorphic in prairie voles. *Proceedings of the National Academy of Sciences USA, 93*(21), 11980–11984.

Donchin, Y., Constantini, S., Szold, A., Byrne, E. A., & Porges, S. W. (1992). Cardiac vagal tone predicts outcome in neurosurgical patients. *Critical Care Medicine, 20*(7), 942–949.

Donchin, Y., Feld, J. M., & Porges, S. W. (1985). The measurement of respiratory sinus arrhythmia during recovery from isoflurane-nitrous oxide anesthesia. *Anesthesia and Analgesia, 64*(8), 811–815.

Dorn, L. D., Susman, E. J., & Petersen, A. C. (1993). Cortisol reactivity and anxiety and depression in pregnant adolescents: a longitudinal perspective. *Psychoneuroendocrinology, 18*(3), 219–239.

Doussard-Roosevelt, J. A., Porges, S. W., Scanlon, J. W., Alemi, B., & Scanlon, K. B. (1997). Vagal regulation of heart rate in the prediction of developmental outcomes for very low birth weight preterm infants. *Child Development, 68*(2), 173–186.

Elder, G. H. (1974). *Children of the Great Depression.* Chicago: University of Chicago Press.

Erikson, E. (1950). *Childhood and society.* New York: W. W. Norton.

Eysenck, H. J. (1983). Stress, disease, and personality: The "inoculation effect." In C. L. Cooper (Ed.), *Stress research* (pp. 121–146). New York: Wiley.

Farrington, D. P. (1989). Early predictors of adolescent aggression and adult violence. *Violence and Victims, 4*(2), 79–100.

Farrington, D. P. (1991). Childhood aggression and adult violence: Early precursors and later-life outcomes. In D. J. Pepler & K. H. Rubin (Eds.), *The development and treatment of childhood aggression* (pp. 5–29). Hillsdale, NJ: Lawrence Erlbaum.

Felsman, J. K., & Vaillant, G. E. (1987). Resilient children as adults: A 40-year study. In E. J. Anthony & B. J. Cohler (Eds.), *The invulnerable child* (pp. 289–314). New York: Guilford Press.

Field, T., Morrow, C., Valdeon, C., Larson, S., Kuhn, C., & Schanberg, S. (1992). Massage reduces anxiety in child and adolescent psychiatric patients. *Journal of American Academy of Child and Adolescent Psychiatry, 31*(1), 125–131.

Field, T., Pickens, J., Fox, N. A., Nawrocki, T., & Gonzalez, J. (1995). Vagal tone in infants of depressed mothers. *Development and Psychopathology, 7*(2), 227–231.

Fleming, A. S., Stallings, J., Steiner, M., Corter, C., & Worthman, C. (1997, March). Cortisol and testosterone correlates of affective responses to infant cry and odor stimuli in new parents. Paper presentation at Inaugural Meeting of the Society for Behavioral Neuroendocrinology and the 29th Meeting of the Conference on Reproductive Behavior. Baltimore, Maryland.

Frank, J. D., & Frank, J. B. (1991). *Persuasion and healing: A comparative study of psychotherapy.* Baltimore, MD: The Johns Hopkins University Press.

Freedman, M. (1989). Fostering intergenerational relationships for at-risk youth. *Children Today, 18*(2), 10–15.

Friedman, M. J., Charney, D. S., & Deutch, A. Y. (1995). *Neurobiological and clinical consequences of stress: From normal adaptation to post-traumatic stress disorder.* Philadelphia, PA: Lippincott-Raven Publishers.

Furstenburg, F. F., Brooks-Gunn, J., & Morgan, S. P. (1987). *Adolescent mothers in later life.* Cambridge: Cambridge University Press.

Gaffan, D. (1992). Amygdala and the memory of reward. In J. P. Aggleton (Ed.), *The amygdala: Neurobiological aspects of emotion, memory, and mental dysfunction* (pp. 471–483). New York: Wiley-Liss.

Gardner, H. (1983). *Frames of mind: The theory of multiple intelligences.* New York: Basic Books.

Garmezy, N. (1983). Stressors in childhood. In N. Garmezy & M. Rutter (Eds.), *Stress, coping, and development in children* (pp. 43–84). New York: McGraw-Hill.

Garmezy, N., Masten, A., & Tellegen, A. (1984). The study of stress and competence in children. *Child Development, 55*(1), 97–111.

Gazzaniga, M. S. (1988). *Mind matters.* Boston: Houghton Mifflin.

Gazzaniga, M. S. (1989). Organization of the human brain. *Science, 245*(4921), 947–952.

Gold, P. W., Goodwin, F. K., & Chrousos, G. P. (1988). Clinical and biochemical manifestations of depression: Relation to the neurobiology of stress (in two parts). *New England Journal of Medicine, 319*(7), 348–353, 413–420.

Goleman, D. (1995). *Emotional intelligence.* New York: Bantam Books.

Gonzalez, J., Field, T., Yando, R., Gonzalez, K., Lasko, D., & Bendell, D. (1994).

Adolescent's perceptions of their risk-taking behavior. *Adolescence, 29*(115), 701–709.

Gouchie, C., & Kimura, D. (1991). The relationship between testosterone levels and cognitive ability patterns. *Psychoneuroendocrinology, 16*(4), 323–334.

Grossman, A., Perry, L., Schally, A. V., Rees, L. H., Kruseman, A.C.N., Tomlin, S., Coy, D. H., Schally, A.M.C., & Besser, G. M. (1982). New hypothalamic hormone, corticotropin-releasing factor, specifically stimulates the release of adrenocorticotropic hormone and cortisol in man. *Lancet, 24,* 921–922.

Gunnar, M. (1987). Psychobiological studies of stress and coping: An introduction. *Child Development, 58*(6), 1403–1407.

Gunnar, M. (1992). Reactivity of the hypothalamic-pituitary-adrenocortical system to stressors in normal infants and children. *Pediatrics, 90*(3 Suppl. 2), 491–497.

Gunnar, M., Marvinney, D., Isensee, J., & Fisch, R. O. (1989). Coping with uncertainty: New models of the relations between hormonal, behavioral, and cognitive processes. In D. S. Palermo (Ed.), *Coping with uncertainty: Behavioral and developmental perspectives. The Penn State series on child & adolescent development.* (pp. 101–129). Hillsdale, NJ: Lawrence Erlbaum Associates, Inc.

Gunnar, M., Tout, K., de Haan, M., Pierce, S., & Stansbury, K. (1997). Temperament, social competence, and adrenocortical activity in preschoolers. *Developmental Psychobiology, 31*(1), 65–85.

Halpern, R. (1993). Poverty and infant development. In C. H. Zeanah (Ed.), *Handbook of infant mental health* (pp. 73–86). New York: Guilford Press.

Henggler, S. W., Rodick, J. D., Hanson, C. L., Watson, S. M., Borduin, C. M., & Urey, J. R. (1986). Multisystemic treatment of juvenile offenders: Effects on adolescent behavior and family interaction. *Developmental Psychology, 22*(1), 132–141.

Hofer, M. A. (1984). Relationships as regulators: A psychobiological perspective on bereavement. *Psychosomatic Medicine, 46*(3), 183–197.

House, J. S., Landis, K. R., & Umberson, D. (1988). Social relationships and health. *Science, 241*(4865), 540–545.

Huffman, L. C., Bryan, Y. E., Pedersen, F. A., & Porges, S. W. (1988, May). Infant temperament: Relationships with heart rate variability. Paper presented at the Annual Meeting of the Society for Behavioral Pediatrics, Washington, D.C.

Huizinga, D., Loeber, R., & Thornberry, T. P. (1993). Longitudinal study of delinquency, drug use, sexual activity and pregnancy among children and youth in three cities. *Public Health Reports, 108*(1), 90–96.

Hutchings, B., & Mednick, S. A. (1974). Registered criminality in the adoptive and biological parents of registered male adoptees. In S. A. Mednick, F. Schulsinger, J. Higgins, & B. Bell (Eds.), *Genetics, environment and psychopathology* (pp. 215–227). Amsterdam: Basic Books.

Insel, T. R. (1997). A neurobiological basis of social attachment. *American Journal of Psychiatry, 154*(6), 726–735.

Jacobson, L., & Sapolsky, R. (1991). The role of the hippocampus in feedback regulation of the hypothalamic-pituitary-adrenal axis. *Endocrine Reviews, 12*(2), 118–134.

Kagan, J., Reznick, J. S., & Snidman, N. (1987). The physiology and psychology of behavioral inhibition in children. *Child Development, 58*(6), 1459–1473.

Kagan, J., Resnick, J. S., & Snidman, N. (1988). Biological bases of childhood shyness. *Science, 240*(4849), 167–171.

Kendall-Tackett, K., Williams, L., & Finkelhor, D. (1993). The impact of sexual abuse on children: A review and synthesis of recent empirical studies. *Psychological Bulletin, 113*(1), 164–168.

Kendler, K. S. (1997). Social support: A genetic-epidemiologic analysis. *American Journal of Psychiatry, 154*(10), 1398–1404.

Keverne, E. B., & Kendrick, K. M. (1992). Oxytocin facilitation of maternal behavior in sheep. *Annals of New York Academy of Sciences, 652,* 83–101.

Kingston, L., & Prior, M. (1995). The development of patterns of stable, transient, and school-age onset aggressive behavior in young children. *Journal of the American Academy of Child & Adolescent Psychiatry, 34*(3), 348–358.

Koehnig, H. G. (1997). *Is religion good for your health?* New York: Haworth Press.

Koehnig, H. G., Cohen, H. J., George, L. K., Hays, J. C., Larson, D. B., & Blazer, D. G. (1997). Attendance at religious services, interleukin-6, and other biological parameters of immune function in older adults. *International Journal of Psychiatry in Medicine, 27*(3), 233–250.

Krystal, J., Kosten, T., Perry, B., Southwick, S., & Mason, J. W. (1989). Neurobiological aspects of post-traumatic stress disorder: Review of clinical and preclinical studies. *Behavior Therapy, 20*(2), 177–198.

LeDoux, J. E. (1995). Setting "stress" into motion: Brain mechanisms of stimulus evaluation. In M. J. Friedman, D. S. Charney, & A. Y. Deutch (Eds.), *Neurobiological and clinical consequences of stress* (pp. 125–134). Philadelphia, PA: Lippincott-Raven.

Lester, B. M., & Tronick, E. Z. (1994). The effects of prenatal cocaine exposure and child outcome. *Infant Mental Health Journal, 15*(2), 107–120.

Levine, S. (1985). A definition of stress? In G. B. Moberg (Ed.), *Animal stress* (pp. 51–69). Bethesda, MD: American Physiological Society.

Levine, S., & Wiener, S. G. (1989). The physiology of stress and behavioral development. In D. S. Palermo (Ed.), *Coping with uncertainty: Behavioral and developmental perspectives* (pp. 1–16). Hillsdale, NJ: Lawrence Erlbaum.

Levine, S., Lyons, D. M., & Schatzberg, A. F. (1997). Psychobiological consequences of social relationships. In C. S. Carter, I. I. Lederhender, & B. Kirkpatrick (Eds.) *The integrative neurobiology of affiliation* (pp. 210–218). New York: New York Academy of Sciences.

Lewis, D. O. (1992). From abuse to violence: Psychophysiological consequences of maltreatment. *Journal of the American Academy of Child & Adolescent Psychiatry, 31*(3), 383–391.

Liberzon, I., & Young, E. A. (1997). Effects of stress and glucocorticoids on CNS oxytocin receptor binding. *Psychoneuroendocrinology, 22*(6), 411–422.

Lightman, S. (1996, August) Anti-stress effects of lactation. Paper presented at Wenner-Gren Foundations International Symposium: "Is There a Neurobiology of Love?" Stockholm, Sweden.

Linnemeyer, S. A., & Porges, S. W. (1986). Recognition memory and cardiac vagal tone in 6-month-old infants. *Infant Behavior, 9*(1), 43–56.

Livingston, R., Lawson, L., & Jones, J. G. (1993). Predictors of self-reported psychopathology in children abused repeatedly by a parent. *Journal of the American Academy of Child & Adolescent Psychiatry, 32*(5), 948–953.

Loeber, R. (1982). The stability of antisocial and delinquent child behavior: A review. *Child Development, 53*(6), 1431–1446.

Loeber, R., & Stouthamer-Loeber, M. (1986). Family factors as correlates and predictors of juvenile conduct problems and delinquency. In N. Morris & M. Tonry (Eds.), *Crime and justice* (pp. 29–149). Chicago: University of Chicago Press.

Lonigan, C. J., Shannon, M. P., Taylor, C. M., Finch, A. J., Jr., & Sallee, F. R. (1994). Children exposed to disaster. II: Risk factors for the development of post-traumatic symptomatology. *Journal of the American Academy of Child & Adolescent Psychiatry, 33*(1), 94–105.

Lundy, B., Field, T., & Pickens, J. (1996). Newborns of mothers with depressive symptoms are less expressive. *Infant Behavior and Development, 19*(4), 419–424.

Luthar, S. S., & E. Zigler. (1991). Vulnerability and competence: A review of research on resilience in childhood. *American Journal of Orthopsychiatry, 61*(1), 6–22.

MacLean, C.R.K., Walton, K. G., Wenneberg, S. R., Levitsky, D. K., Mandarino, J. P., Waziri, R., Hillis, S. L., & Schneider, R. H. (1997). Effects of the Transcendental Meditation program on adaptive mechanisms: Changes in hormone levels and responses to stress after 4 months of practice. *Psychoneuroendocrinology, 22*(4), 277–295.

Masten, A. S. (1986). Humor and competence in school-aged children. *Child Development, 57,* 461–473.

Masten, A. S., Garmezy, N., Tellegen, A., Pellegrini, D. S., Larkin, K., & Larsen, A. (1988). Competence and stress in school children: The moderating effects of individual and family qualities. *Journal of Child Psychology and Psychiatry, 29*(6), 745–764.

McCaul, K. D., Gladue, B. A., & Joppa, M. (1992). Winning, losing, mood and testosterone. *Hormones and Behavior, 26*(4), 486–504.

McEwen, B. S., Angulo, J., Cameron, H., Chao, H. M., Daniels, D., Gannon, M. N., Gould, E., Mendelson, S., Sakai, R., Spencer, R., & Woolley, C. (1992). Paradoxical effects of adrenal steroids on the brain: Protection versus degeneration. *Biological Psychiatry, 31*(2), 177–199.

Mezzacappa, E., Tremblay, R. E., Kindlon, D., Saul, J. P, Arseneault, L., Seguin, J., Pihl, R. O., & Earls, F. (1997). Anxiety, antisocial behavior and heart rate regulation in adolescent males. *Journal of Child Psychology and Psychiatry, 38*(4), 457–469.

Milgram, N. A. (1986). *Stress and coping in time of war: Generalizations from the Israeli experience.* New York: Brunner-Mazel.

Moore-Ede, M. C., Sulzman, F. M., & Fuller, C. A. (1982). *The clocks that time us.* Cambridge: Harvard University Press.

Moskovitz, S. (1983). *Love despite hate: Child survivors of the Holocaust and their adult lives.* New York: Schocken.

Nachmias, M., Gunnar, M. R., Mangelsdorf, S., Parritz, R. H., & Buss, K. (1996). Behavioral inhibition and stress reactivity: Moderating role of attachment security. *Child Development, 67*(2), 508–522.

Nash, J. M. (1997). Fertile minds. *Time, 149*(5), 48–56.

Nelson, E., & Panksepp, J. (1996). Oxytocin mediates acquisition of maternally associated odor preferences in preweanling rat pups. *Behavior and Neuroscience, 110*(3), 583–592.

Oates, R. K., O'Toole, B. I., Lynch, D. L., Stern, A., & Cooney, G. (1994). Stability and change in outcomes for sexually abused children. *Journal of the American Academy of Child and Adolescent Psychiatry, 33*(7), 945–953.

O'Connor, M. J., Sigman, M., & Brill, N. (1987). Disorganization of attachment in relation to maternal alcohol consumption. *Journal of Consulting and Clinical Psychology, 55*(6), 831–836.

Offord, D. R., Boyle, M. H., Racine, Y. A., Fleming, J. E., Cadman, D. T., Blum, H. M., Byrne, C., Links, P. S., Lipman, E. L., MacMillan, H. L. (1992). Outcome, prognosis, and risk in a longitudinal follow-up study. *Journal of the American Academy of Child and Adolescent Psychiatry, 31*(5), 916–923.

Osofsky, J. D., Hann, D. M., & Peebles, C. (1993). Adolescent parenthood: Risks and opportunities for mothers and infants. In C. H. Zeanah (Ed.), *Handbook of infant mental health* (pp. 106–119). New York: Guilford Press.

Paneth, N. S. (1995). The problem of low birth weight. In R. E. Behrman (Ed.), *The future of children: Low birthweight* (pp. 11–34). Los Altos, CA: David & Lucille Packard Foundation.

Parker, G. R., Cowen, E. L., Work, W. C., & Wyman, P. A. (1990). Test correlates of stress-resilience among urban school children. Manuscript submitted for publication.

Pearce, C. M., Martin, G., & Wood, K. (1995). Significance of touch for perceptions of parenting and psychological adjustment among adolescents. *Journal of the American Academy of Child and Adolescent Psychiatry, 34*(2), 160–167.

Pedersen, C. A., & Prange, A. J., Jr. (1979). Induction of maternal behavior in virgin rats after intracerebroventricular administration of oxytocin. *Proceedings of the National Academy of Science, 76*(12), 6661–6665.

Pelcovitz, D., Kaplan, S., Goldenberg, B., Mandel, F., Lehane, J., & Guarrera, J. (1994). Post-traumatic stress disorder in physically abused adolescents. *Journal of the American Academy of Child and Adolescent Psychiatry, 33*(3), 305–312.

Perry, B. D. (1994). Neurobiological sequelae of childhood trauma: PTSD in children. In M. M. Murburg (Ed.), *Catecholamine function in post-traumatic stress disorder: Emerging concepts* (pp. 233–255). Washington, D.C.: American Psychiatric Press.

Porges, S. W. (1986). Respiratory sinus arrhythmia: Physiological basis, quantitative methods, and clinical implications. In P. Grossman, K. Jaansen, & D. Vaitl

(Eds.), *Cardiorespiratory and cardiosomatic psychophysiology* (pp. 101–115). New York: Plenum.

Porges, S. W. (1992). Vagal tone: A physiological marker of stress vulnerability. *Pediatrics, 90*(3, Pt. 2), 498–504.

Porges, S. W. (1997). Emotion: An evolutionary by-product of the neural regulation of the autonomic nervous system. In S. C. Carter, I. I. Lederhendler, & B. Kirkpatrick (Eds.), *The integrative neurobiology of affiliation* (pp. 62–77). New York: New York Academy of Sciences.

Porges, S. W., Doussard-Roosevelt, J. A., & Maiti, A. K. (1994). Vagal tone and the physiological regulation of emotion. *Monograph of the Society for Research in Child Development, 59*(2, Pt. 3).

Porges, S. W., Doussard-Roosevelt, J. A., Portales, A. L., & Greenspan, S. I. (1996). Infant regulation of the vagal "brake" predicts child behavior problems: A psychobiological model of social behavior. *Developmental Psychobiology, 29*(8), 697–712.

Porges, S. W., Doussard-Roosevelt, J. A., Portales, A. L., & Seuss, P. E. (1994). Cardiac vagal tone: Stability and relation to difficultness in infants and three-year-old children. *Developmental Psychobiology, 27*(5), 289–300.

Porter, F. L., Porges, S. W., & Marshall, R. E. (1988). Newborn pain cries and vagal tone: Parallel changes in response to circumcision. *Child Development, 59*(2), 495–505.

Raft, D., & Andresen, J. J. (1986). Transformations in self-understanding after near-death experiences. *Contemporary Psychoanalysis, 22*(3), 319–346.

Raine, A., Phil, D., Venables, P. H., & Williams, M. (1995). High autonomic arousal and electrodermal orienting at age 15 years as protective factors against criminal behavior at age 29 years. *American Journal of Psychiatry, 152*(11), 1595–1600.

Reddy, L. A., & Pfeiffer, S. I. (1997). Effectiveness of treatment foster care with children and adolescents: A review of outcome studies. *Journal of American Academy of Child and Adolescent Psychiatry, 36*(5), 581–588.

Resnick, H., Yehuda, R., Atman, R., & Foy, D. (1995). Effect of previous trauma on acute plasma cortisol level following rape. *American Journal of Psychiatry, 152*(11), 1675–1677.

Rutter, M. (1978). Early sources of security and competence. In J. S. Bruner & A. Garten (Eds.), *Human growth and development* (pp. 33–60). London: Oxford University Press.

Rutter, M. (1979). Protective factors in children's responses to stress and disadvantage. In M. W. Kent & J. E. Rolf (Eds.), *Primary prevention of psychopathology: Social competence in children, Vol. 3* (pp. 49–74). Hanover, NH: University Press of New England.

Rutter, M. (1985a). Family and school influences on behavioral development. *Journal of Child Psychology and Psychiatry, 26*(3), 349–368.

Rutter, M. (1985b). Resilience in the face of adversity: Protective factors and resistance to psychiatric disorders. *British Journal of Psychiatry, 147*, 598–611.

Rutter, M., Cox, A., Tupling, C., Berger, M., & Yule, W. (1975). Attainment and adjustment in two geographical areas. *British Journal of Psychiatry, 126,* 493–509.

Rutter, M., Dunn, J., Plomin, R., Simonoff, E., Pickles, A., Maughan, B., Ormel, J. Meyer, J., & Eaves, L. (1997). Integrating nature and nurture: Implications of person-environment correlations and interactions for developmental psychopathology. *Development and Psychopathology, 9*(2), 335–364.

Rutter, M., Tizard, J., & Whitmore, K. (1970/1981). *Education, health and behavior.* New York: Krieger.

Sameroff, A. J., & Seifer, R. (1983). Familial risk and child competence. *Child Development, 54*(5), 1254–1268.

Sampson, P. D., Streissguth, A. P., Barr, H. M., & Bookstein, F. L. (1989). Neurobehavioral effects of prenatal alcohol exposure: Part II. Partial least squares analysis. *Neurobehavorial Toxicology and Teratology, 11*(5), 477–491.

Sapolsky, R. M. (1991). Testicular function, social rank and personality among wild baboons. *Psychoneuroendocrinology, 16*(4), 281–293.

Schaal, B., Tremblay, R. E., Soussignan, R., & Susman, E. J. (1996). Male testosterone linked to high social dominance but low physical aggression in early adolescence. *Journal of the American Academy of Child & Adolescent Psychiatry, 34*(10), 1322–1330.

Schneider, R. H., Staggers, F., Alexander, C., Sheppard, W., Rainforth, M., Kondwani, K., Smith, S., & King, C. (1995). A randomized controlled trial of stress reduction in older African-Americans. *Hypertension, 26*(5), 820–827.

Seifer, R., Sameroff, A. J., Baldwin, C. P., & Baldwin, A. (1992). Child and family factors that ameliorate risk between 4 and 13 years of age. *Journal of the American Academy of Child & Adolescent Psychiatry, 31*(5), 893–903.

Seligman, M. (1975). *Helplessness: On depression, development, and death.* San Francisco: W. H. Freeman.

Seligman, M. (1991). *Learned optimism.* New York: Knopf.

Smith, J., & Prior, M. (1995). Temperament and stress resilience in school-age children: A within families study. *Journal of the American Academy of Child & Adolescent Psychiatry, 34*(2), 168–179.

Spangler, G. (1997). Psychological and physiological responses during an exam and their relation to personality characteristics. *Psychoneuroendocrinology, 22*(6), 423–441.

Stifter, C. A., Fox, N. A., & Porges, S. W. (1989). Facial expressivity and vagal tone in five- and ten-month old infants. *Infant Behavior, 12,* 127–137.

Susman, E. J., Dorn, L. D., Inoff-Germain, G., Nottelmann, E. D., & Chrousos, G. P. (1997). Cortisol reactivity, distress behavior, and behavioral and psychological problems in young adolescents: A longitudinal perspective. *Journal of Research on Adolescence, 7*(1), 81–105.

Thomas, A., Chess, S., & Korn, S. J. (1982). The reality of difficult temperament. *Merrill-Palmer Quarterly, 28*(1), 1–20.

Tierney, J. P., Grossman, J. B., & Resch, N. L. (1995) *Making a difference: An impact study of Big Brothers/Big Sisters.* Philadelphia, PA: Public/Private Ventures.

Tolan, P. (1996). How resilient is the concept of resilience? *The Community Psychologist, 4,* 12–15.

Tschann, J. M., Kaiser, P., Chesney, M. A., Alkon, A., & Boyce, W. T. (1996). Resilience and vulnerability among preschool children: Family functioning, temperament, and behavior problems. *Journal of the American Academy of Child & Adolescent Psychiatry, 35*(2), 184–192.

Uvnas-Moberg, K. (1997). Physiological and endocrine effects of social contact. In C. S. Carter, I. I. Lederhendler, & B. Kirkpatrick (Eds.), *The integrative neurobiology of affiliation* (pp. 146–163). New York: New York Academy of Sciences.

Uvnas-Moberg, K., Arn, I., Jonsson, C. O., Ek, S., & Nilsonne, A. (1993). The relationships between personality traits and plasma gastrin, cholescystokinin, somatostatin, insulin, and oxytocin levels in healthy women. *Journal of Psychosomatic Research, 37*(6), 581–588.

Vaillant, G. E. (1971). Theoretical hierarchy of adaptive ego mechanisms: A 30-year follow-up of 30 men selected for psychological health. *Archives of General Psychiatry, 24*(2), 109–118.

Vaillant, G. E. (1977). *Adaptation to life.* New York: Little, Brown and Company.

van der Kolk, B. (1989). The compulsion to repeat the trauma: Re-enactment, revictimization, and masochism. *Psychiatric Clinics of North America, 12*(2), 389–411.

Wallerstein, J. S. (1985). Children of divorce: Preliminary report of a 10-year follow-up of older children and adolescents. *Journal of the American Academy of Child Psychiatry, 28*(5), 545–553.

Wallis, C. (1996). Faith and healing. *Time, 147*(26), 58–63.

Werner, E. E. (1989). High-risk children in young adulthood: A longitudinal study from birth to 32 years. *American Journal of Orthopsychiatry 59*(1), 72–81.

Werner, E. E., & Smith, R. S. (1982). *Vulnerable but invincible: A longitudinal study of resilient children and youth.* New York: Adams, Bannister, Cox.

Werner, E. E., & Smith, R. S. (1992). *Overcoming the odds: High risk children from birth to adulthood.* Ithaca, NY: Cornell University Press.

Widom, C. S. (1989). The cycle of violence. *Science, 244*(4901), 160–166.

Wyman, P. A., Cowen, E. L., Work, W. C., & Parker, G. R. (1991). Developmental and family milieu correlates of resilience in urban children who have experienced major life stress. *American Journal of Community Psychology, 19*(3), 405–426.

Wyman, P. A., Cowen, E. L., Work, W. C., Raoof, A., Gribble, P. A., Parker, G. R., & Wannon, M. (1992). Interviews with children who experienced major life stress: Family and child attributes that predict resilient outcomes. *Journal of the American Academy of Child & Adolescent Psychiatry, 31*(5), 904–910.

Zimrin, H. (1986). A profile of survival. *Child Abuse and Neglect, 10*(3), 339–349.

Zuckerman, M. (1991). *Psychobiology of personality.* New York: Cambridge University Press.

Chapter 4

Making Sense of Senseless Youth Violence

James Garbarino

After years of studying family violence (Garbarino, Eckenrode, & the Family Life Development Center, 1997) and experiencing the senselessness of violence in war zones from the Middle East to Central America (Garbarino, Kostelny, & Dubrow, 1991), I have begun examining senseless violence closer to home, specifically focusing on youths incarcerated for murder or other severely violent acts. This interest began with a visit to a North Carolina youth prison in 1994, when I accompanied an NBC *Dateline* crew to film a segment on violent youth. In the prison, we met three boys, all of whom had shot people. Two of them will probably spend the rest of their lives in prison; the one boy who will be released will probably come back. While consulting with news anchor Stone Phillips, I realized how shallow my expertise was. Serving as an expert witness in several recent youth homicide trials—with children's lives and futures on the line—further reinforced the point for me (Garbarino, 1999). Out of that feeling of inadequacy came an impulse to understand violent youth in a deeper way and to make sense of senseless youth violence (Garbarino, 1999).

GAINING PERSPECTIVE

American society currently mirrors my personal crisis of inadequately understanding youth violence. We do not know what to make of the phenomenon of children who shoot and stab other children and adults. We have invented a new vocabulary of terms such as *superpredator* to refer to children whose aggressive behavior baffles, mystifies, and terrifies us.

The current crisis of these children is not historically new, however. In *Juvenile Justice Update,* Robert Shepherd (1997) cites several historical examples, including a 140-year-old *New York Times* editorial lamenting the "number of boy burglars, boy robbers and boy murderers is so astoundingly large as to alarm all good men" (p. 10). In a 1954 *Saturday Evening Post* article, a child psychiatrist working in Manhattan for the Juvenile Court wrote: "At first it comes as a shock to meet youngsters under 16 who rob at the point of a gun, push dope, rape and kill. I've seen boys of 7 so small they could barely clear the desk who had sold themselves to sex perverts. Others had shot out children's eyes or had clubbed or knifed them, just for the fun of it" (p. 12).

Although the current situation has historical dimensions, some aspects of the problem are distinctly contemporary. The magnitude of the problem is much greater; per capita aggravated assault rates have increased sevenfold since 1956, particularly among adolescents. Historians of childhood have traced the development of the modern concept of the child as different from adults and needing protection from the adult world. But in what seems a macabre return to the medieval conception of children as small adults, children are often tried as adults and incarcerated accordingly.

There are further parallels. The homicide rate in the city of Amsterdam in the year 1450 is estimated to have been 150 per 100,000 people. By 1850, when Amsterdam had been "civilized," the rate dropped to 2 per 100,000. This rate might be taken as a kind of base line for the minimum expectable homicide rate (the lowest rate countries report), the rate we find in most of the truly civilized countries in the world. However, among "medieval" countries such as the United States, rates of 25 per 100,000 are common, and in the most medieval social environments in our world, we find rates of 160 per 100,000 population (Garbarino, 1999). The most medieval environments in our society are those with the most primitive conditions where brutality is at its peak.

Having drawn those historical comparisons, however, my central purpose is to approach this topic psychologically. My mentor Urie Bronfenbrenner maintained this as his prime directive (borrowing from Harry Stack Sullivan): Human behavior is more simply human than otherwise (Garbarino, 1999). Nothing is more important than remembering this point, particularly when we feel the impulse to use dehumanizing descriptions (e.g., "superpredator"), policy (e.g., trying children as adults and sentencing them to life in prison or to death), and practice (e.g., creating barbaric prison conditions to "teach them a lesson"). We deny ourselves the important tool of empathy if we classify another person as monstrous, or if we demonize their behavior. If we cannot empathize with someone else, we will not be able to understand them or their behavior. The question, however, still remains: What and where is the human sense in senseless youth violence?

LISTENING TO BOYS WHO MURDER

My colleague Claire Bedard and I launched a collaboration to address this issue. We began from somewhat different perspectives: myself as an American psychologist, she as a Canadian human rights activist. This difference meant that she came to the topic from a more civilized society than I did, as in my opinion, Canada has less economic inequality, a stronger commitment to human rights in practice and in principle, no death penalty, and greater civility. Her primary concern was the issue of human dignity. Out of this collaboration came an attempt to make sense of senseless youth violence by constructing narrative accounts—the memoirs of violent youth—based on long, detailed, and nonjudgmental interviews with them. We interviewed youths incarcerated for murder and other violent acts in New York State youth prisons.

Giving Voice

We framed our collaboration with three goals. The first goal was to give narrative voice to a previously inarticulate group: boys who have exhibited violent behavior and who have been in the human services system for much of their lives. Bert Cohler (1982) elaborated a concept of narrative coherence as a way of giving meaning to events; early negative life events and the ultimate quality of life are connected primarily by the quality of the narrative account about one's own life that a person can develop. The boys with whom we talked consistently said that prior to our interviews with them, no one had ever asked them to tell their whole story before.

Seeking Justice

The second goal of this project was to understand thoroughly that almost all acts of violence express a need for justice. This insight comes from the work of James Gilligan (1996), a psychiatrist who worked for many years with violent and dangerous men in the Massachusetts prison system. He concluded that acts of violence almost universally result from a powerful need to redress injustice. Such behaviors may be warped and distorted and difficult to fathom from the outside, but if we dig deeply enough and listen openly enough, we may hear of the need to restore justice by personally acting on the feelings of shame that come from being rejected, denied, abused, and deprived. We often hear the terms *respect* and d*isrespect*. Those terms resonate with an individual sense of justice.

Untreated Trauma

The third goal of our study was to remember that inside virtually every violent youth is an untreated, traumatized child. Our legal system blocks out this message over and over. Recent work by research psychiatrists Perry, Pollard, Blakley, Baker, and Vigilante (1995) and van der Kolk (1994) illuminates the neurological processes that shape early trauma into later dangerous behavior through brain development and neurochemistry (see Chapter 3 in this volume). Child abuse and community violence are rampant in the lives of children who become violent youths.

If you spend some time in a nonjudgmental relationship with a violent youth, you may glimpse this. One of the boys I listen to has admitted to six or seven murders. He is as tough as they come. On our fourth or fifth visit, I brought him a book based on an interest he expressed in a previous session. When he realized the book was for him with no strings attached, a tear rolled down his cheek. In subsequent sessions, I heard about the shameful abuse and deprivation he suffered as a child and about the traumatic encounters he had with community violence.

Five "Dark Secrets" of Violence

Beyond our three goals of giving voice, understanding, and remembering, we had a series of operating principles that guided our efforts. These principles constitute five "dark secrets" of violent trauma. The first of these dark secrets I call "Peter's Secret." Peter's life reveals to us that in a socially toxic environment, vulnerable children can choke on violence. From his early experience and his early temperament, Peter seemed programmed to be a psychological asthmatic. When he was dumped into areas of Los Angeles where violence and drug-related violence and gangs are endemic, he succumbed to what that environment teaches; at thirteen, he was tried as an adult on first-degree murder charges.

Peter's secret. The idea of the socially-toxic environment has a parallel in the idea of physical toxicity (Garbarino, 1995). The social environment can have psychological and social poisons, just as there are physical poisons in the physical environment. We know that in physically toxic environments, individual and groups vary in vulnerability. For example, during a smog alert, public health officials and private citizens would worry particularly about children with asthma or old people with emphysema—individuals with some special vulnerability to the environmental poisons. The same applies to social toxicity as well. This observation suggests an explanation for some of the changes that professionals have witnessed during the past forty years in the "troubled" population of children and youth.

A few years ago, the director of a day treatment school for emotionally disturbed children asked me for help. The director said:

> We need help. I started this program in 1970 and I've run the program since then continuously. I've always used the same program models. I've trained the staff the same way. We used the same diagnostic criteria to admit children into the program. We take children from the same neighborhoods we always have. But this program used to work.

Having spent some recent time working with the program, I agree that the program does not work any more. I believe that over the years, these highly vulnerable children have been exposed to increasingly toxic social environments; they have soaked up the aggression, the violence, and the ugliness that flourishes unchecked around them. As a result, the program's effectiveness decreases yearly.

This is a story that many professionals in the field could tell. These vulnerable children need to be understood as "psychological asthmatics" living in an intensifying socially polluted environment. Their distress is an indicator of that environment and a measure of their own vulnerability.

That we live in a gun-oriented culture—with nearly half of all households owning one or more guns—is part of the toxicity (Gabarino, 1999). All of us live in this culture. A few years ago, I interviewed white, middle-class, suburban eight-year olds who explained to me how they could get a gun if they needed it. While most of these relatively sheltered and privileged children will never get a gun because they will never feel a need for it, children who know Peter's secret believe they need a gun. While interviewing a nine-year-old boy who lived in a dangerous Californian neighborhood, I asked what would make him feel safer. He thought briefly and replied, "If I had a gun of my own."

In addition to our gun culture, racism is also a problem. Crime statistics verify that many of the affected children live with the cultural shame of being less than perfect because they are predominantly black or Hispanic. They live with racism, and they live in the sick economy that comes out of it. These children have told me, "If you call 911 in my neighborhood, they don't come." Or, "Pizza Hut won't deliver in my neighborhood." Few of us experience such community alienation and the shame accompanying it directly. Some of the more insightful children understand that others look on them with passive pity and little true understanding. In his memoir, one of the incarcerated boys said,

> People on the outside, they go on TV and they say, "Damn, look at them just killing each other," but they don't know what this stuff is about. They think it's really stupid stuff but to us it's big stuff 'cause we live in that environment and we've got to learn how to survive. You place any one of them people outside, you put them in that predicament and they are going to do the same thing. They're not always going to call and try the cops, they're not gonna. They're not gonna. They're gonna try to handle it themselves cause they're gonna fear for their lives.

Snowden's secret. The second dark secret of violent trauma that we contend with is Snowden's secret, a reference taken from Joseph Heller's (1961) novel *Catch 22* about American bomber crews in World War II. During a mission, Yossarian (the main character) attempts to help Snowden, a crew mate hit by anti-aircraft fire. When he opens up Snowden's flak jacket, Snowden's insides fall out. This is what Yossarian calls Snowden's secret: The human body is not strong, powerful, and tough; it is a fragile bag filled with gooey stuff and lumps.

In a psychological parallel, Snowden's secret means facing both human vulnerability in the natural world and the capacity for evil in human nature (Herman, 1992). Each person eventually learns about the trauma and horror that can happen to human beings, but how and when this lesson is learned seems particularly important. To learn it vividly, visually, and experientially in childhood is traumatic—an event from which full recovery is not possible. We must understand that violent children have learned Snowden's secret early in life, witnessing shootings, stabbings, and beatings inside the home and out.

Dantrel's secret. The third, and perhaps most damaging secret of violent trauma, is Dantrel's secret. Dantrel Davis was a little boy who lived in Chicago. Dantrel walked with his mother to school one morning; 100 feet from the school's front door, she let go of his hand. He turned to walk up the steps where some of the teachers were waiting. Police stood on the street corners. Despite the presence of his mother, the police, and his teachers, as he walked the last few feet to school, Dantrel was shot in the back of the head and killed. The dark secret that other children learned from Dantrel's death is that adults cannot protect them.

The recognition that adults cannot or will not protect them marks a dramatic psychological moment in the lives of violent youth. One boy we interviewed shared an incident that occurred on his school playground when he was eight. As he watched helplessly, a friend was badly beaten while the teachers—preferring not to get involved—turned and walked away. Over and over again, the boys speak of this sense of betrayal by adults. We know from generations of research that the breakdown of child protection in war zone situations is crucial to understanding the psychological effect of these situations on children (Apfel & Simon, 1996).

When children understand that adults cannot protect them, that they are left to protect themselves, they often take up weapons and relationships substituting for adult protection in "juvenile vigilantism." A Michigan boy said to me, "If I join a gang, I'm 50 percent safe. If I don't join a gang, I'm zero percent safe." Adults do not enter into the equation. In Chicago, I once visited a school at the invitation of a school social worker who wanted to show me the special program she had for young adolescents. She loved these children, and they loved her. She even spent her own money to buy things for the children. But when she left the room at one point, one of the children said to me, "You know, Mrs. Smith is a lovely lady, but you wouldn't put your life in her hands." Mrs. Smith was shocked to discover that two of those children had guns in their lockers that day, not because they didn't love her or she them, but because they didn't think she was powerful enough to protect them. They knew Dantrel's secret.

These specific experiences of trauma and betrayal do not occur in a vacuum; they happen in the larger context of American social toxicity. An example of the bigger problem is the declining trust reported by children in our country. In 1972, 35 percent of American seventeen year olds agreed that "most people can be trusted" (National Survey of Youth, 1993). By 1992, only 19 percent agreed with that statement. Similarly, in 1972, 30 percent of the youths said that dealing with people required care and caution. That number increased to 60 percent in 1992 (Garbarino, 1995). The children we talked to in prison demonstrated this lack of trust. One of the boys was asked, "Suppose you picked up a newspaper and the headlines said, 'Most people can be trusted.' What would you think?" His response was, "What idiot wrote that?" These children profoundly distrust adult capacity and motivation for protecting them.

Milgrim's secret. The fourth dark secret is Milgrim's secret, based on Milgrim's famous psychological study of the Eichmann Effect (Garbarino, 1995). In the study, ordinary people were brought into a laboratory in the role of "teacher" after seeing a second person, the "learner." The learner sat behind a partition, answering questions, while the teacher administered electric shocks of increasing severity to the learner every time he or she made a mistake. *Normal* people complied and administered escalating shocks. Milgrim's secret is that with violence, anything is possible—as many incarcerated boys know first hand. In other words, any act of violence that is physically possible is psychologically possible as well. There are no limits.

At Cornell, we made a film called *I Still Can't Say It,* about a child abuse prevention program. In a chilling scene in this film, a teacher looks into the camera and tells her story. She says,

> You know, when I was a little girl, my momma used to beat me, and one day somebody called the police and the police came to our house. And the police asked me, they said "Is your momma beating you?" and I said "no" and the police went away. Then later my momma came home and she said, "Why didn't you tell the police that I'd been beating you?" And I looked her in the eye and said, "Because you could kill me."

This child understood Milgrim's secret at an early age. The primary developmental issue is what children do with this knowledge. This girl used her knowledge as the starting point for building a positive life to replace the void she knew as a child. But for some children, this knowledge becomes a license to kill.

One of our young interviewees spoke recently about how he learned Milgrim's secret when he was eight. He awoke one night to see his mother's boyfriend beating her. Blood was all over the house. He and his ten-year-old brother used baseball bats to drive the boyfriend out of the house. He understands Milgrim's secret. Milgrim's secret happens because of desensitization and depersonalization—processes that psychologically bridge what is physically possible and psychologically possible.

Desensitization must be understood in order to understand Milgrim's secret. Children almost never go from innocence to violence in one step but gradually progress to this behavior. A recent review by two military psychologists (Grossman & Siddle, 1999) reveals a disturbing fact about current youth socialization. They point out that in the past soldiers were rather inefficient. Even as late as World War II, only about 20 percent of American soldiers—foot soldiers and riflemen—were able to point their weapons at the enemy and shoot them. The authors believe despite their basic training, a fundamental inhibition against using violence toward others restrained the soldiers. The military discovered that this reluctance could be overcome by changing the training procedures. Originally, soldiers were trained to shoot at targets. The soldiers could get very good at shooting targets, but most of them could not pull the trigger when shooting at a human. The military changed the training after

World War II. By the time of the Vietnam War, 95 percent of American soldiers were able to shoot their weapons at the enemy (this is one reason the kill ratios in the Vietnam War increased dramatically, as compared with earlier wars).

The military used the process of desensitization, training soldiers to shoot at human figures through simulations and human dummies, rather than at abstract targets. Why is this relevant to risk and resilience in children? Grossman and Siddle (1999) argue that

> with the advent of interactive point and shoot arcade and video games there is a significant concern that society is aping military conditioning but without the vital safeguard of discipline. There is strong evidence to indicate that the indiscriminate civilian application of combat conditioning techniques as entertainment may be a key factor in the worldwide skyrocketing violent crime rates including a seven-fold increase in per capita aggravated assault. (pp. 148–149)

For example, violent video games desensitize the impact of violence in ways similar to military training—without the prosocial structure and discipline that soldiers are taught. Despite the prevalence of post-traumatic stress disorder among Vietnam-era veterans, their actual homicide rates are lower than their nonmilitarized peers because their training and discipline buffers this lowered inhibition (Grossman, 1999).

Marshall's secret. Brigadier General S. L. A. Marshall was the official U.S. military historian of World War II in Europe. He discovered that 98 percent of the American soldiers in combat continuously for sixty days became psychiatric casualties, needing treatment and rehabilitation before they could return to the front lines. The remaining 2 percent were psychopaths—not from their wartime experience, but as a pre-existing condition (Grossman, 1999).

Youth violence is similar. One of the boys said, "You place any one of them people outside, you put them in that predicament and they are going to do the same thing." The "war zone mentality" found among inner-city gang members is but an extreme form of an increasingly common pattern in which kids develop the capacity for witnessing—and in the case of Littleton, Colorado, and Paducah, Kentucky—committing lethally violent assaults.

Resilience is not absolute; some settings overwhelm human capacities to cope. Psychologist Pat Tolan (1996) did a study on how many children growing up in the war zone neighborhoods of Chicago are resilient. Tolan defined a resilient child as one who needed neither mental health intervention or remedial education. Over a two-year period, none of the children were found to be resilient. By age fifteen, none of the children had escaped either significant academic deficiency or mental health impairment. The relentless pressure on children who come from that nexus of community violence, family disruption, and personal experience of trauma is overwhelming.

We must be particularly concerned about Tolan's results because the concept of resilience, developed by researchers and clinicians, has become a policy explanation or excuse. Policy makers have argued that intervention or prevention programs are unnecessary because children are resilient. I remember one particular court case in which a prosecutor asked a boy on trial for first-degree murder, "What's wrong with you that you weren't resilient growing up in the environment that you did? Other children seemed to survive. What's wrong with you?"

One of the consequences of learning Marshall's secret is the deterioration of "future orientation," which refers to a person's sense of security about the future. Lenore Terr's 1990 study of the Chowchilla kidnapping, in which a group of children were kidnapped and buried underground, exemplifies this. A year after the kidnapping, the children involved believed they would live six or seven years less than did other children unaffected by the event. At the extreme, traumatized future orientation produces "terminal thinking." An example of this is when a fifteen-year-old is asked, "What do you expect to be when you are thirty?" and he responds, "Dead." Terminal thinking impedes any good work that can be done with teenagers because helping them depends heavily on their future orientation. Why should they study? Why should they stay in school? Why should they drive carefully, avoid drugs, practice chastity or safe sex? What does it matter, if they can't envision a future for themselves?

On my fiftieth birthday, I talked with a sixteen-year-old incarcerated boy. The boy looked at me wistfully and said, "Wow, fifty years old. I might make it to thirty, maybe." And then he added, "You know if I wasn't here in prison, I'd be dead today." A few weeks before, his girlfriend—six months pregnant with his child—was gunned down on the street; because the shooters could not get to him, they killed his family instead. He sits in prison, knowing that when he is released, those same guys will be waiting to take their revenge.

Terminal thinking is an extreme form of fear common in American children. A few years ago, a survey of U.S. sixth to twelfth graders found that 35 percent worry they will be shot and not live into old age. Among black and Hispanic children, the number was greater than 50 percent (Garbarino, 1995). Eroding future orientation is a widespread social phenomenon, with terminal thinking being the most extreme form.

DOING SOMETHING ABOUT VIOLENCE

When we laid out these five dark secrets, we wondered how a child can unlearn or transcend them. Pat Tolan and Nancy Guerra (1994) reviewed violence prevention and reduction programs. They concluded that the two crucial elements to reduce violence and aggression were simultaneous cognitive restructuring and behavioral rehearsal, thus changing ideas about violence, as well as changing practices and behavior. Research shows that by age eight, patterns of aggressive behavior and ideology appear to crystallize and correlate. That crystallization correlates with subsequent adult aggressive violent behavior (Garbarino, 1999).

Cognitive Restructuring

Cognitive restructuring and the rehearsal of behavioral alternatives needs to occur before the onset of adolescence. To that end, we wrote a book for children called *Let's Talk about Living in a World with Violence* (Garbarino, 1993). Evaluations done in Chicago, Illinois, and Ithaca, New York, revealed that when a competent and sympathetic teacher uses the book in a violence reduction program, aggression declines within six months of the program (Bolger, Collins, Darcy, & Garbarino, 1998).

Religious Transformation

What about teenagers currently sitting in prison? If narrative coherence is about retelling the story of one's life, then in a shallow materialist culture such as ours, what are the stories of a life? The basic story is "you're born, you live, you die." If you live in the affluent portion of our world, the story goes like this: "You're born, have a nice day, go shopping, and then you die." If you live in a socially toxic war zone, your story is, "You're born, life sucks, you go to jail, and then you die." Without some transcendent element, where do you go for an alternative narrative? That is why religious transformation is a powerful impetus to nonrecidivism.

We interviewed boys in a maximum-security youth prison with an unusual, safe environment. These children over and over again talked about how—for the first time in their lives—they do not have to watch their backs every minute. At the same time, they are immobilized by their situation. They do not have access either to girls or to drugs; they have no jewelry, guns, cars, expensive stereos, or designer clothing. What is left for them? What can they do? They can only go upward and inward, through a process of reflection, introspection, meditation, religious involvement, spiritual concern, and reading. What kind of environment in our cultural history is characterized by physical immobility, reflection, and an absence of material possessions? In monasteries and convents, vows are made to obedience, poverty, and chastity—to some degree, these boys live a monastic life.

Perhaps creating a monastic life is a key to transforming these children, giving them hope and a chance to start over. Not even this radical refocusing can guarantee permanent change because eventually they go back into the socially toxic environments from which they came. But this process of transformation may be a great opening for them. So rather than boot camps, which shout and push and bully, we should consider monasteries.

STRENGTHENING CHILDREN WHO LIVE WITH VIOLENCE

Children who live with violence can teach many lessons, particularly lessons that point toward improved practice by mental health, education, and social work professionals. First among these is a renewed understanding of the limitations of resilience. Both the experiences of soldiers in chronic combat and inner-city boys indicate that some environments are so traumatic and corrosive they exceed the coping abilities of almost anyone. Resilience is not absolute.

Knowing this, professionals must realize that addressing individual psychological issues alone is not enough. Rather, they must take as a central task of their professional roles the detoxification of psychologically harmful social environments. This requires a systematic effort—a public health approach—that maps and assesses social environments as the basis for allocating resources to support families, schools, neighborhoods, and communities in ways that reduce social toxicity (Garbarino, 1995). With respect to violence, this means a coordinated effort to promote stability, security, affirmation, mentoring, economic equality, community integration, and human rights–based policies as part of a larger effort to reduce experiences and influences that stimulate, promote, reinforce, and rationalize violence (Garbarino, 1999). The eventual goal is to detoxify the social environment and provide a more supportive setting, particularly for psychologically vulnerable individuals, replacing the dark secrets of violence with the enduring truths of love and peace.

REFERENCES

Apfel, R., & Simon, B. (Eds.) (1996). *Minefields in their hearts: The mental health of children in war and communal violence.* New Haven, CT: Yale University Press.

Bolger, K., Collins, C., Darcy, J., & Garbarino, J. (1998). *Evaluation of a violence prevention program for children.* Ithaca, NY: Family Life Development Center.

Cohler, B. (1982). Personal narrative and the life course. *Life Span Development and Behavior, 4,* 205–241.

Family Life Development Center. (1986). *I still can't say it: A documentary about preventing child abuse* [videocassette]. (Available from author, Martha Van Rensselaer Hall, Ithaca, NY 14853).

Garbarino, J. (1993). *Let's talk about living in a world with violence.* Chicago: Erikson Institute.

Garbarino, J. (1995). *Raising children in a socially toxic environment.* San Francisco: Jossey-Bass.

Garbarino, J. (1999). *Lost boys: How our sons become violent and what we can do to save them.* New York: The Free Press.

Garbarino, J., & Bedard, C. (1996). Spiritual challenges to children facing trauma. *Childhood, 3*(4), 467–478.

Garbarino, J., Eckenrode, J., & the Family Life Development Center. (1997). *Understanding abusive families.* San Francisco: Jossey-Bass.

Garbarino, J., Kostelny, K., & Dubrow, N. (1991). *No place to be a child: Growing up in a war zone.* Lexington, MA: Lexington Books.

Gilligan, J. (1996). *Violence.* New York: Putnam.

Grossman, D. (1999). *Stop teaching kids to kill.* New York: Random House.

Grossman, D., & Siddle, J. (1999). Psychological effects of combat. In L. R. Kurtz (Ed.), *Encyclopedia of violence, peace, and conflict.* New York: Academic Press.

Heller, J. (1961). *Catch-22.* New York: Simon & Schuster.

Herman, J. (1992). *Trauma and recovery.* New York: Basic Books.

National Survey of Youth: University of Michigan. (1993). *Monitoring the future 1975–1992.* Ann Arbor, MI: National Survey of Youth, University of Michigan.

Perry, B., Pollard, R., Blakley, T., Baker, W., & Vigilante, D. (1995). Childhood trauma, the neurobiology of adaptation, and "use-dependent" development of the brain: How "states" become traits. *Infant Mental Health Journal, 16*(4), 271–291.

Rittwagenmd, Marjorie. (1954, March 27). Child criminals are my job. *Saturday Evening Post.*

Shepherd, R. (1997). Doing justice to juvenile justice: What changes does the system really need? *Juvenile Justice Update, 3*(4).

Terr, L. (1990). *Too scared to cry.* New York: Harper & Row.

Tolan, P. (1996). How resilient is the concept of resilience? *The Community Psychologist, 4,* 12–15.

Tolan, P., & Guerra, N. (1994). *What works in reducing adolescent violence: An empirical review of the field.* Boulder, CO: University of Colorado Center for the Study and Prevention of Violence.

van der Kolk, B. (1994). *Trauma and meaningfulness.* Rochester, NY: Rochester Symposium on Developmental Psychopathology.

Chapter 5

Youth Risk and Resilience: Community Approaches to Violence Prevention

Deborah Prothrow-Stith

Violence involving young people, both as victims and as perpetrators, has become one of the greatest challenges ever to face the United States. Youth-related violence has reached alarming levels in this country. The numbers leave little doubt as to the severity of this crisis: in 1995 alone, 7,949 people under the age of twenty-four were murdered. That same year, one violent crime occurred every eighteen seconds, and one murder every twenty-four minutes. Homicide is the second leading cause of death for young people between the ages of fifteen and twenty-four, and the leading cause of death for black youths in the same age group. Since the mid-1980s, the homicide rate for teens ages fourteen to seventeen has more than doubled, increasing 165 percent from 1985 to 1993 (Federal Bureau of Investigation, 1995).

Furthermore, adolescent homicides increased by 6.7 percent from 1979 to 1988 (FBI, 1995). The Centers for Disease Control and Prevention (CDC) estimate that by the year 2003, more Americans will die from firearm-related injuries than from motor vehicle accidents. In eight states, this is already true (CDC, 1994).

The United States has a violence problem unlike any other country in the world. The U.S. homicide rate for young men is eight times that of Italy, the developed country with the next highest rate, and 100 times greater than the developed country with the lowest rate (CDC, 1997). If violence were inevitable—simply part of the human condition—then we could expect the homicide rate to be similar in every country. These statistics reveal an important truth: violence is preventable. We do not have to have this problem.

Over the past fifteen years, public health professionals have identified and developed strategies to prevent the problems that place youths at risk for violent behavior. In large part, this has involved investigating the lives of youths who have already committed violent acts. However, violence prevention activists and researchers have also become very interested in understanding the motivations of "resilient youth." How is it that some youths are able to live healthy and successful lives when faced with the same adverse circumstances that foster violent behavior in others? Efforts to study resilience in youths, to understand how individuals overcome challenges to healthy lives, can guide public health strategies aimed at preventing violence.

SCHOOL VIOLENCE: MORE LETHAL

Violence in schools, while not new, is increasingly lethal. The most recent CDC Youth Risk Behavior Survey surveyed students in the ninth through twelfth grades in the fifty states, the District of Columbia, and the Virgin Islands. Twenty-two percent reported carrying a weapon in the thirty days before the survey, and of that number, 8 percent indicated that they had carried a gun. Seven percent said they had been threatened or injured with a weapon while on school property during the twelve months before the survey. Twelve percent admitted to having carried a weapon onto school property in the month before the survey. Sixteen percent had been involved in a physical fight on the school property within a year of the study (CDC, 1993).

The CDC, the U.S. Department of Education, and the National School Safety Center currently are conducting a study of actual deaths in schools. Preliminary data show that 105 school-associated violent deaths occurred in the school years 1992–1993 and 1993–1994: eighty-one homicides, nineteen suicides, and five unintentional firearm-related deaths. Sixty-six percent of these deaths occurred on school property, and 75 percent of the 105 deaths were committed with a firearm (Satcher, 1985).

Four percent of the students said they missed at least one day of school in the month before because they felt unsafe at school. In 1989, 6 percent of students reported avoiding certain places in school or on the way to or from school because they were afraid of being attacked. A 1993 Metropolitan Life poll of 2,500 students in grades six through twelve revealed that 23 percent of students and 11 percent of teachers had been victims of violence in and around schools. Only 15 percent of the students said they never saw violent incidents at school; 31 percent answered that they sometimes saw violence (Metropolitan Life & Louis Harris & Associates, 1993). This poll showed that 15 percent of students had carried a handgun in the thirty days before the survey, and one in twenty-five said they had taken a handgun to school in the past year. Fifty-nine percent said they could get a handgun if they wanted one (Metropolitan Life & Louis Harris & Associates, 1993).

Contrary to the stereotype of violence as predominantly stranger-related or occurring in the context of criminal behavior (such as racial harassment, robbery, or drug dealing), much of the violence experienced in the United States occurs in the context of personal relationships (Spivak, Prothrow-Stith, & Hausman, 1988). Only 15 percent of homicides occur while a crime is being committed, but 50 percent stem from arguments among acquaintances (CDC, 1982)—in family relationships (e.g., child abuse, elder abuse, spouse abuse) or among friends (interpersonal peer violence).

The perpetrator and victim of violence share many traits. They are likely to be young, male, and of the same race. They are likely to be poor and have been exposed to violence in the past, especially family violence. They may be depressed and use alcohol or drugs (Prothrow-Stith & Weissman, 1991). Unfortunately, most current resources and solutions address only part—possibly the smaller part—of the problem. Although established anti-crime and anti-violence strategies should not be discarded, we must recognize the diversity of violent circumstances to which a broader base of efforts must be built that responds to violent events and addresses particular factors.

A closer look at the demographic characteristics reveals certain predominant factors contributing to a complex picture of adolescent violence. In 1988, homicide rates (deaths per 100,000) were considerably higher among twenty- to twenty-four-year-old youths (19 percent) and fifteen- to nineteen-year-old youths (11.7 percent) compared with ten- to fourteen-year-old youths (1.7 percent). Yet the rates increased among all three groups from 1979 to 1988 (CDC, 1990). In terms of gender, males are much more likely to be victims than females (with the exception of sexual assault) and are also more likely to be violent offenders and witnesses to violence.

RACE AND POVERTY

There appear to be extremely large racial differences in violence rates among young Americans. In 1991, homicide was the primary cause of death for black youths aged fifteen to twenty-four; the homicide rate for black youths of both genders (90 percent per 100,000) was nearly nine times the rate for white youths aged fifteen to twenty-four (10.8 percent per 100,000). National statistics concerning other ethnic minority groups, such as Hispanic, Asian-American, and Native-American youths, are scant.

These racial data are not indicative of any biologic or genetic factor given that they are confounded by socioeconomic status, urban living, gun availability, and racism. Although race appears as a significant social predictor in certain studies, multiple variable studies show a more complex situation. Using family income as the primary indicator of socioeconomic status, the National Crime Survey found an inverse relationship between income and the risk of violent victimization (Bureau of Justice Statistics, 1992). In 1988, the risk of victimization was found to be 2.5 times higher for people in low-income families (less than $7,500 annual income), compared with high-income families (more than $50,000 annual income). However, the exact relationship of violence and social factors is complex and still unclear. For example, multivariate studies have demonstrated a connection between race and socioeconomic status. At low socioeconomic levels, black people have a much higher risk of becoming homicide victims compared with white people; at higher socioeconomic levels, however, the difference disappears.

Other studies have suggested that socioeconomic status is the major predictor and race is merely a marker. One study that used several markers for poverty, including number of people per square foot of housing, disaggregated the race and socioeconomic variables. In this study, overcrowded white people had the same high domestic homicide rates as did overcrowded black people. Less crowded black and white people had the same lower rates (Centerwall, 1992). In 1987, the homicide rate for young black men in the military was one-twelfth the national rate, strongly suggesting the influence of social, structural, cultural, and economic factors.

THE APPLICATION OF PUBLIC HEALTH STRATEGIES

Recently, public health practitioners have begun to recognize the problem of violence and have brought different orientations and techniques to complement and strengthen the criminal justice approach. The public health system has noted that violence stamps its consequences on the nation's health statistics as well as its crime statistics. As noted earlier, violence significantly contributes to mortality and morbidity. In fact, homicide and intentional injury may represent as much as $425 billion in short- and long-term health care costs and lost productivity of those who are injured or disabled by violence in just a single year (Farrell, 1993). These facts alone should warrant attention by public health professionals, as well as the broader spectrum of human services professionals, and gives society even more reason to be concerned about violence.

In addition, the public health community has been drawn to this issue by the growing conviction that its techniques of analysis and prevention might be usefully applied to violence. Public health's analytic approach to problems concentrates on identifying risk factors and important causes that could become the focus of preventive interventions. It also brings a record of accomplishment in controlling "accidental" (unintentional) injuries through both environmental manipulations (e.g., seat belts and childproof caps on medicines) and behavioral change (e.g., laws and educational campaigns to reduce drunk driving).

Identification of Risk Factors

Major risk factors for youth violence have been identified. These factors can be broadly categorized into environmental and psychological risk factors. Among the major environmental risk factors that have been most thoroughly studied are witnessing violence, exposure to media violence, and the availability of firearms and ammunition. Although the demographics of violence suggest a strong social effect of poverty, the precise mechanisms of this interaction have not been elucidated. Psychological models, which describe cognitive and behavioral differences between young people at high risk for violence and their less violent peers, have also been developed.

Witnessing Violence

Besides the young people directly injured by violence, increasing attention is being given to the scores more who are affected indirectly, as witnesses to violent acts or by exposure to chronic violent environments (Groves, Zuckerman, Marans, & Cohen, 1993). Pynoos and colleagues (1987) examined the appearance of post-traumatic stress disorder (PTSD) symptoms in children who endured a fatal sniper attack on their elementary school. They reported a correlation between the type and number of PTSD symptoms and proximity to the violent incident, as well as more severe symptoms in children who knew the deceased child.

In addition to acute incidents, other studies found correlations between exposure to chronic violence and distress symptoms (Fitzpatrick & Boldizar, 1993; Freeman, Mokros, & Poznanski, 1993; Lorion & Saltzman, 1993; Martinez & Richters, 1993; Osofsky, Wewers, Hann, & Fick, 1993). Lorion and Saltzman (1993) also described anecdotal reports from their research participants, including reports from teachers and administrators about children who lived in violent settings and who arrived at school in distress, who were unable to concentrate or maintain appropriate behavior in class and who hid in the classroom, afraid to return home or take the bus. Clearly, the physical threat of violence needs to be addressed, as well as the potential for psychopathological and/or emotional disturbances in both victims and bystanders (Durant, Pendergast, & Cadenhead, 1994; Emde, 1993).

Children and Exposure to Media Violence

Links between childhood exposure to media violence and subsequent youth and adult violence have been firmly established over the past four decades. These data have been accepted as conclusive by the American Psychological Association (American Psychological Association Commission on Violence and Youth, 1993) and have been extensively reviewed in the literature (Dietz & Strasburger, 1991; Sege & Dietz, 1994). Therefore, this review briefly summarizes certain salient experimental evidence that suggests a causal link between childhood exposure to violent television programming and subsequent violent behavior. In short, several types of experimental studies have been performed, each of which suggests that exposure to media violence results in increased risk for future violence and violent crimes. These experimental studies include a full spectrum of experiments, ranging from laboratory studies of individual children to large population studies.

In a series of classic experiments, Bandura and his colleagues (1963a, 1963b) exposed preschool children to stereotypical violent activity in a controlled setting and observed their propensity to repeat these actions. An actor appearing on screen attacked a clown doll. Following this attack, in three separate video sequences, the actor was either praised, ignored, or punished. Those preschool-aged viewers who saw the violent behavior rewarded on screen were more likely than the other two groups to repeat the violent actions when given a clown doll. This experiment demonstrated that children can learn violent behaviors from TV and are especially likely to do so when these activities are depicted as socially acceptable.

Exposure to media violence also significantly influences older children's behavior. Meta-analysis of a series of experiments demonstrates conclusively that school-aged boys have more fights in the days after exposure to violent mainstream movies than they do in the days after exposure to less violent movies (Turner, Hesse, & Peterson-Lewis, 1986; Wood, Wong, & Chachere, 1991). The effects of TV watching was examined further in a landmark cohort study involving children raised in Pennsylvania. Huesmann and Eron showed that preference for violent television programming at age eight, as well as total hours of television viewing, predicted the severity of violent criminal convictions by age thirty (Huesmann, Eron, Lefkowitz, & Walder, 1984). This effect might readily be impacted and modified by parental interventions (Austin, Roberts, & Nass, 1990; Huesmann, Eron, Klein, Brice, & Fischer, 1983; Liebert, 1988; Sang, Schmit, & Tascher, 1993). Further, Centerwall (1992) has found that in the United States, Canada, and South Africa homicide rates doubled approximately ten to twelve years after the introduction of English-language television. In the United States, homicide rates doubled first among those portions of the population exposed to television first (white urban dwellers) and only subsequently among those segments of the population that received TV later. Centerwall attributes approximately 10,000 deaths annually in the United States to the results of exposure to media violence (Centerwall, 1992).

Taken together, these studies meet the criteria for causality set forth in the Surgeon General's 1964 report on smoking and health (U.S. Department of Health, Education, & Welfare, 1964) and established that exposure to media violence places children at risk for subsequent violence. Public debate flourishes concerning the roles of video games and violence-oriented musical lyrics in encouraging violence. Currently, however, no definitive data are available on these issues.

Firearms

The United States has more firearms than other industrialized nations not at war, and the facts regarding the presence and increase in their number are astounding:

- Twice as many children in the United States under ten years of age died as the result of firearm injuries in 1991 as U.S. soldiers were killed in the Persian Gulf and Somalia combined (*The State of America's Children Yearbook*, 1994).
- A child under the age of fifteen in the United States is fifteen times more likely to be killed by gunfire than a child growing up in Northern Ireland (*The State of America's Children Yearbook*, 1994).

- A child dies of gunshot wounds every two hours in the United States, whereas a police officer is killed by a gun every five days (*The State of America's Children Yearbook,* 1994).
- The overall firearm-related death rate among U.S. children under fifteen years of age is nearly twelve times higher compared with children in twenty-five industrialized countries (CDC, 1997).
- The FBI's stolen gun file contains more than two million reports, 60 percent of which are reports of stolen handguns; handguns represent only one-third of all firearms privately owned in the United States (Bureau of Justice Statistics, 1995).
- The number of murders committed with handguns has risen steadily since 1985, paralleling the increase in the rate of firearm production (Wintemute, 1987).
- Of the 20,043 reported homicides in 1995, 82 percent were committed with a firearm. Nearly 56 percent of all firearm-related homicides were committed with a handgun in 1995 (FBI, 1995).
- Suicide is nearly five times more likely to occur in households where a gun is present (Kellerman et al., 1993); approximately 60 percent of all suicides in the United States involve guns (CDC, 1994).
- The Centers for Disease Control and Prevention estimates that in 1995 for every firearm-related homicide, there were 3.3 nonfatal firearm injuries (CDC, 1997).
- Approximately 80 percent of the medical cost for treatment of firearm-related injuries is paid for by taxpayers, and the average cost of treatment for a patient with firearm-related injuries is estimated to be $32,000 per hospital admission (Bureau of Justice Statistics, 1996).
- Black male youths aged fifteen to twenty-four are most at risk of firearm-related death. If the rest of the U.S. population were being killed at the same rate as young black males, more than 460,000 people would die of gunshots every year (Bureau of Justice Statistics, 1996).

Teen and young adult homicide is a uniquely American problem. These high rates of youth homicide in the United States have been attributed to the high rate of gun ownership in this country. An international study of gun ownership and homicide found positive correlations between the rates of household gun ownership and the national rates and proportions of gun-related homicide (Killias, 1993; Lester, 1988).

Handgun availability has an increasingly important role in youth homicides. As an example, the increasing trend seen in the total homicide rate among fifteen- to nineteen-year-old youths for the period 1979–1989 is solely attributable to the increase in firearm homicides; the firearm-related homicide rate increased 61 percent (6.9 to 11.1 per 100,000), while at the same time, non–firearm-related homicide rates actually *decreased* 29 percent (3.4 to 2.4 per 100,000) (see Figure 5.1; Fingerhut, Ingram, & Feldman, 1992). From 1980 to 1989, more than 65 percent of the 11,000 homicides committed by high-school–aged youths were firearm related.

Handguns are widely accessible to adolescents in the United States. The national 1990 Youth Risk Behavior Survey found that about one in every twenty high school students had carried a firearm at least once in the thirty days preceding the survey (with the incidence being even higher among only male youths, particularly among black male youths) (CDC, 1991). In a study of inner-city youths, as many as 35 percent of male youths carried a gun outside of school (Sheley, McGee, & Wright, 1992). Firearms contribute to both the violent victimization of youth and to the violent offenses committed by youth. The presence of a weapon in the home is associated with a threefold increase in the likelihood of homicide compared with matched control subjects drawn from the neighborhood surrounding the victim (Kellerman et al., 1993).

In a regional study on firearms, comparisons of two cities (Seattle,

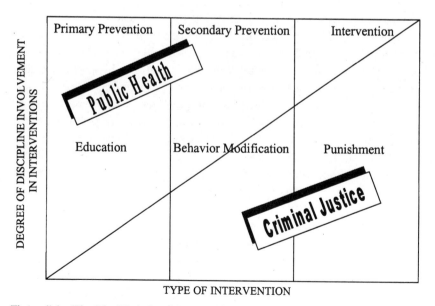

Figure 5.1   The Ideal Relationship Between Public Health and Criminal Justice in Preventing Violence.

Washington, and Vancouver, British Columbia) with similar demographic characteristics revealed that Seattle's excess homicide rate is entirely attributable to firearm homicides. Another study that examined the effect of implementation of gun control legislation showed that enacting tougher gun control laws in the District of Columbia had a positive effect, when compared with neighboring states (Loftin, McDowell, Wiersema, & Cottey, 1991).

All of these studies demonstrate that firearms availability is strongly correlated with increased homicide rates. Logically, this result corresponds with the earlier observation that most homicides result from conflicts among people who know each other well (including friends, acquaintances, and relatives and spouses). In a situation of passionate conflict, handgun availability appears to increase the likelihood of serious injury or death.

Psychological and Behavioral Factors

In pioneering studies conducted in the late 1980s, Slaby and Guerra (1988) demonstrated that adolescents involved in violence have habits of thought that lead them into violent confrontations. The researchers examined the responses of three groups of teenaged boys to a specific scenario. One group of boys was in custody for the commission of violent crimes, the second group was identified by their teachers as being violence-prone, and the third group was identified by their teachers as not being violence-prone. Each boy was presented with the same scenario: He was going to the batting cage after school to work on his batting so that he could make the baseball team. As he arrived, another boy took the last bat. In this scenario, the violence-prone boys were more likely to assign malicious intent to the boy who took the bat than were the less violent boys. In imagining ways to resolve this scenario, the more violent boys could envision fewer alternative means of achieving a resolution.

Slaby and Guerra concluded from this study that the violence-prone boys get into more fights because they were more likely to see harmful intent in a given situation and, having seen such intent, were less likely to come up with a peaceful way to resolve the situation. These results have been confirmed with a larger scale study conducted in the New York City schools (CDC, 1993). Boys who reported having been in serious fights were more likely to suggest that carrying a weapon or threatening to use a weapon were good ways to stay out of fights than the general school population. They were also far less likely to say that one could avoid fighting by apologizing compared with the overall population.

LEVELS OF PREVENTION

Once these risk factors have been identified, the issues of prevention and intervention come into focus. One conceptual framework that can facilitate definitions of roles in addressing the problem and assist developing a broader perspective on programmatic strategies involves breaking the spectrum of violence into levels that reflect different points of intervention. This framework, used frequently in public health circles, structures approaches to problems into three stages: (1) primary prevention, (2) secondary prevention (or early intervention), and (3) tertiary prevention (or treatment and rehabilitation). These distinctions have proved valuable in thinking about intervention efforts even though their boundaries are not discrete. In this discussion, think of these distinctions in terms of concentric circles that widen out in space and time from a central point that is the occurrence of some violent event.

Tertiary prevention is distinguished from secondary and primary prevention in that it lies on the opposite side of the violent event from the other two. Its focus is on trying to reduce the negative consequences of a particular event after it has occurred or on trying to find ways to use the event to reduce the likelihood of similar incidents occurring in the future. Thus, one might think of improved trauma care and increased efforts to rehabilitate or incapacitate violent offenders as tertiary prevention instruments in controlling or responding to violence.

Primary prevention, which by definition addresses the broadest level of the general public, might seek to reduce the level of violence shown on television or to promote gun control. This would be an effort directed toward dealing with the public values and attitudes that may promote or encourage the use of violence. Secondary prevention, on the other hand, identifies relatively narrowly defined subgroups or circumstances at high risk of being involved in or occasioning violence and focuses its attention on them. Thus, secondary prevention efforts might concentrate on urban, poor, and young men at particularly high risk of engaging in or being victimized by violence, educating them in nonviolent methods of resolving disputes or displaying competence and power.

Of course, the relative risk level of groups or circumstances is a continuum—with some people and circumstances at very high risk (e.g., a person who has been victimized by violence in his or her own home, also surrounded by violence in school, entering a bar in which members of a rival gang are drinking) and others at relatively low risk (e.g., a happily married professor, who owns no weapon more lethal than a screwdriver, writing on her computer at home). Generally, the higher risk groups are smaller than the lower risk groups.

Primary prevention instruments are those that can affect larger and larger populations, ideally at relatively low cost. Indeed, the need to reach very large populations requires primary prevention efforts to be low cost per individual reached. Thus, primary prevention instruments tend to include providing information and education on the problem of violence through the popular media (e.g., recruiting Bill Cosby as a spokesperson against adolescent violence [Goldner, 1992] or Sarah Brady's lobbying for gun control laws and educating the public about the risks of hand-guns), rather than providing nonviolence training to the entire population. Long-term primary prevention goals aim to eliminate some of the root causes of violence such as social injustice and discrimination. This public health model can be very useful when applied specifically to the issue of interpersonal violence. In the past, the criminal justice system has addressed each of the three points of intervention to varying degrees. The bulk of criminal justice efforts have focused on the response to serious violent behavior, with moderate attention to early identification and intervention and limited efforts in the area of primary prevention.

The major activities of the criminal justice system historically have involved the roles of the police, the courts, and the prison system in responding to criminal or violent events. Most resources have been directed to investigating and punishing criminal behavior. Tertiary prevention generally has involved incarceration. In the area of secondary prevention, the police have focused efforts on "situational" crime prevention, and the juvenile justice system has made attempts at early intervention with youthful offenders, although youths often were ignored by the courts and probation system until their criminal behavior reached a relatively high level of concern. Primary prevention efforts have focused on controlling "criminogenic" commodities (i.e., guns, drugs, and alcohol) or on elementary school drug and violence prevention education by police. Finally, public health also has applied its analytical expertise to greatly enhance the understanding of risk factors, allowing for a broader vision in the planning and development of preventive approaches (Prothrow-Stith & Weissman, 1991; Spivak et al., 1988).

In the area of secondary prevention, public health has helped develop educational interventions specifically focused on behavior modifications of high-risk individuals, particularly children and youth. A number of curricula currently in use address both the risks of violence in solving problems and conflict resolution techniques (Prothrow-Stith & Weissman, 1991; Spivak et al., 1988).

The criminal justice system has, more recently, increased its involvement with primary and secondary prevention efforts. For example, some criminal justice professionals have become increasingly involved in gun control initiatives. In 1974, the Juvenile Justice and Delinquency Prevention Act gave the Justice Department primary responsibility for delinquency prevention programs. The Office of Juvenile Justice and Delinquency Prevention was designed partly to encourage development of model delinquency prevention programs. One such program is the Boys Clubs of America Targeting Programs for Delinquency Intervention. Other community groups refer at-risk boys to the program who are then recruited. Early evaluations of these programs seem promising. Data indicate that 39 percent of the boys did better at school, and 93 percent who completed the program, have not come back into the juvenile justice system (Boys Clubs of America, 1986). These types of interventions reflect an important connection between the criminal justice and public health professions. The public health system emphasizes prevention, with the criminal justice system focusing on the response to violence, but with both disciplines working together across the spectrum.

PROMISING PROGRAMS

Researchers Joy G. Dryfoos and Lisbeth Schorr both agree that the most effective programs must be comprehensive, family and community oriented, and collaborative in nature (Dryfoos, 1994 & 1997; Schorr, 1997). Some schools, communities, social agencies, and politicians around the country have incorporated this formula for success and have developed strategies to help children and their families prevent or cope with violence. These programs offer the opportunity to learn from their successes and failures.

The Boston Violence Prevention Program

The Boston Violence Prevention Program, an intensive community-based outreach and education effort run by Boston's Department of Health and Hospitals, was launched in 1986 as part of its Health Promotion Program for Urban Youth. Much of the program's early work, supported by foundations, used the *Violence Prevention Curriculum for Adolescents* (Prothrow-Stith, 1987) to train teachers and youth services staff how to teach adolescents about the risks of violence; the program also covered measures that can help to avoid fights. Regular training is offered for teachers, health workers, street outreach workers, and peer workers. The program's peer leaders group is trained and actively participates in training sessions offered by the program. A mass media campaign, "Friends for Life Don't Let Friends Fight," was developed to create a new community ethos supporting violence prevention. The program has been part of the city budget for the past five years and has generated several spin-off activities.

Resolving Conflict Creatively Program

The Resolving Conflict Creatively Program, a holistic school-based conflict resolution program in New York, California, and Alaska, works with the entire school structure to create safe schools. The K–12 curriculum, developed and refined since 1986, requires support from school administration, although it does not mandate that every teacher be trained. Each of the thirty-two school districts in New York City that use the curriculum maintains a certain autonomy, leaving decision making to the school community. After an intense forty-hour training program on the curriculum, teachers incorporate the methods in their classrooms. The program invites and encourages the participation of parents in training. Both teachers and administrators in these schools document fewer fights and a sense of peace. Students become peer mediators and receive special training to negotiate and mediate arguments that break out during school hours.

This program creates a win–win situation. Not only do students develop leadership skills and a sense of responsibility for peace and respect, but teachers and administrators find practical use for conflict resolution skills in their daily lives. The program also offers regular advanced training sessions in topics such as helping students deal with death and grief. For example, a walk through the hallways of Satellite Academy High School in the Bronx gives the sense that despite unsafe surroundings, the school offers an oasis of safety, a place of mutual respect—a place where learning takes place.

Program evaluations show that both teachers and students notice a positive change in the schools. A more comprehensive program evaluation was recently funded through a grant from the Centers for Disease Control and Prevention. Director Linda Lantieri, who co-founded the Resolving Conflict Creativity Program with Tom Roderick of Educators for a Social Responsibility, says that the program instills a sense of profound mutual respect (Lantieri, 1996).

CONCLUSION

The contributions made by public health professionals toward efforts to prevent violence have been tremendous. The continued application of public health strategies to the understanding and prevention of violence ensures success. The public health campaign to reduce smoking took thirty years after the first Surgeon General's report to reduce smoking. Violence reduction can be expected to take at least as long. Violence prevention is much more complex, necessitating the involvement of individual and family factors, as well as the full range of ecological systems in the development of effective intervention strategies.

REFERENCES

Austin, E. W., Roberts, D. F., & Nass, C. I. (1990). Influences of family communication on children's television-interpretation processes. *Communication Research, 17*(4), 545–565.

Bandura, A., Ross, D., & Ross, S. A. (1963a). Imitation of film-mediated aggressive models. *Journal of Abnormal Social Psychology, 66*(1), 3–11.

Bandura, A., Ross, D., & Ross, S. A. (1963b). Vicarious reinforcement and imitative learning. *Journal of Abnormal & Social Psychology, 67*(6) 601–607.

Boys Clubs of America. (1986). *Targeted Outreach Newsletter, Vol. II-1.* Atlanta: Author.

Bureau of Justice Statistics, U.S. Department of Justice. (1992). *Criminal victimization in the United States, 1991* (Agency Report No. NCJ-139563). Washington, D.C.: U. S. Department of Justice.

Bureau of Justice Statistics, U.S. Department of Justice. (1995). *Guns used in crime: Firearms, crime and criminal justice—Selected findings* (Agency Report No. NCJ-148201). Washington, D.C.: U.S. Department of Justice.

Bureau of Justice Statistics, U.S. Department of Justice. (1996). *Firearm injury from crime* (Agency Report No. NCJ-160093). Washington, D.C.: U. S. Department of Justice.

Centers for Disease Control. (1982, November 12). Homicide. *Morbidity and Mortality Weekly Report, 31*(44), 594, 600–602.

Centers for Disease Control. (1990, December 7). Homicide among young black males—United States, 1978–1987. *Morbidity and Mortality Weekly Report, 39*(48), 869–873.

Centers for Disease Control. (1991, October 12). Weapon carrying among high school students—United States, 1990. *Morbidity and Mortality Weekly Report, 40*(40), 681–684.

Centers for Disease Control. (1993, August). *Advance report of final mortality statistics, 1991. Monthly vital statistics report.* Atlanta, GA: Centers for Disease Control.

Centers for Disease Control and Prevention. (1994, January 28). Deaths resulting from firearm- and motor-vehicle-related injuries: United States, 1968–1991. *Morbidity and Mortality Weekly Report, 43*(3), 37–42.

Centers for Disease Control and Prevention. (1997, February 7). Rates of homicide, suicide, and firearm-related death among children in 26 industrialized countries. *Morbidity and Mortality Weekly Reports, 46*(5), 101–105.

Centerwall, B. S. (1992). Television and violence: The scale of the problem and where to go from here. *Journal of the American Medical Association, 267*(22), 3059–3063.

Dietz, W. H., & Strasburger, V. C. (1991). Children, adolescents and television. *Current Problems in Pediatrics, 21*(1), 8–31.

Dryfoos, J. G. (1994). *Full-service schools: A revolution in health and social services for children, youth, and families.* San Francisco: Jossey-Bass.

Dryfoos, J. G. (1997). *Safe passage: Making it through adolescence in a risky society.* New York: Oxford University Press.

Durant, R., Pendergast, R., & Cadenhead, C. (1994). Exposure to violence and victimization and fighting behavior by urban black adolescents. *Journal of Adolescent Health, 15*(4), 311–318.

Emde, R. N. (1993). The horror! The horror! Reflection on our culture of violence and its implications for early development and morality. *Psychiatry, 56*(1), 119–123.

Farrell, C. (1993, December 13). The economics of crime. *Business Week,* pp. 72–80.

Federal Bureau of Investigation, U.S. Department of Justice. (1995). Crime in the United States, 1995. Uniform crime reports. Washington, D.C.: U. S. Department of Justice.

Fingerhut, L. A., Ingram, D. D., & Feldman, J. J. (1992). Firearm and non-firearm homicide among persons 15 through 19 years of age. *Journal of American Medical Association, 267*(22), 3048–3053.

Fitzpatrick, K. M., & Boldizar, J. P. (1993). The prevalence and consequences of exposure to violence among African-American youth. *Journal of the American Academy of Child and Adolescent Psychiatry, 32*(2), 424–430.

Freeman, L., Mokros, H., & Poznanski, E. (1993). Violent events reported by normal urban school-aged children: Characteristics and depression correlates. *Journal of the American Academy of Child and Adolescent Psychiatry, 32*(2), 419–423.

Gentry, J. & Eron, L. (1993). American Psychological Association Commission on Violence and Youth. *American Psychologist, 48*(2), 89.

Goldner, D. (1992, October 2–4). Can TV help save black youth? *Courier-Post,* USA Weekend.

Groves, B. M., Zuckerman, B., Marans, S., & Cohen, D. J. (1993). Silent victims: Children who witness violence. *Journal of the American Medical Association, 269*(2), 262–264.

Huesmann, L. R., Eron, L. D., Klein, R., Brice, R., Fischer, P. (1983). Mitigating the imitation of aggressive behaviors by changing children's attitudes about media violence. *Journal of Personality and Social Psychology, 44*(5), 899–910.

Huesmann, L. R., Eron, L. D., Lefkowitz, M. M., & Walder, L. O. (1984). Stability of aggression over time and generations. *Developmental Psychology, 44*(5), 1120–1134.

Juvenile Justice and Delinquency Prevention Act of 1974, Pub. L. No. 93-415.

Kellerman, A. L., Rivara, F. P, Rushforth, N. B., Banton, J. G., Reay, D. T., Francisco, J. T., Locci, A. B., Prodzinkski, J., Hackman, B. B., & Somes, G. (1993). Gun ownership as a risk factor for homicide in the home. *New England Journal of Medicine, 329*(15), 1084–1091.

Killias, M. (1993). International correlations between gun ownership and rates of homicide and suicide. *Canadian Medical Association Journal, 148*(10), 1721–1725.

Lantieri, L. (1996). *Waging peace in our schools.* Boston: Beacon Press.

Lester, D. (1988). Firearm availability and the incidence of suicide and homicide. *Acta Psychiatrica Belgica, 67*(2), 387–393.

Liebert, R. M. (1988). *Early window: The effects of television on children and youth* (6th ed.). Needham, MA: Allyn and Bacon.

Loftin, C., McDowell, D., Wiersema, B., & Cottey, T. J. (1991). Effects of restrictive licensing of handguns on homicide and suicide in the District of Columbia. *The New England Journal of Medicine, 325*(23), 1615–1620.

Lorion, R. P., & Saltzman, W. (1993). Children's exposure to community violence: Following a path from concern to research to action. *Psychiatry, 56*(1), 55–65.

Martinez, P., & Richters, J. (1993, February). The NIMH community violence project: II. Children's distress symptoms associated with violence exposure. *Psychiatry, 56*(1), 22–35.

Metropolitan Life and Louis Harris & Associates. (1993). *Violence in America's public schools.* New York: Metropolitan Life Insurance.

Osofsky, J., Wewers, S., Hann, D. M., & Fick, A. C. (1993). Chronic community violence: What is happening to our children? *Psychiatry, 56*(1), 36–45.

Prothrow-Stith, D. (1987). *Violence prevention curriculum for adolescents.* Newton, MA: Education Development Center.

Prothrow-Stith, D., & Weissman, M. (1991). *Deadly consequences: How violence is destroying our teenage population and a plan to begin solving the problem.* New York: HarperCollins.

Pynoos, R. S., Frederick, C., Nader, K., Arroyo, W., Steinberg, A., Eth, S., Nunez, F., & Fairbanks, L. (1987). Life threat and post-traumatic stress in school-age children. *Archives of General Psychiatry, 44*(2), 1057–1063.

Sang, F., Schmit, B., & Tasche, K. (1993). Developmental trends in television coviewing of parent-child dyads. *New England Journal of Medicine, 329*(15), 1084–1091.

Satcher, D. (1985, April). The public health approach to violence. Paper presented at the National Education Association National Conferences, Los Angeles, California.

Schorr, L. B. (1997). *Common purpose: Strengthening families and neighborhoods to rebuild America.* New York: Anchor Books.

Sege, R., & Dietz, W. (1994). Television viewing and violence in children: The pediatrician as agent for change. *Pediatrics, 94*(4, Pt. 2), 600–607.

Sheley, J., McGee, Z., & Wright, J. (1992). Gun-related violence in and around inner-city schools. *Journal of Diseases of Childhood, 146*(6), 677–682.

Slaby, R. G., & Guerra, N. G. (1988). Cognitive mediators of aggression in adolescent offenders: 1. Assessment. *Developmental Psychology, 24*(4), 580–588.

Spivak, H., Prothrow-Stith, D., & Hausman, A. (1988). Dying is no accident: Adolescents, violence, and intentional injury. *Pediatric Clinics of North America, 35*(6), 1339–1347.

The state of America's children yearbook. (1994). Washington, D.C.: Children's Defense Fund.

Turner, C. W., Hesse, B. W., & Peterson-Lewis, S. (1986). Naturalistic studies of the long-term effects of television violence. *Journal of Social Issues, 42*(3), 51–73.

U.S. Department of Health, Education, & Welfare. (1964). *Smoking and health. Report of the Advisor Committee to the Surgeon General Public Health Service* (PHSP No. 1103). Washington, D.C.: U.S. Department of Health, Education, & Welfare.

Weaver, B., & Barbour, N. B. (1992). Mediation of children's television viewing. *Families in Society, 73*(4), 236–242.

Wintemute, G. J. (1987). Firearms as a cause of death in the United States, 1929–1982. *Journal of Trauma, 27*(5), 532–536.

Wood, W., Wong, F. Y., & Chachere, J. G. (1991). Effects of media violence on viewer's aggression in unconstrained social interaction. *Psychology Bulletin, 109*(3), 371–383.

Chapter 6

Multisystemic Therapy with Serious Juvenile Offenders and Their Families

Scott W. Henggeler
Stephanie W. Hoyt

Multisystemic therapy (MST; Henggeler & Borduin, 1990; Henggeler, Schoenwald, Borduin, Rowland, & Cunningham, 1998) is a family- and community-based treatment that has reduced long-term rates of recidivism and out-of-home placement for violent and chronic juvenile offenders and improved adolescent and family functioning. Such outcomes are significant in light of the myriad personal and social problems presented and experienced by serious juvenile offenders (Sampson & Laub, 1990, 1993) and the immense financial costs associated with their crimes, apprehension, and incarceration (Miller, Cohen, & Rossman, 1993). This chapter will describe the bases of the success of MST, the specific outcomes that can be expected when MST is delivered with integrity, and the principles that guide the design of MST interventions.

BASES OF THE SUCCESS OF MST

The success of MST with a population that has traditionally proven recalcitrant to treatment (c.f., Tate, Reppucci, & Mulvey, 1995) is most likely a result of the integration of three emphases. First, MST directly addresses the known determinants of antisocial behavior while building protective factors. Second, MST interventions are delivered in the natural ecologies of youths and families—in home, school, and community settings. Third, MST programs emphasize quality assurance, including rigorous training and provider accountability for youth and family outcome.

MST Interventions Target Risk and Protective Factors

Decades of research have produced a relatively clear picture of the primary determinants of serious antisocial behavior in youth (Henggeler, 1996). Based on the reviews and longitudinal studies of numerous investigators (Elliott, 1994; Hawkins et al., 1992; Kazdin, 1987; Thornberry et al., 1995), the following is a generic list of identified correlates:

- *Individual:* low verbal skills, favorable attitudes toward antisocial behavior, psychiatric symptomatology, cognitive bias to attribute hostile intentions to others
- *Family:* lack of monitoring; ineffective discipline; low warmth; high conflict; parental difficulties such as drug abuse, psychiatric conditions, and criminality
- *Peer:* association with deviant peers, poor relationship skills, low association with prosocial peers
- *School:* low achievement; dropout; low commitment to education; aspects of the schools, such as weak structure and chaotic environment
- *Neighborhood and community:* high mobility; low support available from neighbors, church, and so forth; high disorganization; criminal subculture

Although these variables place youths at greater risk for antisocial behavior, protective factors enhance the resilience of individuals exposed to risk factors. As described by Hawkins et al. (1992), several sets of protective factors have been identified by investigators:

- *Individual:* intelligence, being firstborn, easy temperament, conventional attitudes, problem-solving skills
- *Family:* attachment to parents, supportive family environment, marital harmony
- *Peer:* bonding with prosocial peers
- *School:* commitment to schooling
- *Community:* strong social support network, ongoing involvement in church activities

In consideration of these known risk and protective factors, MST attempts to address those factors that are pertinent to a particular youth and family on an individualized basis. Hence, MST must have the capacity to comprehensively address a variety of risk factors ranging from individual cognitive biases to the development of indigenous social support networks. However, for reasons of parsimony and efficiency, MST interventions must be individualized to fit the particular strengths and weaknesses of the youth and his or her social ecology (i.e., family, peers, school, neighborhood).

Implement MST Interventions Where the Problems Are Seen

In most MST programs, treatment has been delivered using a home-based model of service delivery. The home-based model (similar to the family preservation model of service delivery) can be extremely effective in getting services to children and families.

- Therapists have low caseloads, which allows for intensive efforts at engaging families and treating families once they are engaged.
- Therapists are available twenty-four hours per day, seven days per week. Availability for evening and weekend appointment enhances access to care.
- Services are provided in homes and other community locations, which removes several important barriers to service access (e.g., lack of transportation, finding a babysitter).
- Services are family based, by definition. Hence, treatment goals are set primarily by family members, which enhances motivation to work on identified problems.

As evidence of the capacity of MST programs to remove barriers to service access, in a recent study with substance-abusing and dependent juvenile offenders and their families, 98 percent (57 of 58) of the families referred to MST received a full four-month dose of MST services (Henggeler, Pickrel, Brondino, & Crouch, 1996). The lone treatment dropout still received more than twenty hours of direct therapist contact.

Rigorous Training and Accountability of Providers for Youth Outcomes

Several important characteristics of MST programs come under the rubric of quality assurance. MST programs include extensive therapist training, ongoing supervision, and ongoing consultation. The thrust of the training, supervision, and consultation is to promote therapist treatment adherence (i.e., fidelity to the MST treatment protocol). Critically, high adherence predicts favorable long-term outcomes, whereas low adherence predicts poor outcomes (Henggeler, Melton, Brondino, Scherer, & Hanley, 1997). Hence, great effort is placed on promoting treatment adherence among therapists and on-site supervisors. These efforts include five days of orientation to the MST treatment model, periodic booster sessions, frequent on-site clinical supervision, and weekly consultation with an MST expert.

In addition, MST programs emphasize high degrees of accountability for engaging families in the treatment process and for achieving favorable youth and family outcomes. Accountability can be operationalized in several different ways. For example, MST programs often have "no reject" policies, which prohibit therapists and programs from choosing the relatively easy cases while avoiding the difficult cases. In addition, in certain MST programs, therapists receive performance bonuses based on the outcome that they have achieved with their families. Likewise, certain MST programs have negotiated reimbursement rates with funding sources that provide financial incentives for achieving favorable outcomes and disincentives for poor outcomes.

LONG-TERM OUTCOMES OF MST WITH SERIOUS JUVENILE OFFENDERS

Several early clinical trials supported the promise of MST with difficult-to-treat clinical populations (Borduin, Henggeler, Blaske, & Stein, 1990; Brunk, Henggeler, & Whelan, 1987; Henggeler et al., 1991, 1986). Three recently published randomized trials of MST with violent and chronic juvenile offenders, however, have documented the capacity of MST to reduce long-term rates of recidivism and incarceration.

The Simpsonville, South Carolina, Study

The Simpsonville study (Henggeler, Melton, & Smith, 1992) was a collaborative project between the South Carolina Department of Mental Health (DMH) and the South Carolina Department of Juvenile Justice (DJJ) that examined MST as an alternative to the incarceration of violent and/or chronic juvenile offenders. The primary goals of the project were to decrease criminal activity, out-of-home placements, and cost of services. Inclusion criteria for the juvenile offenders were (a) arrest for a violent offense or at least three criminal arrests including at least one felony arrest, (b) prediction by DJJ staff that the youth was likely to be incarcerated for his or her recent arrest, and (c) the presence of at least one parent figure in the youth's life.

The project included eighty-four violent and chronic juvenile offenders, of whom 54 percent had been arrested for violent crimes (one-half of the remainder self-reported that they had committed at least one violent crime during the previous six months; Henggeler, et al., 1993a); their mean number of arrests was 3.5; and they averaged 9.5 weeks of prior placement in correctional facilities. The average age of the youth was 15.2 years, 77 percent were male, the vast majority of the families were economically disadvantaged, 26 percent lived with neither biological parent, and 56 percent were black and the remainder were white.

Youth were assigned randomly to receive MST using the home-based model of service delivery (MST; $n = 43$) or usual services provided by DJJ ($n = 41$). MST therapists were three master's-level counselors employed by the DMH with an average of two years' experience and caseloads of four families each. The average duration of treatment was thirteen weeks. Assessment batteries, comprised of standardized measurement instruments, were administered pre-treatment and post-treatment.

Results showed that MST was effective at reducing rates of criminal activity and institutionalization. At the fifty-nine-week postreferral follow-up, youths receiving MST had significantly fewer re-arrests ($Ms = .87$ vs. 1.52) and weeks incarcerated ($Ms = 5.8$ vs. 16.2) than did youths receiving usual services. At posttreatment, juvenile offenders receiving MST reported a significantly greater reduction in criminal activity than did counterparts receiving usual services. Families receiving MST reported more cohesion, whereas reported family cohesion decreased in the usual services condition. In addition, families receiving MST reported decreased adolescent aggression with peers, whereas such aggression remained the same for youths receiving usual services. Moreover, a 2.4-year follow-up (Henggeler, Melton, Smith, Schoenwald, & Hanley, 1993b) showed that MST doubled the percentage of youths who did not recidivate, in comparison with usual services. Thus, this study demonstrated that an intensive home- and family-based service could reduce the criminal activity of violent or chronic juvenile offenders while maintaining these youths in the community.

The Columbia, Missouri Project

Borduin et al. (1995) compared the effectiveness of MST with individual therapy (IT). Participants were 200 twelve- to seventeen-year-old juvenile offenders and their families referred from the local DJJ office and randomly assigned to receive either MST ($n = 92$) or IT ($n = 84$). Twenty-four families refused services. MST therapists were six doctoral students in clinical psychology who provided home-based services, whereas IT therapists were six master's-level therapists who provided outpatient mental health services. The juvenile offenders were involved in extensive criminal activity as evidenced by their average of 4.2 previous arrests ($SD = 1.3$) and the fact that 63 percent had been previously incarcerated. The average age of the youths was 14.8 years ($SD = 1.6$); 67 percent were male; 70 percent, white; 30 percent, black; and 53 percent lived with two parental figures.

Standardized assessment batteries were conducted at pre-treatment and post-treatment. At post-treatment, families receiving MST reported and evidenced more positive changes in their dyadic family interactions than did IT families. For example, MST families reported increased cohesion and adaptability and showed increased supportiveness and decreased conflict-hostility during family discussions compared with IT families. In addition, parents in the MST group showed greater reductions in psychiatric symptomatology than did parents in the IT condition.

Results from a four-year follow-up of recidivism showed that youths who received MST were significantly less likely to be re-arrested than youths who received individual therapy. Specifically, MST completers ($n = 77$) had lower recidivism rates (22.1 percent) than MST dropouts (46.6 percent; $n = 15$), IT completers (71.4 percent; $n = 63$), IT dropouts (71.4 percent; $n = 21$), and treatment refusers (87.5 percent; $n = 24$). Moreover, MST dropouts were at lower risk of re-arrest than IT completers, IT dropouts, and refusers. Examination of recidivists from each group revealed that MST youths arrested during follow-up were arrested less often and for less serious offenses than IT youths arrested during follow-up. Follow-up data also revealed that MST youths had a significantly lower rate of substance-related arrests than IT youths (4 percent vs. 16 percent) (Henggeler et al., 1991). Significantly, MST youths were less likely to be arrested for violent crimes (e.g., rape, attempted rape, sexual assault, aggravated assault, and assault and battery) after treatment than were IT youths.

The Dissemination Study

One of the primary purposes of this multisite study (Henggeler et al., 1997) was to determine whether MST treatment effects could be maintained if certain quality assurance procedures were eliminated. Specifically, weekly monitoring and consultation by an MST expert regarding therapist fidelity to the MST treatment protocol was discontinued. The role of the MST expert was to provide a consistent voice in promoting adherence to the MST treatment principles and to help therapists and supervisors design interventions needed to overcome barriers to obtaining favorable clinical outcomes. If this ongoing and relatively intensive consultative service was not critical to achieving favorable outcomes, our belief was that the dissemination of MST could be expedited. That is, the weekly involvement of an MST expert distal to treatment sites would not be necessary, which would simplify the adoption of MST programs by provider organizations.

The study included 155 violent or chronic juvenile offenders and their families who were referred at random to either MST or usual juvenile justice services. Inclusion criteria were imminent risk of incarceration, as judged by juvenile probation staff; arrest for a serious offense or at least three criminal offenses; and age from eleven to seventeen years. The youths averaged 15.2 years of age; 82 percent were male; and 81 percent were black and 19 percent were white. In general, the families were economically disadvantaged (e.g., median annual family income was between $5,000 and $10,000). Treatment was provided by ten master's-level therapists in two community mental health sites. Thus, the project reflected a partnership between the South Carolina DMH and DJJ, with full collaboration of the family court.

Standardized assessment batteries were administered to family members pre-treatment and posttreatment, and a 1.7-year follow-up was conducted on archival indices of re-arrest and incarceration. In addition, standardized measures of treatment fidelity were obtained at two points during treatment from the perspectives of the parents, adolescents, and therapists.

Outcome analyses showed two MST treatment effects. MST significantly reduced youth psychiatric symptomatology and the average number of days incarcerated in comparison with usual services. However, rates of re-arrest were reduced at only half (i.e., a 26 percent reduction) of the rate that had been obtained in the early trials of MST that included all the quality assurance mechanisms aimed at promoting treatment fidelity. Moreover, in contrast with findings of numerous previous trials of MST, favorable changes in family relations were not observed. Overall, these findings suggested that the present outcomes were modest in comparison with the outcomes MST has achieved previously with similar samples of serious juvenile offenders.

In consideration of these modest outcomes, the association between adherence to the MST treatment protocol and key outcomes was examined. The essential question was whether outcomes improved when treatment fidelity was high. The results showed that therapist adherence to the MST treatment principles was an important predictor of the adolescents' criminal activity and incarceration during the 1.7-year follow-up. Parent and adolescent ratings of treatment adherence predicted low rates of re-arrest, and therapist ratings predicted decreased self-reported index offenses and low rates of incarceration. Thus, MST was relatively successful when implemented with integrity.

The results of this study highlight the importance of treatment fidelity in obtaining favorable outcomes and of quality assurance mechanisms in promoting treatment fidelity. Although quality assurance mechanisms add an expense to treatment programs, this expense is quickly offset by achieving better outcomes. For example, preventing one incarceration of an offender can fund rigorous training and quality assurance programs, assuming that the treatment program captures the fiscal savings.

Summary

Evidence supporting the effectiveness of MST with serious juvenile offenders and their families is compelling. Three rigorous studies have shown that MST can improve the short-term psychosocial functioning of youths and families as well as decrease long-term rates of re-arrest and incarceration. Moreover, when considered with the favorable outcomes of MST trials with other clinical populations, the case is strong for the viability of MST as treatment for children and adolescents presenting serious clinical problems and their families.

MST CLINICAL PROCEDURES

MST is operationalized through nine treatment principles that are detailed in a clinically oriented volume intended for practitioners (Henggeler et al., 1998). Adherence to these principles defines MST, and as noted previously, high adherence is associated with favorable long-term outcomes (Henggeler et al., 1997). MST training, supervision, and consultation all aim to promote fidelity to the principles. Brief descriptions of the principles follow, and then a case example is presented.

The MST Treatment Principles

Principle 1. The primary purpose of assessment is to understand the fit between the identified problems and their broader systemic context. MST assessment endeavors to understand how identified problems fit or make sense in light of the child and family's ecological context. Hence, the therapist obtains the perspectives of family members, teachers, peers, and members of the support network to determine the strengths and weaknesses of each system in which the youth is embedded (family, peer, school, neighborhood, and support network). The goal of the assessment is to determine the specific factors that exacerbate behavioral problems (e.g., ineffective parental discipline, sibling drug abuse, association with deviant peers, living in a high-crime neighborhood) as well as protective factors that can be used to attenuate identified difficulties (e.g., a father who loves his child, academic competence, skill in extracurricular activities). This ecologically oriented functional analysis sets the direction for treatment and is a continuous ongoing process throughout treatment.

Principle 2. Therapeutic contacts emphasize the positive and use systemic strengths as levers for change. Family members will not be engaged in the treatment process unless they perceive the therapist as understanding their perspective and valuing the strengths that they bring to the therapeutic context. Emphasizing family strengths promotes engagement and family therapeutic efforts, both of which are essential for achieving favorable outcomes. Moreover, strengths provide the key for designing interventions that fit the competencies and motivations of family members and other participants in the treatment process.

Principle 3. Interventions are designed to promote responsible behavior and decrease irresponsible behavior among family members. Therapists should not lose sight of the overarching purpose of treatment. Parents are helped to become more effective—meeting their children's needs for nurturing, guidance (e.g., monitoring and discipline), and physical care—while children and adolescents are helped to contribute positively to their social contexts (e.g., helping around the house, treating others with respect, not harming others, extending efforts in school or in vocational training). Stripped to the essence, the goals of treatment are to increase rates of responsible parent and child behavior.

Principle 4. Interventions are present-focused and action-oriented, targeting specific and well-defined problems. The task of MST is to address well-specified problems in the here and now. Thus, for example, MST interventions aim to have children attend school, come home before curfew, complete their chores, cease association with deviant peers, and engage in certain prosocial extracurricular activities. The value of well-specified goals is that ambiguity regarding treatment progress is minimized. Hence, all participants in the therapeutic process are clear regarding what is trying to be accomplished and whether efforts are being successful.

Principle 5. Interventions target sequences of behavior within and between multiple systems. The thrusts of interventions are to change intrafamily interactions and the family's relations with extrafamilial systems in ways that promote the adaptation of family members. Regarding intrafamily behavior, for example, the MST therapist may emphasize the development of more effective discipline practices by the parents and improved marital communications. Regarding extrafamilial relations, MST might focus on improving the degree of collaboration between the parents and school personnel or on developing an indigenous support network composed of neighbors, extended family, and friends for the family.

Principle 6. Interventions are developmentally appropriate and fit the developmental needs of the youth. Because an overriding goal of MST is to produce long-term change in developmental trajectories of high-risk youth, interventions must be developmentally appropriate. For example, intensive efforts to empower parents to gain control over their child's behavior may be more appropriate for young adolescents than for older adolescents who are near the stage of emancipation. Similarly, MST treatment should always incorporate the goal of developing prosocial peer relations because the development of friendships is a central task of adolescence.

Principle 7. Interventions are designed to require daily or weekly effort by family members. Youths referred to MST programs have serious clinical problems, and intense efforts by key members of the youth's social ecology are needed to ameliorate those problems. By building intensive family efforts into the treatment plan, therapists can track the work of family members continuously. Such tracking allows early identification of barriers to clinical change (e.g., parent has a drug problem that interferes with therapeutic progress; a key player is not "on board" regarding the treatment plan).

Principle 8. Intervention effectiveness is evaluated continuously from multiple perspectives. The continuous evaluation of outcome allows the clinician to determine whether (a) the functional analysis of the targeted problem is valid, and (b) the participants are working as agreed. If favorable outcomes are not emerging, one or both of these areas must be reconsidered. Thus, the effectiveness of MST interventions is examined and re-examined throughout the course of treatment, and lack of progress indicates that re-analysis of the therapist's plan and/or the participants' motivations is immediately required. New or modified interventions then follow that re-analysis, with re-evaluation of effectiveness.

Principle 9. Interventions are designed to promote treatment generalization and long-term maintenance of therapeutic change. Throughout treatment, practitioners must consider the implications of their work for long-term outcomes. Hence, emphasis is placed on helping and empowering parents as the vehicle to improve the functioning of children rather than on the clinician developing a "therapeutic relationship" with the child to effect change. Similarly, the therapist helps the family build an indigenous support network to promote the maintenance of therapeutic gains rather than linking the family with state agencies. Thus, changing the natural ecology of the child and family in ways that support favorable functioning in the long term is viewed as a key and ongoing emphasis of MST.

CASE EXAMPLE

The case of Michael provides an example of the types of serious difficulties treated by MST programs, the conceptual processes underlying the delineation of MST treatment goals, and the types of intervention strategies used to meet these goals.

Referral

Michael is a thirteen-year-old child who lives alone with his mother. He was referred by the school after two months of relatively serious problems including extreme verbal aggression at home and school, fighting at school, mood irritability marked by crying spells and suicidal ideation, and refusal of outpatient therapy and medication for his attention deficit hyperactivity disorder.

Systemic Strengths and Weaknesses

Several important strengths were identified for Michael and others in his systemic context.

- *Individual:* Michael enjoyed sports, had average intelligence, liked school, and responded well to behavioral contingencies.
- *Family:* His mother genuinely cared about him; extended family lived in the neighborhood and were willing to support the mother; and the family had a phone and owned a car.
- *Peers:* Michael had a girlfriend who supported him.
- *School:* Certain teachers were willing to support therapeutic efforts to help Michael.
- *Community:* Organized athletic opportunities were available.

However, several weaknesses were also identified across these systems.

- *Individual:* Michael had two previous psychiatric hospitalizations and presented significant symptoms associated with internalizing and externalizing disorders. He was verbally and physically abusive toward individuals in multiple contexts (e.g., girlfriend, mother, teachers).
- *Family:* Mother's parenting was permissive and inconsistent, and her psychiatric (i.e., she attended a day-treatment program) and drug abuse (i.e., she was a heavy marijuana user) problems interfered with her capacity to parent effectively. Michael's father, who lived two miles away, had serious drug problems, was physically abusive toward Michael, and consistently undermined therapeutic efforts.
- *Peers:* Michael had no friends other than his girlfriend and consequently was socially isolated.
- *School:* Several school personnel were not supportive of therapeutic efforts to help Michael, and school staff were not consistent in their handling of his medication adherence and behavioral problems.
- *Community:* The family lived next door to a crack house, and other types of criminal activity were rampant in the neighborhood.

General Fit

In general, Michael's array of antisocial behavior and mental health problems fit with his biological vulnerabilities (e.g., attention deficit hyperactivity disorder, parents with mental health and substance abuse problems), family context (e.g., significant parental problems that limited effective parenting, modeling of abusive behavior), and neighborhood context (e.g., criminal activity). In this case, difficulties with peers and school most likely reflected these vulnerabilities and family and neighborhood contexts. In other cases, peer and school difficulties might be seen as driving identified problems (e.g., associating with gang members, contributing to criminal activity).

Treatment Goals

The overarching goal of treatment was for Michael to reduce rates of antisocial behavior and internalizing symptoms so that he could remain in his home and school settings. As suggested previously, several key factors contributed to these problems: inconsistent parenting, paternal undermining of treatment objectives, refusal to take medication, lack of cooperation between the family and school systems, and limited coping skills on Michael's part. Although intervention strategies were developed for each of these barriers to behavior change, the present example focuses on inconsistent parenting.

Fit for Inconsistent Parenting and Corresponding Interventions

Despite changes in other systems, if Michael's mother continued to be extremely permissive and to provide little structure for her son, problems were likely to continue. Although the mother lacked basic knowledge regarding effective limit setting and discipline for adolescents, simply providing "parent training" would have little effect in this case. Rather, interventions needed to focus first on those factors that presented barriers to the effective implementation of monitoring and discipline strategies.

Several key barriers to effective parenting were identified. One set of barriers pertained to the mother's personal psychiatric difficulties and substance abuse, which were exacerbated by her lack of medication compliance. To address these difficulties, the therapist, with the mother's consent, organized key adults in the mother's ecology into a working alliance. These individuals included the mother's mental health workers at the day-treatment program, the mother's parents, a friend of the mother, the leader of mother's Tough Love support group, and one of Michael's teachers. This "team" met conjointly to increase and coordinate their supports for the mother's medication compliance and adherence to mental health and substance abuse treatment protocols. Members of the team communicated regularly with each other while planning and implementing interventions. This alliance ensured that all key players were on the same wavelength regarding the interventions needed to stabilize the mother and promote her capacity to parent effectively.

A second set of barriers pertained to the level of support or nonsupport of key individuals in the family's social ecology. The father actively undermined Michael's treatment compliance. The mother had contentious relations with school personnel, which attenuated the success of school-based interventions. In addition, the family had a minimal social support network.

The therapist attempted to engage the father in facilitating treatment goals, but these attempts usually met with failure. After an incident in which the father visited the family's home while intoxicated and was subsequently arrested by the police for threatening Michael and his mother, the therapist and family decided that the father's role in the therapeutic process should be minimized.

The therapist used several procedures to decrease the level of conflict between school personnel and the mother and to eventually open communication channels. The therapist helped the teachers develop a consistent and effective in-school behavioral contingency plan for Michael. With the success of this plan, the therapist convinced the school to eliminate the threat of suspension as their prevailing discipline strategy. When the threat of suspension was eliminated, the mother became less emotionally volatile in her interactions with school personnel and was willing to implement contingencies at home based on Michael's behavior in school. Hence, a system was arranged whereby the school contacted the mother on a daily basis to report good as well as poor behavior. Thus, with both parties (mother and the school) getting something they desired, they were able to focus on their long-standing mutual goals—improved behavioral and academic performance for Michael in school.

Even in the best of circumstances, handling the difficulties presented by Michael would be taxing. For a single parent with personal problems and minimal social support, these difficulties would often be overwhelming. Hence, the development of a strong indigenous support system for the family was a high priority. An examination of the family's social ecology revealed few friends and neighbors who could serve a supportive function, and the family was not involved in organized activities such as church. Michael's grandparents on his mother's side, however, possessed significant interpersonal strengths. Although the grandparents were reluctant to become involved in a supportive role because of frustrations with their daughter's past mental health and substance abuse problems, the grandparents eventually agreed to provide respite for their daughter by caring for Michael on weekends, as needed. Unfortunately, the availability of instrumental support from the extended family was cut short when the grandfather had a stroke and was hospitalized. Further efforts to develop indigenous support were thwarted when a family friend died. Nevertheless, in light of the importance of social support for promoting long-term outcomes, a network of formal and informal social supports was in place by the termination of treatment. On the formal side, this network included the professionals at the mother's day-treatment program. Informal (indigenous) supports included the grandparents as feasible, the mother's Tough Love support group, and another friend identified by the mother. Finally, the therapist endeavored to ensure that the mother provided some quid pro quo for each informal support so that the probability of continued support would be increased.

Outcomes

The preceding section described interventions that directly or indirectly aimed to promote the mother's effectiveness at parenting. This set of interventions, in addition to others not described (e.g., mainstreaming at school, medication to treat an underlying mood disturbance in Michael, decreasing Michael's social isolation by helping him to join a soccer team), combined to produce several positive outcomes. Michael remained free from harm. Although Michael's suicidal ideations persisted throughout treatment, they were manifested as feelings of hopelessness rather than as specific plans to harm himself. Michael's compliance with rules increased; he successfully mainstreamed into regular classes that emphasized academic achievement rather than classroom behavior management; and he began to develop a friendship network of prosocial peers.

On the other hand, interventions were not fully successful with regard to the mother. She continued to have periods of noncompliance with her mental health and substance abuse treatment protocols. During these periods, her affective and instrumental relations with Michael deteriorated. Although the therapist attempted to build a "support team" around the mother, the team concept was never fully realized. This failure threatens the long-term viability of the case. The therapist's hopes, however, are that Michael's involvement with prosocial peers, mainstream classes at school, competent grandparents, and local mental health professionals for ongoing psychopharmacological and support needs will counterbalance the periods of difficulty experienced by his mother.

CONCLUSION

The primary contention of this chapter is that serious clinical problems presented by children, adolescents, and their families can be treated successfully when therapists (a) address the known causes of problems and build protective factors within the child's social ecology, (b) provide services where the problems occur, and (c) assume high levels of accountability for engaging families in treatment and in attaining child outcomes. MST provides one example of a treatment model that has these characteristics. Findings from controlled studies evaluating the effectiveness of MST provide strong support for its capacity to improve child and family functioning and reduce long-term rates of antisocial behavior and out-of-home placement. Importantly, outcomes are linked with therapist adherence to the MST treatment protocol, suggesting that mental health services provide increased attention to training and treatment fidelity.

NOTE

Preparation of this chapter was supported by National Institute of Mental Health Grant MH-51852 and National Institute on Drug Abuse Grants DA10079 and DA08029.

REFERENCES

Borduin, C. M., Henggeler, S. W., Blaske, D. M., & Stein, R. (1990). Multisystemic treatment of adolescent sexual offenders. *International Journal of Offender Therapy and Comparative Criminology, 34*(2), 105–114.

Borduin, C. M., Mann, B. J., Cone, L. T., Henggeler, S. W., Fucci, B. R., Blaske, D. M., & Williams, R. A. (1995). Multisystemic treatment of serious juvenile offenders: Long-term prevention of criminality and violence. *Journal of Consulting and Clinical Psychology, 63*(4), 569–578.

Brunk, M., Henggeler, S. W., & Whelan, J. P. (1987). A comparison of multisystemic therapy and parent training in the brief treatment of child abuse and neglect. *Journal of Consulting and Clinical Psychology, 55*(2), 311–318.

Elliott, D. S. (1994). *Youth violence: An overview.* Boulder, CO: University of Colorado, Center for the Study and Prevention of Violence, Institute for Behavioral Sciences.

Hawkins, J. D., Catalano, R. F., & Miller, J. Y. (1992). Risk and protective factors for alcohol and other drug problems in adolescence and early adulthood: Implications for substance abuse prevention. *Psychological Bulletin, 112*(1), 64–105.

Henggeler, S. W. (1996). Treatment of violent juvenile offenders—We have the knowledge: Comment on Gorman-Smith et al. (1996). *Journal of Family Psychology, 10*(2), 137–141.

Henggeler, S. W., & Borduin, C. M. (1990). *Family therapy and beyond: A multisystemic approach to treating the behavior problems of children and adolescents.* Pacific Grove, CA: Brooks/Cole.

Henggeler, S. W., Borduin, C. M., Melton, G. B., Mann, B. J., Smith, L., Hall, J. A., Cone, L., & Fucci, B. R. (1991). Effects of multisystemic therapy on drug use and abuse in serious juvenile offenders: A progress report from two outcome studies. *Family Dynamics of Addiction Quarterly, 1*(3), 40–51.

Henggeler, S. W., Melton, G. B., & Smith, L. A. (1992). Family preservation using multisystemic therapy: An effective alternative to incarcerating serious juvenile offenders. *Journal of Consulting and Clinical Psychology, 60*(6), 953–961.

Henggeler, S. W., Melton, G. B., Brondino, M. J., Scherer, D. G., & Hanley, J. H. (1997). Multisystemic therapy with violent and chronic juvenile offenders and their families: The role of treatment fidelity in successful dissemination. *Journal of Consulting and Clinical Psychology, 65*(5), 821–833.

Henggeler, S. W., Schoenwald, S. K., Borduin, C. M., Rowland, M. D., & Cunningham, P. B. (1998). *Multisystemic treatment of antisocial behavior in children and adolescents.* New York: Guilford Press.

Henggeler, S. W., Melton, G. B., Smith, L. A., Foster, S. L., Hanley, J. H., & Hutchinson, C. M. (1993a). Assessing violent offending in serious juvenile offenders. *Journal of Abnormal Child Psychology, 21*(3), 233–243.

Henggeler, S. W., Melton, G. B., Smith, L. A., Schoenwald, S. K., & Hanley, J. H. (1993b). Family preservation using multisystemic treatment: Long-term follow-up to a clinical trial with serious juvenile offenders. *Journal of Child and Family Studies, 2*(4), 283–293.

Henggeler, S. W., Pickrel, S. G., Brondino, M. J., & Crouch, J. L. (1996). Eliminating (almost) treatment dropout of substance abusing or dependent delinquents through home-based multisystemic therapy. *American Journal of Psychiatry, 153,* 427–428.

Henggeler, S. W., Rodick, J. D., Borduin, C. M., Hanson, C. L., Watson, S. M., & Urey, J. R. (1986). Multisystemic treatment of juvenile offenders: Effects on adolescent behavior and family interactions. *Developmental Psychology, 22,* 132–141.

Kazdin, A. E. (1987). Treatment of antisocial behavior in children: Current status and future directions. *Psychological Bulletin, 102,* 187–203.

Miller, T. R., Cohen, M. A., & Rossman, S. B. (1993). Victim costs of violent crime and resulting injuries. *Health Affairs, 12,* 186–197.

Sampson, R. J., & Laub, J. H. (1990). Crime and deviance over the life course: The salience of adult social bonds. *American Sociological Review, 55*(5), 609–627.

Sampson, R. J., & Laub, J. H. (1993). *Crime in the making: Pathways and turning points through life.* Cambridge: Harvard University Press.

Tate, D. C., Reppucci, N. D., & Mulvey, E. P. (1995). Violent juvenile delinquents: Treatment effectiveness and implications for future action. *American Psychologist, 50*(9), 777–781.

Thornberry, T. P., Huizinga, D., & Loeber, R. (1995). The prevention of serious delinquency and violence: Implications from the program of research on the causes and correlates of delinquency. In J. C. Howell, B. Krisberg, J. D. Hawkins, & J. J. Wilson (Eds.), *A sourcebook: Serious, violent, & chronic juvenile offenders* (pp. 213–237). Newbury Park, CA: Sage.

Chapter 7

Disaster, Trauma, and Children's Resilience: A Community Response Perspective

Lawrence B. Rosenfeld
Mooli Lahad
Alan Cohen

Any attention paid to the variety of news media confirms that disasters are common occurrences throughout the world. The stories fascinate us, whether of the destructive power of natural disasters, such as floods and fires; technological disasters, such as plane crashes, and nuclear reactor accidents; or disasters of human design, such as wars and terrorism. We want to understand what happened, to learn how victims are responding, and to be assured that something is being done to help. It is easy to commiserate with the families and children suffering from the effects of a disaster.

Studying the psychosocial aspects of disasters, for example, learning what conditions mediate a child's and family's responses, and understanding why some children are resilient and experience a quick return to their everyday life while others may never return to normal functioning has several benefits (Raphael, 1986). For instance, studying disasters can increase counter-disaster effectiveness, such as prediction, disaster management, rescue and recovery, and long-term adaptation and can help uncover the causes of psychological and social problems associated with disasters. Increases in violent crime rates (Fitzpatrick & Boldizar, 1993), wars (Rosenblatt, 1983; Solomon, 1995), and civilian casualties in wars (Boyden, 1994) make it essential to understand what factors put children and families at risk of suffering some form of lasting psychopathology and what factors serve to protect them and enhance their resiliency.

DEFINING AND CATEGORIZING DISASTERS

Historically, labeling an event as a "disaster" means that it has several characteristics in addition to the destruction of property, loss of life, and widespread injury. According to Saylor (1993b), the event also "has an identifiable beginning and end; adversely affects a relatively large group of people; is 'public' and shared by members of more than one family; is out of the realm of ordinary experience; and, psychologically, is traumatic enough to induce stress in almost anyone" (p. 2). Vogel and Vernberg (1993) add three characteristics to this list: Disasters are "events that are relatively sudden, highly disruptive, [and] time-limited (even though the effects may be longer lasting)" (p. 465).

One useful approach to developing a typology of disasters considers the origin or etiology of the event. Raphael (1986) discussed two broad classifications, "natural" and "man-made," and Vogel and Vernberg (1993) subdivided the latter category into two parts, "acts of human violence, such as sniper shootings" and "failures of technology or results of human error, such as plane crashes and toxic contamination" (p. 465). Parson (1995a) divided disasters into three categories: natural disasters, "disasters of human unintentional occurrence," and "disasters of intentional human strategy" (pp. 164–165). Classifying disasters into three categories, natural (earthquakes, tornadoes, fires, floods, and hurricanes), technological (events in which any type of apparatus made by humans and for human use becomes defective with little or no warning, and is psychologically or physically detrimental to human lives; Breton, Valla, & Lambert, 1993; Erickson, 1994; Handford et al., 1986; Vernberg & Vogel, 1993), and "complex" (the result of human design or motivation), allows consideration of the broad range of events covered in the literature on disasters.

MEDIATING EFFECTS ON CHILDREN'S
REACTIONS TO DISASTERS

The significance of a disaster for a child depends upon his or her developmental stage, which influences his or her ability to cognitively grasp the impact of the event (Parry-Jones & Parry-Jones, 1994). A child's age affects the way in which she or he processes, responds to, and copes with a disaster. Specifically, age affects the child's focus of concern, conceptual understanding, and coping mechanisms (Garbarino & Kostelny, 1996; Gudas, 1993; Handford et al., 1986). For example, until a child is approximately nine or ten years old, and is in Piaget's "concrete operations or operational thinking" stage, thoughts about a disaster are likely to be egocentric and limited by the child's direct experiences (Piaget's "preoperational" stage). Prior to about age nine, unless the disaster disrupts family life in clearly identifiable ways, the child is not likely to understand what is happening or to think about it logically (Monaco & Gaier, 1987); for example, Handford et al. (1986) found that children under age eight were unaware of the danger associated with the Three Mile Island nuclear accident. By about nine, there is a reduction in egocentrism and an increase in recognizing the effects of a disaster from the perspective of others; cause-and-effect reasoning helps the child analyze the situation and her or his own thoughts about it. Usually, by age fourteen, a child comprehends a disaster in ways similar to the adults with whom she or he interacts. For example, numerous aspects of the problem may be considered, abstract thinking may take place (the lessons learned from the disaster), and a critical perspective may be adopted (criticizing how the press report the disaster).

As early as 1943, Freud and Burlingham reported that children evacuated and taken from their parents during World War II had fears that were related to their stage of development (Handford et al., 1986). Since then, multiple articles consider the utility of understanding the stages of child cognitive development Piaget presented in the 1950s. Piaget reasoned that the younger a child is, the less likely she or he is cognitively able to gather and interpret information about a given situation (Handford et al., 1986; Monaco & Gaier, 1987). Supporting the perspective that age (a) affects how children understand disasters and (b) largely determines which post-disaster coping skills they employ, Katz (1989) stated:

> Coping usually requires thinking through the alternatives at hand and trying to make the best of stressful circumstances. However, a preschooler's capacity to analyze and formulate strategic plans is very limited. Getting help is therefore highly dependent upon an adult recognizing warning signs in youngsters struggling with stress. (p. 2)

Some studies, for example, have shown that preschool children respond to disasters with less global psychological distress than older children (Green et al., 1991):

> The very young child's experience of a disaster is undoubtedly limited by his or her cognitive capabilities. The traumatic experience is probably not

understood in a coherent conceptual way, thus producing a more gener-
alized, disorganized post-traumatic state, which is likely to be strongly
influenced by how the parents react to the event, and how they interact
with the child after the event. The older child will be able to "understand"
what happened in a more cognitively sophisticated way, have some appreciation of present and future consequences, and experience more sophisticated reactions, which include attempts to fend off reminders and the
meaning of the event. (p. 949)

Young children tend to verbalize simple and less thoughtful responses
to a disaster and to display more physical manifestations of stress. Specifically, younger children, such as preschoolers, tend to have a high incidence of specific behavioral difficulties, including trauma and general-
ized fears, regressive toilet habits, and aggressiveness (Green et al., 1991).
In contrast, children over ten years of age usually grasp that a major disaster threatens their lives, and "young teenagers often report a sense of
foreshortened future" (Yule, 1992, p. 201). For example, Handford et al.
(1986) found that younger children's responses to the Three Mile Island
nuclear plant accident disaster were "vague and undifferentiated" (e.g.,
Three Mile Island "might be dangerous"), while older students were
more focused and explicitly talked about fear of death (for themselves
and others), anger related to Three Mile Island interfering with their play
space, concern about other people's feelings (e.g., mother and father
being worried), and worry about future consequences.

According to Handford et al. (1986; cf. Monaco & Gaier, 1987), children under eight years of age do not recognize the initial danger of a
disaster, while children between the ages of nine and twelve begin to
understand the different dangers involved. Older children, nine to
twelve years of age, also use skills that help them conceptualize and make
sense of the situation.

The type of disaster affects children's responses. Looking specifically
at natural disasters, children from birth to two may become irritable or
cry and want to be held and cuddled more than usual after a natural disaster (Federal Emergency Management Agency, 1996b). These small
children can often remember the sights, sounds, and smells associated
with the trauma (Federal Emergency Management Agency, 1996b). Very
young children, under age four, have an underdeveloped level of con-
sciousness that prevents them from fully appreciating the extent of a natural disaster. Because of this factor, natural disasters rarely cause these
young children to develop mental disorders. Instead, the most important factor for children this age is their mother's reaction to the natural
disaster, for example, if she becomes chronically depressed, is absent, or
is unable to function normally.

Preschoolers (ages two to six) tend to feel helpless and powerless after a natural disaster (Federal Emergency Management Agency, 1996b). Because of their age and small size, they do not feel capable of protecting themselves or others. They are overcome with fear and insecurity and cannot comprehend the nature of permanent loss. Mental disorders become more differentiated and frequent in preschoolers than in younger children.

School-aged children (six to ten years), on the other hand, can comprehend the concept of permanent loss and other complex issues (Federal Emergency Management Agency, 1996b). They may become preoccupied with the details of the trauma and experience a variety of reactions, including guilt, failure, or fantasies of "playing rescuer." This age group is 1.5 times more likely than preschoolers to develop a permanent mental disorder.

Preteens and adolescents, between the ages of 11 and 18, typically react in a manner that contains both childlike and adult elements (Federal Emergency Management Agency, 1996b). Teenagers may survive a natural disaster with a feeling of invulnerability, which leads to an increase in reckless behavior. Other teenagers may be overwhelmed by their wide range of emotions following a natural disaster and feel unable to discuss these emotions with their family.

Sitterle and Gurwitch's (1999) study of the Oklahoma City bombing, a complex disaster, found responses associated with different age groups that were not found with natural disasters, especially for very young children:

> The parents of infants and infant care staff reported more sleep difficulties, more clingy behavior, and more difficulty with soothing and consoling a crying infant. In the toddler room, children also showed these behaviors as well as a heightened response to loud noises and more irritability. . . . In children between 3 and 5 years of age . . . regressive behaviors such as a return to a pacifier and toileting accidents were noted. . . . Startle responses were similarly observed in older children. (p. 175)

In addition to a child's age and cognitive stage of development, his or her sex shapes perceptions of and responses to a disaster. For example, Yule (1992) studied the psychopathology of child survivors of a sea disaster involving an accident between a ship, the Jupiter, carrying schoolchildren and a tanker and found that all the children involved in the sinking had significantly higher depression scores than a control group. However, only girls scored higher in the category of anxiety. Other studies have shown that boys may be more prone to stress reactions than girls. Some researchers hypothesize that cultural norms teach boys to behave stoically, while girls may have more freedom to display their emotion.

Although such social norming is difficult to prove, it may account for the differences in reactions to disasters (Katz, 1989).

Sex differences in reaction to the space shuttle Challenger disaster were studied by Wright, Kunkel, Pinon, and Huston (1989). Because boys seem to be more interested in space travel than girls, the researchers tried to discern if sex made a difference in fourth-, fifth-, and sixth-grade children's desire to follow media coverage of the shuttle explosion and in their emotional reaction to the disaster. Overall, findings indicated that boys knew more about the space program than girls and, prior to the disaster, had watched more programs concerning space-oriented topics. Girls, on the other hand, scored higher than boys did on all of the measures concerning negative affect and emotional upset. The boys were generally distressed by this major setback in space exploration; girls worried about the danger another teacher may face on future missions.

How particular children are likely to process and respond to a disaster and its after-effects requires understanding the influence of their parents and other close adults. Aptekar and Boore (1990) noted that "children's symptoms have been found to be dependent on how their significant adults react, and to be exaggerated when the children are separated from those adults" (p. 83). Children tend to react to natural disasters in a manner similar to their parents; a child's distress positively correlates with the distress level of her or his parents (Vogel & Vernberg, 1993). Green et al. (1991) found in their study of the Buffalo Creek Flood disaster that older children may be more affected by parental reactions because they endure the strongest effects of their parents' emotional imbalance. In other words, if parents are emotionally ill-equipped to cope with a technological disaster, such as the Buffalo Creek Flood, older children tend to take on parenting roles for younger siblings. Additionally, children may be more likely to relate to their parents' feelings of survivor guilt or need to rectify the situation. Aptekar and Boore (1990) labeled this transference of feelings from adults to children "communicated anxiety."

In order to understand how children will probably react to a disaster, and thus how to proceed with interventions, requires cultural sensitivity, the recognition and understanding of the influences of culture in a given context. Two case studies—a bus and train collision in Israel (on June 11, 1985, a train collided with a lead bus that was taking a group of seventh graders on an end-of-year outing; nineteen children, one parent, the homeroom teacher, and the bus driver were killed while children and adults in the buses following the lead bus watched the incident;

Klingman, 1987), and the Chernobyl nuclear accident (on April 26, 1986, at 1:23 a.m., the world's worst nuclear disaster occurred at the Chernobyl nuclear power station in Belarus, in the northern part of the Ukraine, diffusing 190 tons of highly radioactive uranium and graphite into the atmosphere; *Chernobyl Children's Project Fact Sheet,* 1996)—provide excellent examples of how familiarity with a community's culture is essential for understanding how children are affected by and respond to a disaster and how interventions may best be conducted.

A community's grieving rituals are an integral part of its culture, and the lack of understanding of these rituals hampered the implementation of an effective intervention in Israel after the train and bus collision. For instance, the Jewish religion requires a traditional seven-day period in which family members stay at home to mourn the loss of their family member, after which they resume daily activities. During this period, help from strangers is not usually welcome. The way in which the intervention for the Israel bus and train wreck was handled interrupted this sacred period of mourning in three ways (Toubiana, Milgram, Strich, & Edelstein, 1988, p. 238):

1. The strangers may have been unwelcome and looked upon as intruders, especially if the families were religiously observant and the professional visitor failed to appreciate or perform the appropriate rituals.
2. The family was not left to use its own resources and other natural support resources.
3. Though there is no social mandate to do so, mourning families often feel obliged to provide refreshments (through the help of nonimmediate family members) for all visitors, an amenity that becomes burdensome with multiple visitors.

In addition, feedback offered after the intervention process revealed that "teachers complained that well-meaning outsiders were intrusive in the corridors and classrooms of the school and usurped the teacher's authority, thereby undermining the self-confidence of the school's primary helpgivers" (Toubiana et al., 1988, p. 237).

Intervention after the Chernobyl nuclear accident also demonstrates the importance of understanding a community's culture. Greenpeace (based out of Canada) traveled to Kiev to help children living in the affected area. In this situation, the Greenpeace tour experienced immediate difficulties in the foreign culture. Although the U.S.S.R. desperately needed extra help, this crisis exposed the country's "critical shortage of

food and medicine, outdated information and bureaucracy based on isolation and mistrust" (Lailey, 1993, p. 15). Allowing foreigners in at this
time of need was a humiliating moment in U.S.S.R. history, and the government offered little cooperation. "General challenges [of the Greenpeace tour] included understanding the medical system, the medical
training, the economy and the political state of the country, and the
effects of previous humanitarian aid projects. Daily challenges included
communication, human resources and supplies" (Lailey, 1993, p. 6). For
example, understanding local medical practices was important for chan-
neling and directing energy to those in need. Soviet practices differed
markedly from Canadian procedure in everything from the protocol of
how patients are seen in medical facilities to ordering and fixing equip-
ment and machinery (Lailey, 1993).

CONSEQUENCES OF DISASTERS
AND CHILDREN'S RESPONSES

The elements influencing a child's post-disaster reactions are complex and interdependent. When looking at the literature on how disasters affect children, two primary models are represented. These two
models offer a framework for looking at the effects of a particular disaster and can be used to compare and contrast effects across different
types of disasters. The older model, post-traumatic stress disorder
(PTSD), considers children more or less "passive victims" of a disaster.
Resiliency, the newer model, sees children as active, resourceful agents
possessing qualities or having access to environmental resources that
make them less prone to suffering ill effects. Other models, typically
developed for particular types of disasters (political violence or war) are
broader than either the PTSD or resiliency models and can be interpreted as including them.

PTSD

PTSD requires "the experience of a traumatic event that is 'outside
the range of usual human experience' [and which] is so extreme that
almost anyone would experience significant psychopathology and subsequent problems in adjustment" (Keppel-Benson & Ollendick, 1993,
p. 31). The fact that such an event has occurred does not warrant an
automatic PTSD diagnosis. Instead, the American Psychiatric Association requires (a) at least one of the symptoms that displays a re-experi-
encing of the event (a child may repeatedly act out what happened in
the disaster when playing with toys), (b) at least three of the symptoms

of avoiding aspects of the event or showing a general numbing of responsiveness (a child may avoid activities that remind her or him of the disaster, or be unable to remember parts of the disaster), and (c) at least two of the symptoms that display hyperarousal in the presence of relevant stimuli (a child may have difficulty falling or staying asleep, be irritable, have difficulty concentrating, or startle more easily) (La Greca, Silverman, Vernberg, & Prinstein, 1996; Saylor, 1993a). Additional characteristics of children with PTSD include a refusal to return to school and clinginess toward parents; endless fears about the disaster; feeling like she or he is unlucky; "spacing out" when people talk to him or her; sleep disturbances that last longer than a few days, such as nightmares, bedwetting, and screaming during sleep; behavioral problems not typical for that child; physical complaints such as stomachaches, headaches, and dizziness; and listlessness (American Academy of Child and Adolescent Psychiatry, 1996; Greenwald & Rubin, 1999). Some PTSD symptoms become more severe over time, such as feelings of shame, thought suppression, splitting off of emotions from disturbing memories, misperceptions, death dreams, perceptions of a shortened future, and repetitive play and re-enactment (Raphael, 1986).

PTSD rarely occurs during the stressful event; instead, symptoms begin to appear either right after the event or several months or years later (American Academy of Child and Adolescent Psychiatry, 1996). Keppel-Benson and Ollendick (1993) cited the extensiveness of the event, previous experiences, premorbid functioning, developmental considerations, and other variables as factors influencing the probability that a child will experience PTSD. Shaw et al. (1995) listed several risk factors, both internal and external to the child, that are linked to a vulnerability for PTSD: proximity to the high impact area, personal injury or the injury or death of a family member, parental response/parental psychopathology, degree of life threat, family structure, age, sex, pre-existing anxiety and depression, and early separation from parents. Lonigan, Shannon, Taylor, Finch, and Sallee (1994) reported that a child is more prone to develop PTSD if he or she has anxiety or negative emotionality, high levels of sadness, worry, fear, or feelings of loneliness. In addition, girls seem to be at greater risk than boys for developing long-term symptoms of PTSD, including being nervous, having stomachaches, fearing another natural disaster, or feeling lonely (La Greca et al., 1996). In her review of recent research on PTSD in children, Pfefferbaum (1997) divided predictors of children's PTSD responses into six areas: (1) physical proximity (e.g., direct exposure) and emotional proximity (e.g., a close family member or friend is affected) to the traumatizing event; (2) biological sex; (3) age and developmental level; (4) previous exposure, prior conditions, and initial response; (5) family influences; and (6) socio-economic and cultural factors (e.g., access to medical attention).

Resiliency

Studies of PTSD that fall into the area of resiliency research focus on children's personal characteristics and the attributes of their several ecosystems that predispose them to PTSD (Boyden, 1994; Rutter, 1987). "Resiliency is the child's capacity to bounce back from [or not succumb to] traumatic childhood events and develop into a sane, integrated, and socially responsible adult" (Apfel & Simon, 1996c, p. 1). In defining resiliency, researchers have considered what characteristics of a child and a child's environment constitute *risk factors,* "influences that increase the probability of onset, digression to a more serious state, or maintenance of a problem condition" (Kirby & Fraser, 1997, pp. 10–11), and what characteristics constitute *protective factors,* "internal and external forces that help children resist or ameliorate risk" (Kirby & Fraser, 1997, p. 16).

For example, Jeney-Gammon, Daugherty, Finch, Belter, and Foster (1992) found a relationship between children's means of coping with disaster and the development of depressive symptoms. Hypotheses drawn from three different theories were supported: psychoanalytic theory (H: children with feelings of anger and self-blame about a disaster are more likely than other children to develop depressive symptoms); Levinson's behavioral theory (H: children who withdraw from social interactions after a natural disaster develop higher levels of depressive symptoms than children who seek social support); and cognitive theory (H: children who positively reframe circumstances have less depression than children who blame themselves for the negative outcomes of disasters).

Children seem to be more resilient to psychological problems after a natural disaster if (1) they have family support systems able to respond to their needs; (2) their daily routine is quickly restored (including a return to school); and (3) they are given the opportunity to discuss and work through their fears and disaster experiences in a structured environment (Galante & Foa, 1986). Additionally, hardiness concept theory asserts that adaptive mechanisms within individual children, such as having an internal locus of control, a high level of dedication to tasks, and a perception of change as positive and challenging, can improve their ability to cope with natural disasters (Kiser et al., 1993).

Assessing the impact of war on children, Macksoud, Aber, and Cohn (1996) argued that a variety of variables affect the relationship between war-related stress and outcomes. For example, children who feel secure and who are trusting (often the result of having responsive parents) appear more adaptive to stressors than those who are insecure and not trusting, and children who feel empowered and competent to deal with stress are more likely to cope effectively.

In his discussion of children and political violence, Cairns (1996) reviewed the literature on children and disasters in an attempt to identify resiliency factors. For example, passive, withdrawn children appear to be more vulnerable to the effects of political violence, whereas extroverted children are more likely to respond with aggressive behavior; also, social support appears to be a resilience protective factor. However, Cairns recognized two problems with studies focusing on children's resilience to political violence that are not unique to research with this one type of disaster: Experts are still unsure why some children have strong protective factors, while other children bend under the slightest strain. "A major problem with this whole area is the almost complete lack of studies in which children have been seen both before and after their exposure to political violence. . . . Studies in this area often lack adequate (or any) control groups, while samples may be biased when they are obtained from clinical sources" (p. 69).

Regardless, the conceptualization of the child as active (resiliency) rather than passive (PTSD) is a compelling one. Gibbs (1994) never used the word *resiliency* but asked readers to reframe the child as an active subject with the ability and motivation to break patterns of trauma induced by exposure to warfare (described most frequently in PTSD models). In Mozambique, Gibbs found that "children do not perceive themselves, nor are they perceived as passive, vulnerable, or being unable to work. This is not to say that they have not suffered during the war and its aftermath, only that they have suffered just as everyone else has suffered" (p. 272).

GENERAL MODELS: REACTIONS AND INTERVENTIONS

Two general models for looking at children's reactions to disasters, one developed specifically for acts of political violence (Gibson, 1989) and the other applied to natural disasters (Vernberg, La Greca, Silverman, & Prinstein, 1996) conceptualize relationships among the disaster, the experience of the disaster, the children's personal characteristics, and the children's ecological systems. Gibson's (1989) model, developed for looking at the effects of political violence on children, takes a dynamic-interactionist approach. The model consists of five levels of considerations: (1) the immediate stressful event; (2) interpersonal factors, such as the child's sex, temperament, and coping strategies; (3) interpersonal and contextual variables, such as family support and the support available from others; (4) wider contextual variables, such as social, political, and economic conditions; and (5) the link between ideological structures of the society—the society's cultural beliefs—and factors on the other four levels.

Vernberg et al.'s (1996) integrative conceptual model enumerated four factors that determine a child's reaction after a natural disaster and described how these factors interact to affect the child as a whole. The model is broad and although developed for natural disasters, it may be logically extended to both technological and complex disasters.

The first factor in the Vernberg et al. model considers the amount of exposure to traumatic events. This is the most crucial factor in determining whether a child will develop PTSD symptoms. For example, La Greca et al. (1996) found that a child's level of exposure to a natural disaster was a significant factor leading to PTSD symptoms seven to ten months after the natural disaster. A natural disaster also may influence a child's access to social support and his or her ability to use coping strategies (Vernberg et al., 1996).

The second factor in the model considers the individual characteristics of a child, such as sex, ethnicity, and age (Vernberg et al., 1996), and the third examines the characteristics of the social environment, such as access to social support networks, the availability of natural disaster–related interventions, and the functional ability of the adults in the child's life. Children with strong social support networks typically cope better with trauma than isolated children, and although parents offer the most significant source of support to children, peers and teachers serve vital roles (Vernberg et al., 1996).

The fourth aspect of the Vernberg et al. model is based on the coping skills of children. Coping efforts are found to be highest among children with greater psychological distress (La Greca et al., 1996). The four different variables of coping strategies used in the model—positive coping, blame-anger, wishful thinking, and social withdrawal—are all associated with PTSD symptomatology (Vernberg et al., 1996). Research findings indicate that children generally use several of these coping strategies, positive and negative, to deal with a specific traumatic event. However, use of the negative coping strategy of blame-anger has been shown to be a strong predictor of PTSD symptomatology (La Greca et al., 1996); in contrast, wishful thinking is a harmless coping strategy typically used after a major natural disaster (Vernberg et al., 1996). (La Greca et al., 1996, add a fifth factor to the model: intervening stressful life events in a child's life. Traumatic life events unrelated to the natural disaster, such as the death of a family member or a divorce in the family, negatively effect a child's post-disaster reaction.)

As depicted in Figure 7.1, the four factors of the Vernberg et al. model interact with each other, such that a child's response to a disaster depends on a consideration of all four factors simultaneously. While one factor may be more important than others in a particular circumstance, it is only after consideration of all four factors that a child's reactions may be understood fully.

In addition to models that focus on children's reactions to disasters, there are models for planning interventions. For example, Vogel and Vernberg (1993) presented a four-stage model for planning interventions, both before and after a natural, technological, or complex disaster. The first stage is the pre-disaster preparation phase. During this stage, it is important that plans accommodate children's mental health needs. The second stage, disaster impact, starts the moment the disaster

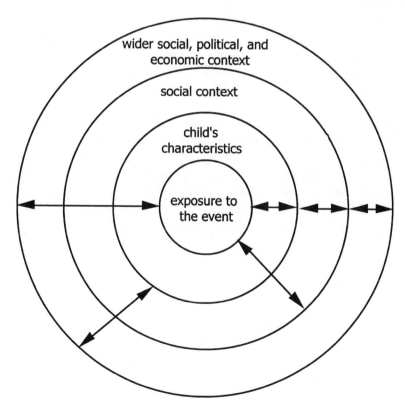

Figure 7.1   Interacting Elements in Children's Response to Disaster.

begins and lasts through its completion. Vernberg and Vogel (1993) advised that this time is well spent "providing support and advice to administrators and other adults in leadership positions, gathering and providing information regarding disaster events to children and families directly affected by the disaster, and managing acute distress among witnesses of the traumatic events" (p. 486).

The third stage, short-term adaptation, lasts from twenty-four hours to several months postdisaster. During this stage intervention strategies are introduced into classroom activities and family and individual treatment. Klingman (1987), for example, described events the day after the bus and train disaster in Israel: (a) informing teaching staff about different reactions they might see children display, (b) working with children who saw the crash occur, (c) checking in with children who were in a near-miss group because they had opted not to attend the end-of-year celebration, (d) observing children who were close friends of children killed in the crash, (e) allowing teachers to take a break while mental health professionals held class discussions, (f) pursuing children who displayed signs of extreme shock (e.g., wandering the halls aimlessly), (g) assigning peers to visit children who refused to return to school, (h) setting up a crisis hotline so parents and other concerned individuals could call for help, (i) consulting with school officials to plan daily school schedules (e.g., length of day, planning memorials), and (j) coordinating mental health teams.

Vernberg and Vogel's (1993) stage four is long-term adaptation. The time frame of this stage usually begins three months after a disaster occurs and lasts for an unspecified amount of time. Activities during this time include "individual, family and small group interventions and public ceremonies and other disaster-related rituals" (p. 486).

A second intervention model, one used for soldiers suffering from combat stress (Klingman, 1987; Toubiana et al., 1988), provides a different perspective from Vernberg and Vogel's (1993) time-oriented model. This model, which deals specifically with how to implement interventions, specifies four parts: (1) immediacy—the intervention should take place as soon as possible, (2) proximity—optimal intervention happens close to the scene of disaster, (3) community—the intervention is done in a setting shared by the population involved (e.g., a school), and (4) expectancy—the intervention should take place in an atmosphere where the people involved believe that the explanations provided, and the behavior required of them, ensure that their stress reactions are normal and that they will recover shortly.

NATURAL DISASTERS: REACTIONS
AND INTERVENTIONS

A child undergoes two different kinds of experiences when a natural disaster occurs. The first experience is the trauma of the natural disaster—the type of disaster, whether or not there was forewarning and time to prepare, the level of impact on the community, the amount of the family's direct exposure, and the length of time the disaster lasts (Lystad, 1990). The second experience involves the disruptions to daily life that result from the natural disaster—disruptions in living conditions, relationships, roles, and routines (Lystad, 1990). Both of these experiences serve as stressors for the child and can lead to psychological stress reactions. Typical reactions include the following:

a. fear—of any physical reminder of the event (Raphael, 1986), that the disaster will recur (University of Illinois at Urbana-Champaign, 1995), of the dark (Miller, Kraus, Tatevosyan, & Kamenchenko, 1993)

b. anxiety about the safety of loved ones, about the destruction of home and school (Kiser et al., 1993)

c. depression stemming from the inability of overwhelmed family members to provide support to their children (Goenjian et al., 1995)

d. poor school performance (Pynoos, Steinberg, Manoukian, Tavosian, & Fairbanks, 1993; Shannon, Lonigan, Finch, & Taylor, 1994)

e. behavioral symptoms—aggression (Durkin, Khan, Davidson, Zaman, & Stein, 1993; Raphael, 1986), avoidance of activities that remind them of the traumatic event (Miller et al., 1993)

f. separation anxiety—fears about dying and losing their parents (Goenjian, 1993), difficulty separating from their parents and going to school because they do not want to leave their parents' sight (University of Illinois at Urbana-Champaign, 1995)

g. PTSD (Garrison et al., 1995; Raphael, 1986; Shaw et al., 1995; Vogel & Vernberg, 1993; University of Illinois at Urbana-Champaign, 1995)

h. regression—thumb sucking and wanting to be held (University of Illinois at Urbana-Champaign, 1995), enuresis (Durkin et al., 1993)

i. somatic complaints—gastrointestinal complaints, sleep disturbances, headaches (Azarian, Skriptchenko-Gregorian, Miller, & Kraus, 1994)

j. guilt (Azarian et al., 1994; Goenjian et al., 1995; Pynoos et al., 1993)
k. concern for others (Saylor, Swenson, & Powell, 1992).

Interventions

Pre-disaster interventions. Ponton and Bryant (1991) described two phases of pre-disaster mental health interventions that can be used to strengthen children and their families. During the long-term pre-disaster phase (i.e., a natural disaster is not imminent), they recommend that child mental health professionals help with disaster planning activities in their community—educating community leaders about potential psychological effects of natural disasters on children and raising community awareness of children's potential mental health needs. During the acute pre-disaster period, when a natural disaster is imminent, all community leaders, including mental health professionals, should disseminate information to the public about impending danger and address the specific needs of children and families (Ponton & Bryant, 1991).

The Federal Emergency Management Agency (1997) recommended that parents should create a family disaster plan before a natural disaster occurs and provided details about how to develop such a plan.

La Greca et al. (1996) described classroom activities that could help teachers prepare their students for future natural disasters. These activities are designed to help children develop feelings of control over natural disasters, which can help them overcome feelings of helplessness and anxiety in the face of natural disasters.

Post-disaster interventions: individual. After natural disasters, individual therapeutic interventions with children have proven useful for children experiencing a great deal of post-disaster distress. The Children's Psychotherapy Center (Azarian et al., 1994) suggested the following interventions for childhood victims of natural disaster: individual psychotherapy; group psychotherapy; and cognitive-behavioral treatment, such as muscle and cognitive relaxation training, systematic desensitization, and occupational therapy. The Federal Disaster Law of 1974 mandated mental health services as part of disaster planning and recovery in the United States (Ponton & Bryant, 1991).

Systematic initial screening of children after a natural disaster is necessary to evaluate the severity of children's traumatic experiences, their losses, their level of post-traumatic stress reactions, their grief reactions, their level of depression, and their level of separation anxiety disorder.

This screening should be followed by periodic screening for potential secondary reactions in children not present during the initial screening (Goenjian, 1993). Evaluation results can be used to direct casework and treatment modalities. Children with post-traumatic stress reactions need early clinical intervention in order to prevent chronicity and secondary depression. Goenjian (1993) advised clinicians to use a variety of different techniques when treating children after natural disasters, with full awareness of the variations in onset, course, and risks of comorbid stress reactions in children.

An important aspect of individual therapy with children after a natural disaster is understanding their defense mechanisms (Miller et al., 1993). Therapists need to process the trauma with the children and help reconstruct their coping abilities. Muscle and cognitive relaxation training, cathartic figure drawing, dance, occupational therapy, and systematic desensitization should be considered for children suffering from post-disaster reactions (Miller et al., 1993). Massage therapy, used with grade-school children after Hurricane Andrew, represents an additional possibility (Field, Seligman, Scafidi, & Schanberg, 1996).

Because post-disaster disorders can be reinforced and increased by others similarly suffering, orphaned children should be placed with a new family or in children's homes with a small group of residents, rather than in large boarding houses (Kozlovskaia et al., 1991). Although small doses of tranquilizers and antidepressants when combined with therapy can be used to stop mental disorders (Kozlovskaia et al., 1991), most researchers do not recommend medication for children after natural disasters. Therapists must address issues of bereavement when working with children after a natural disaster; children with high levels of negative emotionality, especially sadness, should be encouraged to re-establish emotionally supportive relationships instead of withdrawing from social support (Lonigan et al., 1994).

Mental health professionals should respond not only to the immediate victims of a natural disaster, but also to children living in surrounding communities (Shaw et al., 1995). Children in areas peripheral to the impacted area suffer as well, and they are often overlooked by mental health professionals who leave these areas to provide aid to children directly affected.

After the Armenian earthquake, the Armenian Relief Society of the Western United States, in collaboration with the government of Soviet Armenia, organized and implemented a mental health treatment program for survivors (Goenjian, 1993). This program encompassed both individual and community interventions, with the following goals:

- to evaluate and provide psychological first-aid to about 10,000 victims in two years, and to offer brief individual and group therapy to people in great distress
- to train local therapists and teachers to provide mental health services to victims
- to open two mental health clinics in the earthquake zone
- to advise government officials and other relief organizations in assigning priorities to the various relief efforts.

The relief organization introduced therapeutic modalities into Soviet Armenia that focused on brief crisis-oriented individual and group psychotherapy (Goenjian, 1993). The therapy consisted of exploratory, supportive, and educational techniques, as well as behavioral interventions, such as progressive relaxation and systematic desensitization. The therapy encouraged the free expression of feelings and open communication between the therapist and client, which proved to be effective for this population.

Mental health professionals also met with teachers and provided them with information about psychological trauma and effective ways to cope with children's post-disaster distress (Goenjian, 1993). They also evaluated children in their schools, which helped identify those who needed individualized treatment (Goenjian, 1993).

Post-disaster interventions: family. Supportive relationships with family members, teachers, and friends are important means for helping children cope with the impact of natural disasters. Often, however, children try to hide their distress from their parents since they do not wish to add to their parents' stress (Sleek, 1998). Further, parents do not necessarily know how to detect signs of post-traumatic stress in children. Belter, Dunn, and Jeney (1991) found that parents reported significantly fewer symptoms of PTSD in their children than their children did.

Most family interventions focus on supporting parents and educating them about children's psychological needs following a natural disaster. Specific advice is available from ICES Disaster Resources (University of Illinois at Urbana-Champaign, 1995), and a Federal Emergency Management Agency (1996a, 1996b) publication, *Helping Children Cope with Disaster.* In addition, Konkov (1991) suggested that family psychotherapy is the most effective treatment for children after a natural disaster.

Post-disaster interventions: school. La Greca, Vernberg, Silverman, Vogel, and Prinstein's (1994) workbook, *Helping Children Prepare for and Cope with Natural Disasters: A Manual for Professionals Working with Elemen-*

tary School Children, details a variety of post-disaster strategies to use with children in a school setting. *Children, Stress, and Natural Disasters: School Activities for Children* (University of Illinois Cooperative Extension Service, 1995) offers guidelines and classroom activities for teachers to use under headings such as "Learning about Disasters," "Examples of Activities that Promote the Sharing of Experiences and the Expression of Feelings," and "Classroom Activities to Help Children Express Feelings." Galante and Foa (1986) provided a description of a treatment program used in an Italian elementary school for children after an earthquake.

Post-disaster interventions: community. Rubin and Sapirstein (1985) wrote about community recovery from a natural disaster. In the second chapter of their book, the authors conceptualized a framework for the communal recovery process that encompasses all domains of community life: residential, business, public services and facilities, the general population, and mitigation.

In her chapter "Community and Political Dynamics," Raphael (1986) discussed how a community's nature and culture influence the way that the community reacts to a natural disaster. She noted that the most influential variables in determining how a community will respond to a natural disaster are its degree of poverty, deprivation, underdevelopment, and socioeconomic vulnerability. She also claimed that a community's willingness or preparedness to cope with a natural disaster depends on its sense of vulnerability to the threat of natural disasters, the trust of its citizens in public authorities, its communication system, and the costs of preparedness and response.

Also in this chapter, Raphael (1986) discussed the phases a community undergoes in response to a natural disaster. Immediately after a natural disaster, a community experiences an initial shock and numbness, which leads to a spontaneous but uncoordinated response (typically, people flock to the disaster area to help but are not coordinated in their actions). After a period of time, the formal organizational structures of the community develop action plans to cope with the damage. However, these various organizational systems often conflict with one another over who has responsibility for what tasks, thereby making their roles ineffective.

Child and adolescent mental health professionals responding to the 1989 Loma Prieta earthquake in San Francisco developed a "hands on" approach to dealing with the community and served as consultants to community members after the disaster (Ponton & Bryant, 1991). They answered calls to a crisis hotline, developed widely disseminated educational materials on children and disasters, and provided consultation to the media, members of the community (e.g., teachers and parents), and members of other communities confronting natural disasters. Shannon et al. (1994) argued that professional education and public awareness about children's possible reactions to natural disaster are an important means of ensuring a rapid, normalized community recovery.

TECHNOLOGICAL DISASTERS: REACTIONS AND INTERVENTIONS

Technological disasters occur when something made by humans and intended for human use becomes defective with little or no warning, resulting in psychological and/or physical harm, such as when a building collapses, a plane crashes, a train derails, or air becomes poisonous following an industry mishap. Toxic spills and accidents at nuclear plants—relatively recent events—differ from many other types of disasters because of their important long-term consequences for human health and environmental welfare (Breton et al., 1993).

Specific stressors associated with the Chernobyl disaster, for example, were (a) evacuations (over 400,000 people became "environmental refugees"); (b) current and future food contamination—people had limited access to clean food, and the contaminated soil that grew the grass eaten by cattle and the vegetables eaten by people ensured continuing cycles of illness; (c) not being able to play outside—radiation, spread in the summer through forest fires, made many areas radioactive zones (bans still exist on children walking in the surrounding forests, playing in the parks, and picking wild vegetation, such as berries and flowers, due to possible high radiation content); (d) loss of family members, peers, and other significant relationships as a result of immediate and long-term radiation exposure or cancers; (e) future birth defects—there is a 250 percent increase in congenital birth defects and in infant mortality; and (f) greater risk of developing cancers—the greatest increase is in bone and connective tissue cancer, up 62 percent (Chernobyl Children's Project Fact Sheet, 1996; Connor, 1998).

Stressors similar to those after Chernobyl occurred after the March 28, 1979, meltdown at the Three Mile Island nuclear reactor in Middletown, Pennsylvania: (a) evacuations—children under the age of five and pregnant women within a five-mile radius were required to leave the area, as per the governor of Pennsylvania's order, while numerous other families evacuated by choice; (b) few families evacuated permanently, and many did not evacuate at all, increasing emotional stress for those who chose to remain in the area; (c) threat of possible plant explosion; (d) possibility of long-term effects of radiation exposure; (e) interruption of daily activity, including disruptions in school schedules and the ability to use contaminated play areas (Three Mile Island residents faced fewer problems with food than those near Chernobyl, since food was readily accessible from other parts of the country); and (f) continual dangers associated with exposure to decontamination procedures (Breton et al., 1993; Handford et al., 1986).

Unlike nuclear accidents and toxic spills, major transportation crashes, like the bus and train incident in Israel, are relatively common. The specific stressors associated with this disaster were (a) watching the accident unfold and not being able to do anything about the situation; (b) the death of peers and friends—including having to participate in the process of grieving and bereavement by helping to plan the funeral and bury the young deceased; (c) the death of a teacher; (d) the loss of routine in school-related activities; and (e) the initial fear of returning to school (Klingman, 1987).

Second-hand exposure to technological disasters also may be a problem, as when the space shuttle Challenger exploded on the morning of January 28, 1986. Terr et al. (1996) interviewed 153 third and tenth graders from Concord, New Hampshire, who watched the Challenger explosion on television, and from Porterville, California, who heard about the explosion, at two different times: five to seven weeks after the disaster and then again after fourteen months. The majority of the children's memories were clear, consistent, and detailed; they were able to talk about where they were, who else was there, and personal occurrences linked to the event. (Those less emotionally involved demonstrated significantly less ability to recall.)

The specific stressors associated with second-hand exposure to the Challenger disaster included the following: (a) the initial shock of watching the disaster, followed by substantial emotional distress, especially because of its repetitive broadcast over the media (Stevenson, 1986), although distress reportedly subsided approximately six days after the explosion (Wright et al., 1989); (b) sadness at the loss of a teacher and friend by the children at the school in Concord, New Hampshire, where astronaut Christa McAuliffe taught—it is arguable that the rest of the nation's reaction was less severe, although still significant, than that felt by people in Concord; and (c) anger at not knowing who to blame for the deaths of the crew—young children particularly expressed anger, needing someone to blame, whereas older children saw the explosion partially as a technical error and not necessarily the result of human error.

Interventions

Children's responses to technological disasters are mediated by risk and protective factors. For example, Handford et al. (1986) found that the intensity of children's responses to the Three Mile Island nuclear accident was affected by their parents' reactions (e.g., when the parents' reactions were different from each other, the children's reactions were more intense), and children with a psychiatric disorder were either more reactive or less reactive to the trauma than the normal children. Several studies confirm that proximity to a disaster affects reactions. Little, however, is known about risk, resiliency, and children's reactions to technological disasters because of the lack of attention to individual, as opposed to group, variations in responses.

Unlike natural disasters, with which children often have some familiarity and some coping mechanisms, technological disasters present a challenge to those trying to help children cope (Wright et al., 1989). Children typically have little or no guidance as to how they should react or what their feelings mean when an unfamiliar disaster occurs (Wright et al., 1989). For example, children had no previous examples of how to react to or make sense of the Challenger explosion (Wright et al., 1989). Similarly, after a toxic spill, children have a difficult time processing the disaster since such accidents have no definitive end; children are left in a state of constant anxiety and fear (Erickson, 1994).

Too often, communities do not adequately plan for possible technological disasters. However, differences in types of technological disasters make any uniform or generalizable plan difficult to formulate. Depending on the disaster—whether natural, technological, or complex—some interventions are best geared toward group work, while others should focus on individual counseling. A combination of both approaches is most often used. Since technological disasters affect more than one family, initial group interventions are best; individual sessions can be accommodated as the need arises.

Community interventions. The collective decisions a community makes concerning whether and how to proceed with an intervention significantly determines children's mental health wellness after a technological disaster. When studying a sea disaster involving an accident between the Jupiter, a ship carrying schoolchildren, and a tanker, Yule (1992) found that some schools supported the quick organization of mental health teams, while other schools decided not to pursue help until nearly a year later. Yule compared the different approaches and found that the schools that pursued immediate help fared better than those choosing to wait.

The strength of a community's bonding is another determinant of the recovery of its citizens. For some, a traumatic event is a bonding experience, whereas others find their relationships deteriorating. Erickson

(1994) wrote about community bonding with respect to two types of communities, "corrosive" and "therapeutic." In a corrosive community, people divide themselves into the "hurt" and "unhurt"; the unhurt "try to distance themselves from those touched, almost as if they are escaping something spoiled, something contaminated, something polluted" (p. 236). A therapeutic community, however, is one in which "the shared experience becomes almost like a common culture, a source of kinship" (p. 237). As Erickson stated: "It is the *community* that offers a cushion for pain, the *community* that offers a context for intimacy, the *community* that serves as the repository for binding traditions. And when the community is profoundly affected, one can speak of a damaged social organism in almost the same way that one would speak of a damaged body" (p. 234).

Planning interventions in response to technological disasters almost always involves large groups of people in the decision-making process and takes place on the community level. As Toubiana et al. (1988) pointed out, maintaining agreement between the organizations involved (e.g., school personnel, emergency crews, government officials) requires continual discussion. To implement intervention with minimum complications, governments, politicians, and administrators should be included in all planning stages. Their authority is needed in order to implement and direct public policy (Apfel & Simon, 1996a). In addition, keeping lines of communication open and intact will repress subsequent difficulties from arising. For instance, once the initial chaos subsided, the intervention plan for the Israeli bus and train disaster called for a coordination of interdisciplinary teams. This decision was adopted to avoid duplication of services, contradictions in plans, disagreements about what type of approach should be used (e.g., clinical versus psychoeducational), and rivalries among the adults working together (Klingman, 1987).

Yule (1992) offered the following suggestions for the most effective intervention. First, it is paramount to get children to "make sense of what happened to them and to gain mastery over their feelings" (p. 224). According to Yule, the most efficient way to go about this process is to treat the children in small groups and to ask them to write out their complete recollection of the disaster.

Besides writing, letting children talk about their experience in a safe environment—especially to their parents—is extremely beneficial (Wright et al., 1989; Yule, 1992). Whether performing a communitywide intervention or working with children on an individual basis, children need to verbalize their feelings and emotions (Breton et al., 1993). Teachers can facilitate discussion by encouraging children to bring in photos and newspaper articles in order to commemorate the dead and allowing them to hear information they may need in order to process the event (Monaco & Gaier, 1987). Children also can profit from talking to other children who have lived through the disaster. The dialogue between these children can help put into perspective feelings of anxiety, survival guilt, sadness, and shame (Yule, 1992).

Interventions may be necessary for those involved in, but not necessarily directly affected by the disaster. In the case of the bus and train disaster, intervention protocol was needed for the parents, surviving teachers, and children. After the Jupiter experience, some teachers indicated that children who were friends of students who had survived the ordeal seemed to have been impacted by the tragedy, as witnessed by a marked decline in their end-of-year examination scores (Yule, 1992).

Although valid post-disaster psychological assessments of children are important, the literature on children and disasters provides little information on how to conduct them. Handford et al. (1986) recommended that children be given a standardized disaster-specific questionnaire and a standardized mental status examination. In addition, mental health professionals should take histories, establish a child behavioral anxiety scale, and give a psychiatric diagnosis. Finally, the parents should be given the same disaster-specific questionnaire and mental status test to get their impression of their child's mental health.

COMPLEX DISASTERS: REACTIONS AND INTERVENTIONS

The range of events included under the heading "complex disaster" is much broader than the range that defines natural and technological disasters. Community violence, civil war, government-sponsored terrorism, terrorism between nations, and war between nations are all examples of complex disasters, of events that are the result of human design or motivation. In the introduction to their book, *Minefields in Their Hearts,* Apfel and Simon (1996b) write:

> In this book, we and other mental health professionals speak of children wounded by war, persecution, and communal violence. The wounds are caused by direct bodily injury, by witnessing violence done to others, and by separation from loved ones. . . . Their effects may be felt into the next generations. (p. 1)

Fitzpatrick and Boldizar (1993) estimated both the physical (e.g., the murder rate for black youths is seven times greater than for white youths) and psychological (e.g., victims of a violent crime often experience depression) effects of community violence on 221 low-income black youth. Their findings indicate that being a victim of and a witness to violence were strong predictors of PTSD symptomatology and that men were more likely to be witnesses to and victims of violent acts. Results also suggested that "older children and those living with both parents or at least one primary female reported fewer symptoms than did younger children or those living in households without the presence of primary females" (p. 428).

Looking at community violence in a different context, Aber (1994) studied the effects of Lebanon's civil war on children, a war that lasted from 1975 until 1991. Based on his work with UNICEF, Aber suggested a useful model of the effects of war-related stress and trauma on children, discussed classifying children according to their level of involvement in the war—from active, such as being a victim, to limited, such as emigration—and presented information on outcome possibilities, such as PTSD. Using the PTSD model to organize the effects he observed, Aber analyzed how different variables (e.g., father's occupation) may influence children's reactions.

Melville and Lykes (1992) provided another perspective on the effects of civil war on children in their study of the sociocultural and psychosocial effects of government-sponsored terrorism on Guatemalan Indian children. Their comprehensive research projects in Guatemala and Mexico (where there are more than 46,000 Guatemalan refugees) were conducted separately during the summer of 1988. In addition to addressing the situated context of a thirty-year civil war, their discussion of effects ranged from the physical, such as sleep disturbances, to the sociocultural, such as changes in traditional dress (e.g., there was a decline in attachment to traditional dress by the children in Mexico), language use (e.g., the children had either not learned Mayan or had discontinued its use), and sex-related work (e.g., whereas the boys in Guatemala received better preparation for peasant life in Guatemala, for the boys in Mexican refugee camps, farming was not feasible). Analyzing what factors enabled children's survival—what they call "resources for survival"—the researchers found that the children thought support from parents and close relatives, or if these support providers were not available, from friends or caretakers, was most helpful in their recovery.

Summarizing numerous studies of the effects of war—including the Yom Kippur War in Israel, and the war in Lebanon—and political violence on children—including Palestinian children; children in South Africa, Mozambique, and Central America; and children in a Cambodian concentration camp—Swenson and Klingman (1993) offered a guide for looking at direct, long-term, and indirect effects. For example, many children exposed to the war in Lebanon had "symptoms of post-traumatic stress . . . and feelings of betrayal that altered their sense of trust" (p. 139), and children exposed to the political violence in Cambodia who lived "in foster care were more likely to have a psychiatric diagnosis than children living with their family" (p. 148). Long-term effects pertain to the adult survivors of childhood war experiences, and indirect effects consider the effects on children of survivors. Swenson and Klingman (1993) also summarized interventions following conventional war and note general findings. For example, psychotherapy alone is often inadequate, so interventions at the community, school, and family levels must be used. (Solomon, 1995, discussed several empirical studies of different responses of Israeli children to the Gulf War. Age, sex, and levels of exposure are among the variations she analyzes.)

Interventions

Not all children succumb to the horrors of complex disasters; some are resilient. Apfel and Simon (1996b, pp. 9–12, and 1996c, pp. 3–4), summarizing research across a variety of types of complex disasters and considering data from interviews with survivors and clinicians, outline the factors they see as contributing to resiliency:

1. *resourcefulness,* the ability to extract warmth and kindness in the worst of circumstances; including the ability to attract and use adult support, which enhances feelings of power and competence
2. *curiosity and intellectual mastery,* which includes being knowledgeable about the crisis around them and being active rather than passive, seeking rather than denying
3. *ability to conceptualize,* to gain a broader view of the disaster, a view that makes it more than a personal struggle
4. *compassion—but with detachment*
5. *conviction of one's right to survive*
6. *ability to remember and invoke images of good and sustaining figures,* usually parents, who offer standards and ideals that provide a sense of security, of order
7. *ability to be in touch with a variety of feelings and emotions, and not denying or suppressing major affects as they arise*—including the ability to compartmentalize the pain and postpone affect until it is safe to express and the ability to laugh and to stay calm in trying circumstances

8. *a goal to live for; a vision of the possibility and desirability of the restoration of a civilized moral order,* which includes recognizing that "a need to act in order to restore moral order may take precedence over the need to get even" (p. 11)

9. *the need and ability to help others, to be altruistic*—recognizing that helping others also helps oneself and that being helpless to stop the disaster does not mean being helpless in dealing with its consequences.

Focusing on risk rather than protective factors, Parson (1995a) discussed two different types of risk factors. The first type is "intraself" risk factors, such as absence of emotional support, low educational attainment, and prior traumatic exposure. The second type is "socioenvironmental" risk factors, such as the suddenness of onset of the disaster, degree of destruction and social network disruption, and the post-disaster community resources available. Within the context of intraself risks, socioenvironmental risks, and protective factors, interventions are developed to help the victims of complex disasters.

Perhaps the single most useful source for looking at interventions for complex disasters is Saylor's (1993a) text, *Children and Disasters,* which contains three chapters summarizing interventions with children: Gillis's "Individual and Small-Group Psychotherapy for Children Involved in Trauma and Disaster," Klingman's, "School-Based Intervention Following a Disaster" (cf. Walz & Bleuer, 1992), and Joyner and Swenson's "Community-Level Intervention after a Disaster." These chapters address when and where caretakers should get involved, what the children might be feeling (from PTSD to revenge fantasies), how everything from theory to hotlines to free writing activities might help, and why some children may be harder to reach than others (e.g., ethnic differences in responses to help and problems associated with victim mistrust).

Focusing on individual-oriented therapy, Wall and Levy (1996) presented a unique approach to working with families and children. Children who suffer the death of a significant other because of homicide, or who witness a homicide, often withdraw and become rude and argumentative, and their trust in human relationships may be shattered. By suggesting the use of narrative theory as part of an intervention, Wall and Levy move beyond the usual alternatives associated with working with victims.

Although they specifically focus on clinical applications of narrative theory to children, families, and communities exposed to homicide,

Wall and Levy's approach may be useful in other contexts. They described narratives as:

> symbolized accounts of actions that have temporal dimensions. Narratives are not literal accounts of events, since they incorporate the narrator's perspective and evaluation. . . . Narratives are used to evaluate the past in the light of the present, as models to guide current behavior, as well as to anticipate future events and experiences. (1996, p. 404)

Children who construct coherent narratives typically are those able "to maintain a sense of personal meaning when confronted by unpredictable events and adversity." In contrast, children who construct incoherent narratives may be revealing their "lack of interpersonal security, self-fragmentation, and a loosening of ties to a social environment" (p. 405). One of the goals of an intervention-employing narrative is to help children develop narrative coherence; to do so, caregivers should pay attention "to both the structure and content of the narratives and their potential to provide avenues for enhancing a sense of self-efficacy" (p. 405). (Wall and Levy describe an in-depth case study of how to use this intervention with a nine-year-old black child who survived the death of his brother, a victim of gang violence.)

Based on their analysis of effective interventions designed for children who are victims of a complex disaster, Apfel and Simon (1996b) observed nine aspects they had in common:

> (1) genuine and nonjudgmental caring for the child survivors; (2) respect for the child . . . and for the strengths of the survivor while providing for his or her needs; (3) recognition of the complexity of the child's experience and nonpartisan empathy with the child's struggle; (4) willingness to try nontraditional approaches derived from the particular culture, child, or situation; (5) willingness to try another intervention when something is not working . . . ; (6) attentiveness to the caregiver's needs . . . ; (7) encouragement of acts that help build or restore community—especially acts of altruism and helpfulness; (8) development of approaches that progressively empower and encourage . . . ; [and] (9) awareness of the political dimensions of violence, so that one can help the child form an age-appropriate understanding of the larger political and social context. (p. 13)

Many of the interventions offered in the literature on children and disasters have an individual or small group focus, but sometimes because the disaster is too large and all-encompassing to manage or the resources available are severely limited, the approach needs to be on a larger scale. Boothby (1996), based on his unique experience working in Cambodia, Mozambique, and Rwanda, argued that:

given the scale of need associated with war and refugee crises, and the severe lack of financial and professional resources, a primary mental health approach may be a more effective way of mounting sustainable responses to the social and psychological needs of children and their families. (p. 152)

For example, communities using relief workers, paraprofessionals, teachers, social workers, nurses, and community agencies and religious organizations can be mobilized to respond to crises in useful and cost-effective ways. These individuals and groups can establish support networks, and enhance parental coping skills.

At the community level, psychosocial programs may be integrated with other programs, such as employment initiatives and job training, to impact more fully the needs of children and families. Using the Project on Children and War in Mozambique as an example, Boothby described how government and nongovernment agencies were brought together to develop a family reunification program, locate unaccompanied children (i.e., children who left or were forced to leave their parents, or children whose parents died), and search for lost family members. Water and agricultural programs, community-based foster care, and primary health programs were developed for communities that took in large numbers of orphans and unaccompanied children.

CASE STUDY OF A COMPLEX DISASTER: THE OKLAHOMA CITY BOMBING

On Wednesday, April 19, 1995, at 9:02 A.M., an explosion caused by a 4,800-pound explosive blasted through the Alfred P. Murrah Federal Office Building in Oklahoma City, Oklahoma. "Reverberations from the blast shattered windows throughout the city; and glass fell like sharp rain over whole sections of the city, literally covering the streets for blocks and blocks throughout the downtown area. . . . All over Oklahoma City, people felt the force of the blast" (Sitterle & Gurwitch, 1999, p. 161). One hundred sixty-eight people were killed, including 19 infants and children, 614 were treated in outpatient clinics, and 82 were hospitalized (Krug, Nixon, & Vincent, 1996). In addition to the people who were directly wounded, an immeasurable number of people were indirectly harmed. Thirty-eight percent of the population of the area knew someone who had been killed or injured in the blast, and people who were in areas near the blast, such as children in nearby schools, also were traumatized by the disaster (Krug et al., 1996).

Children not living in Oklahoma City or not knowing anyone harmed in the bombing also were affected by the disaster. Peterson (1995) writes that children living in New Haven, Connecticut, felt fear and sadness after the Oklahoma City bombing:

> Young children tend to internalize traumas, whereas adults are able to sep-
> arate themselves from faraway crises. . . . "I'm scared. It could happen
> here," one student said. "I dreamed that I lost my mother and father in a
> bombing," [another] said. Another boy said his mother told him to watch
> coverage of the bombing because "it could happen to you." "I feel scared
> because that could have happened in New Haven, and we could have been
> dead," another child added. (p. 1)

The Oklahoma City bombing strongly affected children's sense of safety throughout the United States: "The school's social worker said the discussion gave counselors a glimpse at how students react to catastrophes. 'It's a stressful situation, and we definitely get a sense of what the children are going through,' she said" (Peterson, 1995, p. 1).

Unlike natural and technological disasters, responses to complex disasters, such as domestic terrorism, reflect the reality that there is someone or something to blame. Parson (1995a) explained the difference in people's responses to disasters that are caused by a human who intends harm, as opposed to those caused by accident or by nature. Complex disasters, according to Parson (1995a), cause individuals to lose their sense of trust and meaningfulness in life: "Most people do not expect to suffer unspeakable psychological horror, anguish, and pain from the purposive acts of another human being" (p. 167). Timothy McVeigh, as a domestic terrorist, added a frightening dimension to the disaster (Romano & Kenworthy, 1997).

Children's responses to the Oklahoma City bombing included the following signs of anxiety (American Psychological Association, n.d.b; Belshe, 1995; Sitterle & Gurwitch, 1999): nightmares, decrease in grades, heightened aggression, bedwetting, hyperactivity, withdrawal from family and friends, eating and sleeping problems, sensitivity to loud sounds, withdrawal from other people, and being unusually quiet. The American Psychological Association (n.d.a) urged parents to seek the help of a mental health professional if their child exhibited frequent nightmares, extreme aggression, complete withdrawal, constant "war games," and an inability to perform daily activities.

Interventions

An important aspect of intervention is "meaning management," which involves the "explorations, decisions, actions, and programs geared to identify, highlight, and restructure shattered, distorted meaning systems in victims" (Parson, 1995b, p. 269). The Oklahoma City bombing destroyed people's trust and left them wondering why such a horrific nightmare would happen to them; interventions were needed to address this perception and attempt to restore each survivor's sense of psychosomatic and social equilibrium (Parson, 1995b).

Parson (1995b) listed nineteen service-delivery principles that supported intervention efforts in the Oklahoma City bombing. The first principle states that "services take into account the local customs, practices, desires and values of Oklahoma City victims" (p. 269). Other principles highlight the interdisciplinary and integrative nature of services and the need for service deliverers to be inclusive and not overlook certain people, to reinforce positive attitudes, to enhance self-worth, to facilitate self-help and social support groups in the community, and to develop programs for taking care of the caretakers.

Parson (1995a) described the self-efficacy adaptational coping model (SEAC), composed of four phases survivors usually go through after a disaster as they attempt to regain their sense of meaning: (1) turbulence and processing, (2) stasis and reappraisal, (3) immersion and transition, and (4) self-efficacy and adaptational coping. During the turbulence and processing phase, which lasts from zero to three months, children often suffer from "separation anxiety, school avoidance, disturbed sleep patterns, hyperarousal, and even bed wetting and encopresis" (p. 275). During stasis and reappraisal, which lasts from three to six months, victims (Parson does not distinguish between adults and children) "feel trapped and lost in a new and strange world of fears, anxieties, and helplessness" (p. 282). Victims feel vulnerable and a strong need to find meaning in what has happened to them. During the third phase, immersion and transition, which lasts from six to eighteen months, victims still have symptoms of PTSD, feelings of vulnerability, and intense rage. The last phase, self-efficacy and adaptational coping, lasts from eighteen to twenty-four months and is marked by feelings of incompetence and inability to manage events and deal with the environment. Parson presented a detailed description of each phase, including the goals of intervention and general intervention strategies.

Post-disaster interventions: assessment. Parson (1995a) suggested the need for a post-disaster assessment of all victims of terrorism. In order to determine the specific needs of each survivor, this assessment ideally should take place before intervention strategies are developed:

Though all victims may appear homogeneous in levels of exposure their response patterns may differ significantly based upon such variables as personality, coping capacities, temperament, and the nature of the recovery socioecology. Post-disaster assessment attempts to create a true victim-service fit through systematic data gathering from the following sources: (1) personal history and dynamics before the disaster . . . (2) objective and subjective perceptions and stress behavior during the disaster . . . and (3) the specific stresses and responses after the incident (e.g., disruption of basic needs: food, shelter, water, medicines, and loss of personal resources). (pp. 168–169)

Assessment takes place in several stages, beginning with classifying victims into one of several categories, such as "direct impact victims," "direct contact victims," or "peripheral victims" (people affected by the suffering of family and friends, but who have no personal injuries or property loss). Second, instruments and questionnaires (e.g., structured clinical interviews, validated instruments to assess mood, anxiety, coping, and social support) are used to assess post-disaster functioning. Diagnosis and the development of intervention strategies complete the assessment process, although Parson argues that assessment is ongoing, as victims' status changes.

Post-disaster interventions: family. The American Psychological Association (n.d.b) on-line publication, *Helping Children Cope: A Guide to Helping Children Cope with the Stress of the Oklahoma City Explosion,* offered recommendations to parents interested in helping their children cope with the bombing. These recommendations included the following general guidelines: talk to your children about their feelings, be patient, monitor television viewing so that children are not exposed to sensationalism, give children an outlet for their anxiety (such as drawing, writing letters to survivors or to their congressional representative, and donating money or time to the Red Cross), make a preparation plan in case of a future disaster, teach children about conflict resolution, stay calm, and help your children feel protected. The American Psychological Association (n.d.a) also created a Disaster Response Network that offers on-site, free mental health services to disaster survivors and relief workers.

Sitterle and Gurwitch (1999) described the "Compassion Center," an important support intervention for families with missing loved ones. Located at the First Christian Church, this is where the families of the 300 people thought to be missing gathered immediately after the blast to obtain information, provide information (e.g., photographs and medical records of missing loved ones), and receive emotional support and assistance.

During the days following the bombing, literally thousands of volunteers and hundreds of family members passed through the center. The medical examiner's office, the National Guard, the military, police, clergy, the American Red Cross, the Department of Veterans Affairs Oklahoma Medical Center, the Department of Veterans Affairs Emergency Management Preparedness Office, the Department of Veterans Affairs National Center for PTSD, and the Salvation Army integrated and worked in a coordinated fashion to deliver immediate services. (pp. 167–68)

In addition to the Compassion Center, mental health services provided briefings during which accurate and up-to-date information was provided to families and organized death notification teams with personnel from the medical examiner's office, mental health professionals, and clergy.

Post-disaster interventions: community. In the wake of the Oklahoma City bombing, rituals and ceremonies enabled community members to offer support to one another and publicly grieve for their losses: "Ceremonies, vigils, celebrations, and other forms of ritual give people an opportunity to connect at a time when they feel disconnected by affirming identity, relatedness, and the social values of goodness and justice" (Sitterle & Gurwitch, 1999, p. 178). For example, during the national day of mourning, tens of thousands of people, including President and Mrs. Bill Clinton, attended the service entitled "A Time of Healing" (Isaza, 1995). Prayer services were widely used by community members. A crisis and prevention team also held a seminar several days after the bombing to help mourners deal with the stress (Belshe, 1995). On the first anniversary of the disaster, ceremonies were designed specifically for the victims and survivors, who were allowed on the disaster site for the first time.

As part of the ceremony, 168 seconds, one for each of the victims who perished in the blast, were set aside for a period of silence as thousands of people crowded into the few blocks around the Alfred P. Murrah Federal Building site. The whole nation paused while the names of those murdered were read. One by one, name by name, for 20 minutes, a roll call of 168 names was recited. (Sitterle & Gurwitch, 1999, p. 180)

In addition, victims received an outpouring of support from people throughout the country. Potts (1995) wrote:

There was no shortage of help in downtown Oklahoma City Thursday afternoon. In addition to the rescuers, there were people offering food to rescuers, terrified people awaiting news about family members, media workers and other bystanders. In fact, Salvation Army volunteer Heather Hatfield said they had such an oversupply of food that they were throwing out some that had gone bad. "The help is overwhelming," Hatfield said. (p. 1)

Many people donated blood and other resources to the disaster victims (Gallaga, 1995), and many local counseling services offered therapy free of charge (Belshe, 1995). According to Krug et al. (1996), psychologists became a significant part of the communal recovery effort:

> Their roles have been diverse and include serving on notification teams to families with regard to their loved one's status; answering emergency phone lines established for concerned, stressed, and anxious persons in the community; debriefing rescue workers; planning immediate and long-term services for persons who will require care for significant emotional disorders that will arise from this tragedy and for which debriefing and brief counseling are not sufficient; leading research teams to address the effects of this terrorism; and, of major significance, gatekeeping to prevent revictimization by both well-meaning and profit-seeking individuals. (p. 104)

The "gatekeeping" function proved to be a significant role for psychologists in order to prevent the survivors from being abused further (Krug et al., 1996). To achieve this aim, the psychologists convinced Governor Frank Keating of Oklahoma to establish a coordinating group to oversee help and access to the survivors. The State of Oklahoma, Department of Mental Health and Substance Abuse Services, was given complete control for coordinating clinical services, and the University of Oklahoma Health Sciences Center was given responsibility for coordinating research and education concerning the disaster (Krug et al., 1996). The ability of the Oklahoma City community to collaborate in this manner ensured the maximum care and protection of the victims.

The stress experienced by mental health and volunteer workers made "helping the helpers" a necessary part of the post-disaster intervention plan. For example, short defusings lasting less than a half-hour were required of all workers at the end of their shifts each day. Also, members of death notification teams participated in mandatory defusings after each notification and team members were limited to no more than four notifications in total (Sitterle & Gurwitch, 1999, p. 172).

The community affected by the disaster went beyond Oklahoma City to include the entire United States. In addition to the child victims and witnesses of the bombing, children throughout the country were distressed by this bombing event. Schwartz (n.d.) offered advice on how communities nationwide could tell their children about terrorist bombings. Schwartz advised, "We must find a balance on the one hand between helping a child feel safe and on the other acknowledging the existence of violence, evil, and danger in the world" (p. 1). He offered three suggestions for parents and teachers when discussing terrorist bombings with children. First, adults should wait for children to bring up the subject, instead of introducing it to children. Second, adults should think carefully about their own feelings and insights about what happened before sharing their thoughts with children. This will better prepare them to discuss and then explore the topic with children. Third, the discussion should include elements of faith and morality, which allow children to think through the meanings of good and evil.

PREPARING FOR AND RESPONDING TO COMPLEX DISASTERS: A THEORY AND PRACTICE PERSPECTIVE

During the 1970s, the north of Israel was under continuous threat of rocket shelling. These rockets, nicknamed "Katyushas," were fired sporadically from South Lebanon. By the late 1970s and early 1980s, virtually no week went by without an attack, day or night. The town of Kiryat Shmona, a large target situated only four kilometers from the border, was hit most of the time. Usually, structures and properties were destroyed; occasionally there were injuries and fatalities. For example, in 1974 terrorists attacked Kiryat Shmona killing eighteen and injuring sixteen children and adults. Perhaps the most significant damage was psychosocial.

Over the past twenty years, Kiryat Shmona's population has fluctuated between 16,000 and 20,000, although some 250,000 people lived there at one time or another: Massive turnover is one of the psychosocial outcomes of the tense situation. Today, people in this area still live with a general threat of shelling; shellings occur occasionally and without advance warning. Over the years, adults and children have learned to identify precursors of the hazard.

In 1979, when the project leading to the establishment of the Community Stress Prevention Centre began, fewer than ten articles and no books had been written about how civilians cope with critical incidents, such as ongoing shelling, and the most effective coping strategies. The only guidebook available was a collection of activities called *Rescue* (Ayalon, 1976).

The First Project: The Model for Working in Schools

Based on the experiences of Caplan (1975) and Klingman and Ayalon (1977), the first stress prevention and intervention project developed by the Community Stress Prevention Centre was initiated in schools in Kiryat Shmona. An immediate problem was getting principals and teachers to address the subject of crisis intervention and stress prevention in their classes. Superstitious and rational thinkers alike were wary of broaching the subject. Time and further shelling, however, convinced the first principal that the staff and students needed a psychoeducational program to help them deal with the situation. To a large extent, the steps planned in 1979 constitute the basis of the current model used by the Community Stress Prevention Centre for developing preventive and intervention projects.

After convincing principals of the program's value, the next step was to form a team to control the project and to deal with the school's emergencies (even though schools had gone through ten years of shelling without such provisions). The principal, vice principal, a senior head of a department, school nurse, counselor, psychologist, special education teacher, and the teacher responsible for safety and security comprised this team. They worked on developing and testing the school's response readiness to emergencies and participated in developing the psychoeducational program.

A second team was formed with volunteer teachers who agreed to learn a variety of methods and techniques for developing a student-centered program. The primary focus of the program was on how to talk and work through feelings accompanying life on the border and in the shadow of threat. This group met for ten sessions and the result of their work was a program for pupils eventually called "No One Is Alone."

The next step was for a pair of teachers, or a teacher and the school counselor, to pilot the new program. Organized in small groups with a rotating chairperson, students were given various tasks, such as developing their own shelter first-aid box (with games and pencil and paper activities), and designing a system to report if someone is missing so that a squad of adults could be sent to search for the child. Teachers, trained to serve as facilitators, guided and supported the student groups' self-energized process.

The initial project was evaluated by Lahad and Abraham (1983), who reported a reduction in students' anti-social behavior, screaming, and physical symptoms and an increase in their cooperative behavior, such as mutual support. In addition, the groups had a high degree of openness: the children willingly shared personal thoughts and feelings about what was happening in their part of Israel. Although the level of situational anxiety was higher for students in the experimental program than for those in a control group, students in the program also showed an increase in their effective use of coping skills. These outcomes have been corroborated for recent No One Is Alone programs (Shacham, 1996).

BASIC Ph: An Integrative Model of Coping and Resiliency

Children and adults in northern Israel cope effectively with the constant threat to their lives, property, and daily routine. For example, a survey of referrals to the local mental health clinic and school psychology services in Kiryat Shmona showed that they were at the same rate as referrals in the center of Israel (Lahad, 1981)—between 5 and 10 percent. If such a small percentage of the population manifests acute stress reactions following an incident, what helps the rest of the population continue their lives productively?

Responses to two questions, "What helps you to continue living in this situation?" and "What do you do in order to continue?" provide the simple answer: People often are stronger than expected, and momentary disability does not predict pathology; most peoples' responses are simply normal reactions to abnormal situations. Today, using a resiliency framework, the idea that children and adults exposed to critical incidents can successfully survive is a common one, but in the late 1970s this concept was rather new.

Like many other researchers in the field of resiliency, Lahad focused on how people survive and what they do to cope. Based on observations and interviews with hundreds of adults (parents, teachers, and community workers) and students (children and adolescents) living under constant and prolonged threats in Israel and elsewhere, Lahad (1997) and Lahad and Cohen (1997) developed a multi-modal model to explain mental resilience in stressful situations. The model, BASIC Ph, relates to six major characteristics or dimensions that Lahad (1997) argues are at the core of an individual's coping style: *B*eliefs and values (when a person copes by making reference to self-reliance and her or his clear values, views, and beliefs), *A*ffect and emotion (when a person copes by expressing affect of all types), *S*ocial (when a person copes by seeking support in friendships, social settings, and organizations), *I*magination (when a person copes by using his or her imagination, such as creating imaginary playmates or situations), *C*ognition and thought (when a person copes by acting according to his or her knowledge, thoughts, and common sense), and *Ph*ysiology and activities (when a person copes by engaging in physical activity, including eating, dancing, and traveling). Each individual has her or his primary combination of coping activities and resources, a style that reflects a blending of all six dimensions (e.g., a person whose primary coping style is SI (social and imagination) might seek social support from imaginary figures, such as Superman). Although each person can potentially use any of the strategies, each has a preferred mode of coping developed and refined since childhood.

The BASIC Ph model has been used in response to a variety of incidents. For example, Lahad and his colleagues worked with psychosocial teams in Tel Aviv during the Gulf War, during various military operations in the north of Israel, and during the "Intifada" on the West Bank and Gaza Strip; also, they worked with communities and psychosocial services during suicide bomb attacks in 1996 and 1997.

Although planned and controlled studies of crisis interventions are scarce, children's coping styles were studied during two different incidents. The first incident involved the evacuation of children from Kiryat Shmona during Operation Accountability in 1993; the second involved junior high school students in Afula exposed to a suicide car bombing. The bomb exploded at the gates of their school killing three girls and four adults and injuring eight classmates. Results confirmed the structure of the BASIC Ph model and its usefulness in working with children, both for helping them use their natural coping styles and for enhancing and expanding their coping mechanisms to reduce tension and prevent post-traumatic stress reactions.

THE COMMUNITY STRESS PREVENTION CENTRE

The Community Stress Prevention Centre, established in 1981 in northern Israel following a wave of attacks on border settlements, serves the population of Israel's northern border towns, villages, and kibbutzim, Jews and non-Jews, in times of crisis and insecurity. The center aims to prepare the civilian population for coping with crisis and disaster; to train local authorities how to cope with critical situations and handle them effectively before, during, and after they occur; and to train professionals in emergency intervention techniques. The Community Stress Prevention Centre has a psychosocial team to help communities, families, and individuals during crises. Using the integrative BASIC Ph model, it develops models and programs for enhancing resiliency.

The opening of the Community Stress Prevention Centre expanded the focus of preparing for and responding to crises from the education system and the family to the community at large. A community-oriented perspective is important because disasters affect more people than those typically thought of as victims. Disasters affect all those within three "circles of vulnerability," which considers geographical proximity (how close one is physically to the incident), social proximity (how close one is socially to the victims), and psychological proximity (how close one feels psychologically to the victim or the incident). The closer someone is geographically, socially, and/or psychologically, the more likely he or she is to be adversely affected by the event. Every critical incident is akin to a stone cast into a pool of water, the ripples spreading through the pool to its edges. Similarly, the effects of an incident are felt throughout an entire community.

The Community Model

The Community Stress Prevention Centre model provides psychosocial support through an interdisciplinary team. Recognizing that no single service can provide all the help needed in the wake of a critical incident, all psychosocial, educational, community, and medical services must function under one coordinating committee. This committee is headed by the director of social services, who also serves as a consultant to the crisis management team about the major psychosocial aspects of an incident.

During an emergency, psychosocial teams are dispatched to affected areas to perform the following duties: (a) assess the situation and provide immediate support to the affected population, such as food, shelter, and medical and psychological support; (b) open information and relief centers as needed; (c) take charge of evacuation centers and provide both formal and informal education to the evacuees; and (d) have representatives in hospitals to help when patients or relatives need assistance (e.g., securing lodging, finding other relatives, or obtaining emergency funding). Psychosocial teams also take charge of locating and providing help and support to people with special needs.

Perhaps the most difficult tasks are handled by the response team that provides help and support at the site of the disaster and in the mortuary. Response team members, social workers, psychologists, and nurses escort relatives throughout the terrible process of identifying the deceased and follow up later during the mourning period, visiting at home and ensuring continuity of help from other local services.

To ensure an efficient response to a disaster, small groups of professionals receive special training, such as hospital social workers who have to work with the families of the injured and deceased, personnel who deal with the process of identifying bodies, integrated teams that work for the mortuary, and psychosocial notification teams that inform families that their loved ones are dead.

Training local authorities does not end with building the integrated coordinating team; it also is essential to define the roles of all the various people involved in responding to the disaster, such as the mayor and heads of departments and numerous disaster services. Following the basic training, the different groups receive guidance as they write their contingency plans and standard operating procedures. Once an integrated coordinating team is formed, then roles are defined, a contingency plan and operating procedures are written, and a simulation exercise is conducted. Results of the simulation are used to refine training programs and make amendments to the standard operating procedures.

Along with training local authorities, there is a need to train integrated intervention teams. Several reasons exist for this:

1. Most psychosocial professionals are not trained to work in the immediate aftermath and chaos following a disaster; their training is usually along the lines of psychopathology and psychotherapy that stress insight, transference, and psychodynamic approaches, which are difficult to utilize in a crisis situation.
2. In their daily work, the different psychosocial services do not necessarily maintain close contact with each other, do not have the same principles, and do not share the same models and theories. Moreover, overt competition and a presumed hierarchy among services may interfere with crisis management.
3. Crisis intervention methods are active, directive, and specific; "active intervention," "triage," "the needs of the group versus those of the individual," and "normal people suffering from abnormal situations" are ideas that, on the whole, are alien to many health and social work professionals.
4. Leaving the boundaries of the clinic and reaching out into the "battlefield" can be new and scary.

Therefore, Community Stress Prevention Centre personnel train professionals in methods of crisis intervention, teach mental first-aid techniques, and show how to use non-pathological terminology and the language of BASIC Ph to understand how individuals and families perceive the world and their situation. Techniques taught include pacing and leading, bridging continuities, information formulation, critical incident stress debriefing, identifying leadership in a crowd, and communicating with traumatized people. Additionally, information is presented on family crisis intervention and grief reactions.

Outcomes of training include the following:

1. A common language is developed for the integrated team.
2. Members of the team learn about each other and familiarize themselves with each other's strengths and weaknesses, which enables them to support one another during crises.
3. Cooperation develops between and among different services both in their daily work and in maintaining contact for the benefit of their clients.
4. Waiting lists and treatment time shorten as services adapt and adopt short-term crisis intervention methods in their daily work and use a multi-disciplinary approach.

The emergency behavior officer. Decision makers, whether mayors, chiefs of police or fire brigades, army officers, or ministers, typically lack training in understanding the needs of the public when responding to a disaster. In some cases, because of training as military or police officers, they confuse the public with the "enemy." For example, the public may be viewed as helpless, resulting in a decision not to inform citizens about what is happening for fear they will panic. Or, the public may be viewed as unimportant, and thus public reactions are not considered as a factor in decision making. In one particular example, food and mattresses were distributed to the population of a northern Israeli town who had spent a week in air raid shelters. The distribution was made without suitable notification and without considering the stress and distress of the inhabitants. Contrary to the authorities' expectations, nearly all the food and mattresses were taken by those near the distribution point (at one end of a street), leaving those further away (at the other end of the street) with little food and no mattresses. Not only did the authorities fail to convey the message to those further away that someone cared about them, they caused tension between those who received food and mattresses and those who did not.

A second instance occurred when authorities decided not to warn the public of the possibility of heavy rains that might cause flooding. They thought of the panic that might ensue following such an announcement, as well as public embarrassment if the prediction should prove incorrect. The result was flooded homes, people in search of help in the dark, loss of property, feelings of abandonment, and local authority services having to operate under extremely unfavorable conditions.

Examples such as these made clear the need for an expert in the behavioral sciences to act as a consultant to decision makers—an emergency behavior officer. During 1985–1986, the Community Stress Prevention Centre trained the first group of professionals in skills necessary to understand the human aspects of critical incidents and the many factors influencing the public's reaction. The training included presentation of a central behavioral picture, how to predict developments from the point of view of human reactions, how to offer suggestions and recommendations for alternative courses of action, how to use the BASIC Ph model as a paradigm both for understanding how a community copes and as the basis for communicating with decision makers and the public, and how to use the media as a source of support (Lahad, Cohen, & Peled, 1995).

The media and the emergency behavior officer. In recent years, particularly after the Gulf War (Solomon, 1995) and the Dizengoff bus explosion, there has been growing criticism of the media for exposing disasters in a brutal way. The national and international media have adopted what may be called "The CNN Standard": immediate, unedited on-site broadcasting, presenting the news of a disaster without buffering or fully considering the impact of the broadcast on viewers. While people in large countries find it difficult enough to cope with such pictures, in smaller countries there is an added sense of vulnerability: "It could be me, there. I know the place, and the people. I am a potential target, and a near miss survivor."

Working with national and international television stations is very complicated, especially when the goals are to affect how they present a disaster and to get them to serve as a positive force in responding to a disaster. However, along with national and international television stations there are local radio and cable television stations that focus on local news and issues and that are more sensitive and attentive to the needs of the local population. Given their investment in the community, these stations tend to restrict what they broadcast. Importantly, these stations can respond to local needs in times of emergency by providing specific information, answering questions from the public, interviewing local people and authority figures, serving as a focal point for information, increasing morale, and offering reassurance. However, local stations also are influenced by the model of the national and international stations, and they may act according to similar norms and procedures. (In the past, dismembered bodies were shown live on local television and horrific pictures were broadcast unedited.)

To help local media present news in a way that facilitates responding to a disaster, the emergency behavior officer advises on wording and programming, helps presenters prepare their performance, and assists on-air personnel in circumstances when terrible news is first disclosed (Lahad, 1996). The main functions of the consultant to a local television or radio station are to train personnel to (a) use different ways of broadcasting during the different phases of a disaster (e.g., live interviews, information slides, pre-prepared films, programs, activities, and quizzes); (b) build programs for different target audiences (e.g., children, adolescents, adults, immigrants) according to the time of day; (c) use the open studio as a source of reassurance, morale, and information; (d) monitor verbal and nonverbal communications and their influence on viewers; (e) focus on directions and information, rather than giving interpretations and commentary; and (f) balance the harsh news with an understanding of viewers' ability to cope. Also, the consultant provides staff members with information on public reactions to stressful events, how victims and their relatives are likely to think and feel after a disaster, and how people with different developmental needs and ages comprehend messages. The emergency behavior officer, as a consultant and advisor, does not have any control or powers of censorship.

Over the past five years, the Community Stress Prevention Centre has studied the use of local stations in helping the local population cope with critical incidents. The main finding is that when properly prepared, and when the staff accept the norms of *community* television, the impact on the local audience is significant: Local people feel updated, cared for, and that their needs are being met. The issues surrounding how the media report a disaster need further investigation and development, especially when dealing with national and international media.

HELPING THE HELPERS

Helpers are not invulnerable. Evidence indicates that they are affected by their close work with disaster victims and their relatives and that they are prone to "compassion fatigue" (Figley, 1995). This may be a more common problem in Israel than elsewhere because, in many cases, helpers are in the "near miss" category when incidents occur. Even when helpers are not in the vicinity of the incident, because Israel is a small country, helpers are likely to know some of the victims directly or indirectly through relatives, colleagues, or acquaintances. When incidents happen in very famous and central places the familiarity of the place makes the tragedy extremely vivid to many people.

Psychosocial work and rescue operations go on simultaneously; however, because psychosocial workers are not trained to work in the vicinity of disasters while rescue operations are in progress, the Community Stress Prevention Centre developed a set of procedures and activities to use before, during, and after a disaster to support the helpers. Advising local authorities and heads of psychosocial teams to take protective measures for their staff enables them to maintain long-term services to the public and preserves the mental well-being of their employees. A major part of the procedures is Critical Incident Stress Debriefing (Mitchell, 1983), adapted to Israeli conditions (Lahad & Cohen, 1997), together with specific training on how to work in a disaster situation (e.g., methods for organizing shifts and ways of getting into and out of a scene). At the same time, activities to promote creativity and relaxation are combined, and group support and team building are enhanced. Today, Community Stress Prevention Centre methods of helping the helpers are used by the Israeli Police Force, hospital personnel, local authority psychosocial and crisis intervention teams, and the Israeli Home Front.

A unique opportunity to expand on the procedures and activities designed to help the helpers was afforded the Community Stress Prevention Centre in 1993 when UNICEF asked the center to plan and conduct a course for professionals from the countries of former Yugoslavia (Ayalon & Lahad, 1996; Gal, Ayalon, & Lahad, 1995; Gal & Lahad, 1996). All of the professionals were distressed, fatigued, and heavily traumatized. All had been subjected to the war atrocities, the loss of friends and family members, and the destruction of homes and workplaces but, nonetheless, still were trying to work with and for the population of all these countries, particularly the children.

The course, using the BASIC Ph as a central model for coping and regaining resiliency, included art and bibliotherapy, puppet therapy, drama therapy, and music therapy to elicit a variety of expressions of the trauma. Cognitive aspects of coping, problem solving, conflict resolution, and planning also were part of the project, along with social support, sociodrama, group debriefing, and physical activities. Values clarification was introduced as a way to regain inner conviction and meaning. Course participants learned many ways to cope and to continue their journey from hurt to healing.

Two weeks of intensive workshops were held twice, the first for Croatians and Bosnians and the second for Serbs, Montenegrans, and Macedonians, followed by continuous workshops in their own countries (Lahad, 1994; Shacham & Niv, 1994) and a joint workshop for all former Yugoslavia countries in 1995 (Ayalon & Lahad, 1996). One of the workshop outcomes was the development of local projects for children, families, and schools (Ayalon, Lahad, & Cohen, 1998). Many of the projects use BASIC Ph as either their model for planning and/or as their tool for assessing and developing coping skills.

Summary

The major lesson learned by Community Stress Prevention Centre personnel after two decades of work with individuals, groups, and communities is that with help, communities can develop resiliency and the ability to cope with terrible events and their long-term effects. The Community Stress Prevention Centre model stresses the need to identify, activate, and work toward integration of all the forces in society to enable the process of coping to reverberate in all the circles of vulnerability. Combined efforts of local authorities, community services, community workers, volunteers, education systems, and the family are part of a long process, but one with promising results.

CONCLUSION

To mitigate the negative effects of disasters on families and children, it is necessary to reduce risk factors and maximize protective factors. Many risk factors, however, are not subject to change, including a child's physical and emotional proximity to a disaster; cognitive and social development; sex; pre-existing psychological conditions, such as anxiety and depression; personal injury or the injury or death of a family member; and early separation from parents. Other risk factors may be changed but certainly not easily, such as the extent of a disaster's destruction (e.g., a community can build only "earthquake-proof" houses); the structure or climate of the family; and a community's degree of poverty, deprivation, underdevelopment, and socioeconomic vulnerability.

A variety of risk factors, however, such as the extent to which a disaster disrupts daily life, parental responses, and the amount of threat to lives posed by the disaster can be reduced with pre-disaster planning at the community and family levels. Pre-disaster planning includes a variety of different activities, such as developing a "family disaster plan" and a "community disaster plan" that detail who has responsibility for doing what when a disaster strikes; putting together "disaster first-aid" kits; educating community leaders about the potential psychological effects of disasters on children; raising community awareness of children's potential mental health needs; using classroom activities to help children develop feelings of control, as well as to enhance and expand their coping mechanisms; and building effective communication systems to allow for early warning and, during a crisis, the dissemination of disaster-related information.

In addition to reducing risks, helping children develop protective factors increases their resiliency. Several protective factors appear to have as their goal the reduction of uncertainty—uncertainty about self, family, community and, on a more philosophical or spiritual level, people and the world, and the enhancement of feelings of empowerment and control. For example, social support from family, friends, neighbors, and teachers is mentioned prominently as a resilience protective factor. According to Albrecht and Adelman (1987), "the significance of supportive communication that reduces one's perceptions of uncertainty is that it helps the receiver in developing a sense of perceived control over stressful circumstances" (p. 24). Supportive communication reduces ambiguity, complexity, and unpredictability, sources of uncertainty, and thus increases feelings of personal control. Supportive messages may enhance feelings of control by helping the child see realistic alternatives to a stressful situation, gain coping skills, and recognize that help is available from others.

Children who feel empowered and competent to deal with stress are more likely to cope effectively. Protective factors that enhance feelings of empowerment and competence, in addition to social support, include having a family and community support system able to respond to the child's needs, giving the child the opportunity to discuss and work through his or her fears and disaster experiences, and increasing the child's perception of change as something positive and challenging.

Apfel and Simon (1996b) noted that successful interventions have in common the development of approaches that progressively empower and encourage children. Their list of protective factors (Apfel & Simon, 1996b, 1996c) *define* children who feel both empowered and competent: resourceful, curious, knowledgeable, compassionate, able to remember and invoke images of good and sustaining figures, helpful (i.e., see others as important and feel capable of helping), see themselves as having the right to live, and have a goal for which to live. These resilient children, like those in Mozambique about whom Gibbs (1994) wrote, "do not perceive themselves, nor are they perceived as passive, vulnerable, or being unable to work" (p. 272).

A community response perspective of disasters based on a resiliency model can affect the very definition of "disaster." Such a perspective has the potential to reduce the number of individuals who suffer long-term traumatic reactions and to limit the disruptive nature of disasters over time as families and communities come together, refocus, and regain equilibrium.

REFERENCES

Aber, J. L. (1994). Poverty, violence, and child development: Untangling family and community level effects. In C. A. Nelson (Ed.), *Threats to optimal development: Vol. 27. Integrating biological, psychological, and social risk factors* (pp. 229–272). Hillsdale, NJ: Lawrence Erlbaum.
Albrecht, T. L., & Adelman, M. B. (1987). Communicating social support: A the-

oretical perspective. In T. L. Albrecht & M. B. Adelman (Eds.), *Communicating social support* (pp. 18–39). Newbury Park, CA: Sage.

American Academy of Child and Adolescent Psychiatry (1996). Helping children after a disaster [Online]. Available: http://www.psych.med.umich.edu/web/aacap/factsFam/disaster.htm.

American Psychological Association. (n.d.a). *Disaster response network* [Online]. Available: http://www.apa.org/drn.html.

American Psychological Association. (n.d.b). *Helping children cope: A Guide to helping children cope with the stress of the Oklahoma City explosion* [Online]. Available: http://www.apa.org/kids.html.

Apfel, R. J., & Simon, B. (Eds.). (1996a). *Minefields in their hearts: The mental health of children in war and communal violence.* New Haven, CT: Yale University Press.

Apfel, R. J., & Simon, B. (1996b). Introduction. In R. J. Apfel & B. Simon (Eds.), *Minefields in their hearts: The mental health of children in war and communal violence* (pp. 1–17) New Haven, CT: Yale University Press.

Apfel, R. J., & Simon, B. (1996c). *Psychosocial interventions for children of war: The value of a model of resiliency* [Online]. Available: http://www.healthnet.org/MGS/Article3.html.

Aptekar, L., & Boore, J. A. (1990). The emotional effects of disaster on children: A review of the literature. *International Journal of Mental Health, 19*(2), 77–90.

Ayalon, O. (1976). *Rescue! An emergency handbook.* Haifa, Israel: University of Haifa Press.

Ayalon, O., & Lahad, M. (1996). *Report to UNICEF following international mission to former Yugoslavian countries.* Kiryat Shmona, Israel: Community Stress Prevention Centre.

Ayalon, O., Cohen, A., & Lahad, M. (1998). *Bridges of hope and healing: Application of coping skills in former Yugoslavia.* Kiryat Shmona, Israel: Community Stress Prevention Centre.

Azarian, A., Skriptchenko-Gregorian, V., Miller, T., & Kraus, R. (1994). Childhood trauma in victims of the Armenian earthquake. *Journal of Contemporary Psychotherapy, 24,* 77–85.

Belshe, R. (1995). OUHSC readies post-disaster counseling. *The Oklahoma Daily* [Online]. Available: http://www.uoknor.edu/okdaily/april21/ouhsc_trauma.html.

Belter, R., Dunn, S., & Jeney, P. (1991). The psychological impact of Hurricane Hugo on children: A needs assessment. *Advanced Behavioral Research Therapy, 13,* 155–161.

Boothby, N. (1996). Mobilizing communities to meet the psychosocial needs of children in war and refugee crises. In R. J. Apfel & B. Simon (Eds.), *Minefields in their hearts: The mental health of children in war and communal violence* (pp. 149–164). New Haven, CT: Yale University Press.

Boyden, J. (1994). Childrens' experiences of conflict related emergencies: Some implications for relief policy and practice. *Disasters, 18*(3), 254–267.

Breton, J-J., Valla, J-P., & Lambert, J. (1993). Industrial disaster and mental health of children and their parents. *Journal of the American Academy of Child and Adolescent Psychiatry, 32,* 438–445.

Cairns, E. (1996). *Children and political violence.* Oxford: Blackwell Publishers.

Caplan, G. (1975). *Organization of support systems and community mental health.* New York: Behavioral Publishers, Inc.

Chernobyl children's project fact sheet [Online]. (1996). Available: http://www.aardvark.ie/ccp/press/facts0.1html.

Connor, B. (1998, June 27). Children of Chernobyl. *Herald-Sun* [Durham, NC], pp. B1, B2.

Durkin, M., Khan, N., Davidson, L., Zaman, S., & Stein, Z. (1993). The effects of a natural disaster on child behavior: Evidence for posttraumatic stress. *American Journal of Public Health,* 1549–1551.

Erickson, K. (1994). *New species of trouble: Explorations in disaster, trauma, and community.* New York: Norton.

Federal Emergency Management Agency. (1996a, July). *Helping children cope with disaster* [Online]. Available: http://www.fema.gov/fema/children.html.

Federal Emergency Management Agency. (1996b, October). *Helping children cope with disaster* [Online]. Available: http://www.fema.gov/fema/children.html.

Federal Emergency Management Agency. (1997). *Your family disaster plan* [Online]. Available: http://www.fema.gov/fema/famplan.html.

Field, T., Seligman, S., Scafidi, F., & Schanberg, S. (1996). *Alleviating posttraumatic expression of feelings* [Online]. Available: http://www.ag.uiuc.edu/disaster/csndact7.html.

Figley, C. R. (Ed.). (1995). *Compassion fatigue: Coping with secondary traumatic stress disorder in those who treat the traumatized.* New York: Bruner/Mazel.

Fitzpatrick, K. M., & Boldizar, J. P. (1993). The prevalence and consequences of exposure to violence among African-American youth. *Journal of the American Academy of Child and Adolescent Psychiatry, 32*(2), 424–430.

Gal, R., Ayalon, O., & Lahad, M. (1995). *1995 Report to UNICEF following the international mission to former Yugoslavian countries.* Kiryat Shmona, Israel: Community Stress Prevention Centre.

Gal, R., & Lahad, M. (1996). *1996 Report to UNICEF following international mission to former Yugoslavian countries.* Kiryat Shmona, Israel: Community Stress Prevention Centre.

Galante, R., & Foa, D. (1986). An epidemiological study of psychic trauma and treatment effectiveness for children after a natural disaster. *Journal of the American Academy of Child Psychiatry, 25,* 357–363.

Gallaga, O. (1995). Explosion prompts blood drives, donations. *The Oklahoma Daily* [Online]. Available: http://www.uoknor.edu/okdaily/april20/blood_drives.html.

Garbarino, J., & Kostelny, K. (1996). What do we need to know to understand children in war and community violence? In R. J. Apfel & B. Simon (Eds.), *Minefields in their hearts: The mental health of children in war and communal violence* (pp. 33–51). New Haven, CT: Yale University Press.

Garrison, C., Bryant, E., Addy, C., Spurrier, P., Freedy, J., & Kilpatrick, D. (1995). Posttraumatic stress disorder in adolescents after Hurricane Andrew. *Journal of the American Academy of Child and Adolescent Psychiatry, 34,* 1193–1201.

Gibbs, S. (1994). Post-war social reconstruction in Mozambique: Re-framing children's experience of trauma and healing. *Disaster, 18*(3), 268–276.

Gibson, K. (1989). Children in political violence. *Social Science and Medicine, 28*(7), 659–667.

Gillis, H. M. (1993). Individual and small-group psychotherapy for children involved in trauma and disaster. In C. F. Saylor (Ed.), *Children and disasters* (pp. 165–186). New York: Plenum Press.

Goenjian, A. K. (1993). A mental health relief programme in Armenia after the 1988 earthquake. *British Journal of Psychiatry, 163,* 230–239.

Goenjian, A. K., Pynoos, R. S., Steinberg, A. H., Najarian, L. M., Asarnow, J. R., Karayan, I., Ghurabi, M., & Fairbanks, L. A. (1995). Psychiatric comorbidity in children after the 1988 earthquake in Armenia. *Journal of the American Academy of Child and Adolescent Psychiatry, 34,* 1174–1184.

Green, B. L., Korol, M., Grace, M. C., Vary, M. G., Leonard, A. C., Gleser, G. C., & Smitson-Cohen, S. (1991). Children and disaster: Age, gender, and parental effects on PTSD symptoms. *Journal of the American Academy of Child & Adolescent Psychiatry 30*(6): 945–951.

Greenwald, R., & Rubin, A. (1999). Assessment of posttraumatic symptoms in children: Development and preliminary validation of parent and child scales. *Research on Social Work Practice, 9,* 61–75.

Gudas, L. J. (1993). Concepts of death and loss in childhood and adolescence. In C. F. Saylor (Ed.), *Children and disasters* (pp. 67–84). New York: Plenum Press.

Handford, H. A., Mayes, S. D., Mattison, R. E., Humphrey, F. J., Bagnato, S., Bixler, E. O., & Kales, J. D. (1986). Child and parent reactions to the Three Mile Island nuclear accident. *Journal of the American Academy of Child Psychiatry, 25*(3), 346–356.

Isaza, R. (1995). America mourns. *The Oklahoma Daily* [Online]. Available: http://www.uoknor.edu/okdaily/april24/america_mourns.html.

Jeney-Gammon, P., Daugherty, T. K., Finch, A. J., Belter, R. W., & Foster, K. Y. (1992). Children's coping styles and report of depressive symptoms following a natural disaster. *Journal of Genetic Psychology, 154,* 259–267.

Joyner, C. D., & Swenson, C. C. (1993). Community-level intervention after a disaster. In C. F. Saylor (Ed.), *Children and disasters* (pp. 211–231). New York: Plenum Press.

Katz, L. (1989). *Coping with stress* [Online]. ERIC Clearinghouse on Elementary and Early Childhood Education. Available: http://ecrips.ed.uiuc./edu/npin/respar/texts/health/stress.html.

Keppel-Benson, J. M., & Ollendick, T. H. (1993). Posttraumatic stress disorder in children and adolescents. In C. F. Saylor (Ed.), *Children and disasters* (pp. 29–43). New York: Plenum Press.

Kirby, L. D., & Fraser, M. W. (1997). Risk and resilience in childhood. In M. W.

Fraser (Ed.), *Risk and resilience in childhood; An ecological perspective* (pp. 10–33). Washington, D.C.: NASW Press.

Kiser, L., Heston, J., Hickerson, S., Millsap, P., Nunn, W., & Pruitt, D. (1993). Anticipatory stress in children and adolescents. *American Journal of Psychiatry, 150,* 87–91.

Klingman, A. (1987). A school-based emergency crisis intervention in a mass school disaster. *Professional Psychology: Research and Practice, 18,* 604–661.

Klingman, A. (1993). School-based intervention following a disaster. In C. F. Saylor (Ed.), *Children and disasters* (pp. 187–210). New York: Plenum Press.

Klingman, A., & Ayalon, O. (1977). Preparing the education system for emergency. *Israeli Journal of Psychology and Counseling in Education [Chavat Da'at], 15,* 135–148.

Konkov, F. (1991). Primary psychological intervention with families of earthquake survivors in Armenia. *American Journal of Family Therapy, 19,* 54–59.

Kozlovskaia, G. V., Bashina, V. M., Goriunova, A. V., Kireeva, I. P., Novikova, E. V., & Skoblo, G. V. (1991). The effect of the earthquake in Armenia on the mental health of the juvenile population of the affected areas. *Soviet Neurology and Psychiatry,* 11–23.

Krug, R., Nixon, S., & Vincent, R. (1996). Invited editorial: Psychological response to the Oklahoma City bombing. *Journal of Clinical Psychology, 52,* 103–105.

La Greca, A. M., Silverman, W. K., Vernberg, E. M., & Prinstein, M. J. (1996). Symptoms of posttraumatic stress in children after Hurricane Andrew: A prospective study. *Journal of Counseling and Clinical Psychology, 64,* 712–723.

La Greca, A. M., Vernberg, E. M., Silverman, W. K., Vogel, A. L., & Prinstein, M. J. (1994). *Helping children prepare for and cope with natural disasters: A manual for professionals working with elementary school children.* Miami, FL: Children and Natural Disasters Project, Departments of Psychology, University of Miami and Florida International University.

Lahad, M. (1981). *Preparation of children and teachers to cope with stress: A multimodal approach.* Unpublished master's thesis, Hebrew University, Jerusalem, Israel.

Lahad, M. (1997). *BASIC Ph—The story of coping resources.* In M. Lahad & A. Cohen (Eds.), *Community stress prevention, volumes 1 and 2* (pp. 117–145). Kiryat Shmona, Israel: Community Stress Prevention Centre.

Lahad M. (1994). Community mass communication in disasters. *Bulletin of the Israel Emergency Planning Committee [Da Melach], 37,* 9–11.

Lahad M. (1996, June). *Children facing disaster.* Paper presented at the meeting of the Second World Conference of the International Society for Traumatic Stress Studies, Jerusalem, Israel.

Lahad, M., & Abraham, A. (1983). Preparing teachers and pupils for coping with stress situations: A multi-modal program. *Israeli Journal of Psychology and Counseling in Education [Chavat Da'at], 16,* 196–210.

Lahad, M., & Cohen, A. (Eds.). (1997). *Community stress prevention, volumes 1 and 2.* Kiryat Shmona, Israel: Community Stress Prevention Centre.

Lahad, M., Cohen, A., & Peled, D. (1995). *Emergency behavior officer training manual.* Kiryat Shmona, Israel: Community Stress Prevention Centre.

Lailey, J. (1993). *Working with Chernobyl's children* [Online]. Available: http://www.friends-partners.org/oldfriends/health/proj/proj0057.htm.

Lonigan, C. J., Shannon, M. P., Taylor, C. M., Finch, A. J., Jr., & Sallee, F. R. (1994). Children exposed to disaster: II. Risk factors for the development of post-traumatic symptomatology. *Journal of the American Academy of Child and Adolescent Psychiatry, 33,* 94–105.

Lystad, M. (1990). United States programs in disaster mental health. *International Journal of Mental Health, 19*(1) 80–88.

Macksoud, M. J., Aber, J. L., & Cohn, I. (1996). Assessing the impact of war on children. In R. J. Apfel & B. Simon (Eds.), *Minefields in their hearts: The mental health of children in war and communal violence* (pp. 218–230). New Haven, CT: Yale University Press.

Melville, M. B., & Lykes, M. B. (1992). Guatemalan Indian children and the sociocultural effects of government-sponsored terrorism. *Social Science and Medicine, 34*(5), 533–548.

Miller, T., Kraus, R., Tatevosyan, A., & Kamenchenko, P. (1993). Post-traumatic stress disorder in children and adolescents of the Armenian earthquake. *Child Psychiatry and Human Development, 24,* 115–123.

Mitchell, J. T. (1983). When disaster strikes: The critical incident stress debriefing process. *Journal of Emergency Medical Services, 8*(1), 36–39.

Monaco, N. M., & Gaier, E. L. (1987). Developmental level and children's responses to the explosion of the space shuttle Challenger. *Early Childhood Research Quarterly, 2,* 83–95.

Parry-Jones, B., & Parry-Jones, W. (1994). Post-traumatic stress disorder: Supportive evidence from an eighteenth-century natural disaster. *Psychological Medicine, 24,* 15–27.

Parson, E. (1995a). Mass traumatic terror in Oklahoma City and the phases of adaptational coping, part I: Possible effects of intentional injury/harm on victims' post-traumatic responses. *Journal of Contemporary Psychotherapy, 25,* 155–184.

Parson, E. (1995b). Mass traumatic terror in Oklahoma City and the phases of adaptational coping, part II: Integration of cognitive, behavioral, dynamic, existential and pharmacologic interventions. *Journal of Contemporary Psychotherapy, 25,* 267–309.

Peterson, C. (1995). Oklahoma bombing leaves mark on city kids. *The Yale Daily News* [Online]. Available: http://www.yale.edu/ydn/paper/5.3/5.3.95storyno.CC.html.

Pfefferbaum, B. (1997). Posttraumatic stress disorder in children: A review of the past 10 years. *Journal of the American Academy of Child and Adolescent Psychiatry, 36,* 1503–1511.

Ponton, L. E., & Bryant, E. C. (1991). After the earthquake: Organizing to respond to children and adolescents. *Psychiatric Annals, 21*(9), 539–546.

Potts, G. (1995). People from near and far pitch in. *The Oklahoma Daily* [Online]. Available: http://www.uoknor.edu/okdaily/april21/volunteerism.html.

Pynoos, R. S., Steinberg, A. H., Manoukian, G., Tavosian, A., & Fairbanks, L. A. (1993). Post-traumatic stress reactions in children after the 1988 Armenian earthquake. *British Journal of Psychiatry, 163,* 239–247.

Raphael, B. (1986). *When disaster strikes: A handbook for the caring professions.* London: Hutchinson.

Romano, L., & Kenworthy, T. (1997, June 3). Guilty on all counts. *The News and Observer* [Raleigh, NC], pp. 1A, 9A.

Rosenblatt, R. (1983). *Children of war.* Garden City, NY: Anchor Press.

Rubin, C. B., & Sapirstein, M. D. (1985). *Community recovery from a major natural disaster.* Boulder, CO: Institute of Behavioral Science, University of Colorado.

Rutter, M. (1987). Psychosocial resilience and protective mechanisms. *American Journal of Orthopsychiatry, 57,* 316–331.

Saylor, C. F. (Ed.). (1993a). *Children and disasters.* New York: Plenum Press.

Saylor, C. F. (1993b). Children and disasters: Clinical and research issues. In C. F. Saylor (Ed.), *Children and disasters* (pp. 1–9). New York: Plenum Press.

Saylor, C., Swenson, C., & Powell, P. (1992). Hurricane Hugo blows down the broccoli: Preschoolers' post-disaster play and adjustment. *Child Psychiatry and Human Development, 22,* 139–149.

Schwartz, E. (n.d.) *What to tell children about terrorist bombings* [Online]. Available: http://psy.uq.oz.au/dev/disaster/bombing.html.

Shacham, Y. (1996). *Stress reactions and activating coping resources: A comparison between children who remained under Katyusha rocket shelling and children who were evacuated to a safe haven.* Unpublished doctoral dissertation, Newport University, Newport Beach, CA.

Shacham, Y., & Niv, S. (1994). *Report to UNICEF following international mission to former Yugoslavian countries.* Kiryat Shmona, Israel: Community Stress Prevention Centre.

Shannon, M. P., Lonigan, C. J., Finch, A. J., Jr., & Taylor, C. M. (1994). Children exposed to disaster: I. Epidemiology of post-traumatic symptoms and symptom profiles. *Journal of the American Academy of Child and Adolescent Psychiatry, 33,* 80–93.

Shaw, J. A., Applegate, B., Tanner, S., Perez, D., Rothe, E., Campo-Bowen, A. E., & Lahey, B. L. (1995). Psychological effects of Hurricane Andrew on an elementary school population. *Journal of the American Academy of Child and Adolescent Psychiatry, 34,* 1185–1192.

Sitterle, K. A., & Gurwitch, R. H. (1999). The terrorist bombing in Oklahoma City. In E. S. Zinner & M. B. Williams (Eds.), *When a community weeps* (pp. 160–189). Philadelphia, PA: Brunner/Mazel.

Sleek, S. (1998, June). After the storm, children play out fears. *APA* [American Psychological Association] *Monitor,* p. 12.

Solomon, Z. (1995). *Coping with war-induced stress: The Gulf War and the Israeli response.* New York: Plenum Press.

Stevenson, R. (1986). The shuttle tragedy, "community grief," and schools. *Death Studies, 10,* 507–518.

Swenson, C. C., & Klingman, A. (1993). Children and war. In C. F. Saylor (Ed.), *Children and disasters* (pp. 137–163). New York: Plenum Press.

Terr, L. C., Bloch, D. A., Michel, B. A., Shi, H., Reinhardt, J. A., & Metayer, S. (1996). Children's memories in the wake of Challenger. *American Journal of Psychiatry, 153,* 618–625.

Toubiana, Y. H., Milgram, N. A., Strich, Y., & Edelstein, A. (1988). Crisis interventions in a school community disaster: Principles and practices. *Journal of Community Psychology, 16,* 228–240.

University of Illinois at Urbana-Champaign. (1995). *Helping children cope with a disaster* [Online]. ICES Disaster Resources: Disaster Fact Sheets [Online]. Available: http://www.ag.uiuc.edu/disaster/facts/kidscope.html.

University of Illinois Cooperative Extension Service (1995). *Children, stress, and natural disasters; School activities for children: Introduction* [Online]. Available: http://www.ag.uiuc.edu/disaster/csndact1.html.

Vernberg, E. M., & Vogel, J. M. (1993). Task Force Report, part 2: Interventions with children after disasters. *Journal of Clinical Child Psychology, 22,* 485–498.

Vernberg, E. M., La Greca, A. M., Silverman, W. K., & Prinstein, M. J. (1996). Prediction of posttraumatic stress symptoms in children after Hurricane Andrew. *Journal of Abnormal Psychology, 105,* 237–247.

Vogel, J. M., & Vernberg, E. M. (1993). Task Force Report, part 1: Childrens' psychological responses to disasters. *Journal of Clinical Child Psychology, 22,* 464–484.

Wall, J. C., & Levy, A. J. (1996, Winter). Communities under fire: Empowering families and children in the aftermath of homicide. *Clinical Social Work Journal, 24*(4), 403–414.

Walz, G. R., & Bleuer, J. C. (Eds.). (1992). *Developing support groups for students: Helping students cope with crises.* Greensboro, NC: ERIC Counseling and Student Services Clearinghouse.

Wright, J. C., Kunkel, D., Pinon, M., & Huston, A. C. (1989). How children reacted to televised coverage of the space shuttle disaster. *Journal of Communication, 39*(2), 27–45.

Yule, W. (1992). Post-traumatic stress disorder in child survivors of shipping disasters: The sinking of the "Jupiter." *Psychotherapy and Psychosomatics, 57,* 200–205.

Chapter 8

Resilience: Implications for Evidence-Based Practice

Mark W. Fraser
Jack M. Richman

At its core, this book describes an emerging framework for understanding social and health problems and for developing more effective social and health programs. Rooted in concepts such as risk and protection, a resilience orientation to practice permeates each chapter. Children who overcome adversity and function at normative or higher levels are often described as resilient (see, e.g., Garmezy, 1974; Rutter, 1979). From a conceptual perspective, this book tells the story of resilient children first by examining risk factors for conduct problems, including youth violence, and second by exploring the factors that lead some children to resist or adapt to risk. It is only in the recent past that investigators have attempted to understand adaptation in the context of child development, a variety of adjustment outcomes, and the multiplex of factors that influence outcomes. If we can understand these factors—as virtually all chapter authors argue—we may be able to improve the effectiveness of services for children who are at risk of antisocial, aggressive behavior (see also, Coie et al., 1993; Fraser & Galinsky, 1997). Drawing from the chapters and from research evidence on problems in childhood, the purpose of this final chapter is to identify common themes throughout the book and to distill from these themes implications for practice with children at risk.

TOWARD A FRAMEWORK FOR "EVIDENCE-BASED" PRACTICE: A RESILIENCE PERSPECTIVE

In identifying common themes and implications across chapters, we adopt an evidence-based perspective on practice. A concept with European origins, the term *evidence-based practice* is characterized by a process of systematically identifying and employing the best available evidence in making practice decisions. The perspective incorporates the wide range of information often employed by practitioners in developing understandings of problems and devising intervention plans. In the social and health sciences, the best current evidence is defined traditionally as information derived from research; however, in making practice decisions at the case level, empirically derived knowledge is integrated routinely with client preferences, case-specific idiographic information, and the accumulated expertise of the practitioner. An evidence-based perspective places research information in the context of specific case data and experientially based knowledge that accrues with practice.

Using the Best Current Information to Design More Effective Interventions

Evidence-based practice differs from a clinical scientist perspective on practice in the sense that a practitioner is not expected to conjoin day-to-day practice with research methods involving systematic data collection and analysis. Rather the practitioner is expected to understand and use research knowledge in defining practice problems and selecting interventions that optimize outcomes. Using the "best available" information means that interventive strategies with the highest chances of being effective, given current knowledge, are selected. By extension this implies that, in the absence of research related to a specific problem or interventive strategy, the practitioner is expected to use theory with a research basis, knowledge of the etiology of related or similar social and health problems, knowledge gained from clinical supervision, knowledge derived from listening to the client, and knowledge from practice experience.

Evidence-based practice presupposes a hierarchy of knowledge about intervention, but it makes use of a mix of many different sources of information. Historically, the gold standard for evidence was the double-blind controlled study with random assignment. Although they are growing in number, there are too few such studies that inform human services practice. In evidence-based practice, the concept of the *best available evidence* acknowledges the potential contribution of a wider body of evidence—comparison group studies, longitudinal cohort studies, qualitative research, and other systematically collected information. Thus the perspective derives, in part, from the idea that uncertainty is never fully resolved by any single research method and that evidence in different forms is constantly emerging.

Eileen Gambrill (1999) says of evidence-based practice: "Evidence-based practice is the conscientious, explicit, and judicious use of current best evidence in making decisions about the care of clients. It involves integrating individual practice expertise with the best available external evidence from systematic research as well as considering the values and expectations of clients" (p. 6).

Forging Common Conceptual Frameworks based on Resilience

Embedded in this beguiling statement are many knotty problems. How are practitioners supposed to distill the evidence when it is published in a perplexingly broad array of professional journals? When it is founded on dozens of different theories that propose competing constructs and frames of reference? When it makes use of advanced analytic procedures in which few of us have training? When, from a purely practical standpoint, it is so voluminous? The answers to these questions extend beyond the purpose of this chapter (for a discussion, see Sackett, Richardson, Rosenberg, & Haynes, 1998). However, one aspect of the work in this book is particularly relevant to the problems posed by the emerging evidence-based practice model. Largely atheoretical and cross-disciplinary, *a resilience perspective provides a means for conceptualizing social problems and improving the effectiveness of social programs.*

Although the contributors to this book come from a heterogeneity of professions—communications, education, psychiatry, psychology, public health, and social work—they have spoken using a common vernacular. They invoke terms such as *risk factor, protection,* and *resilience* to describe children who have recovered from trauma or who have prevailed over adversity. Through combinations of internal and external resources, these children not only survive significant threat, but they achieve normative or better developmental outcomes. They avoid poor developmental outcomes even though one might have predicted a poor outcome on the basis of their risk exposure. The resilience framework that authors use to describe these successful children—and conversely to discuss children who are not successful and who engage in problematic and sometimes dangerous behaviors—holds the potential to form the basis for a new interdisciplinary connectedness. More importantly, it holds potential for forging new multi-disciplinary preventive and inter-ventive initiatives. In short, this book demonstrates both a framework for understanding conduct problems—including youth violence—and a means for translating disciplinary constructs into cross-disciplinary con-cepts that may promote more effective services for children and families.

RESILIENCE: WHAT DO WE KNOW?

From the language and concepts of risk and protection arises a singu-larly important and engaging construct: resilience. Resilience emerges from the interaction of risk and protective factors. Children who are resilient are characterized by high functioning in the context of adversity. In this sense, they experience unexpected, positive outcomes in the face of threat. Today, scholars discuss three related aspects of resilience:

- Overcoming the odds—being successful in spite of exposure to high risk
- Sustaining competence under pressure—adapting successfully to high risk
- Recovering from trauma—adjusting successfully to negative life events.

The degree to which resilience exists in a population depends both on the magnitude of the adversity—or risk—and the way one defines suc-cessful functioning. In Masten et al.'s (1999, p. 144) sample of 205 urban schoolchildren, they found 43 (57.3 percent) of 75 high adversity chil-dren to be "doing reasonably well on . . . major developmental tasks." These children were defined as resilient by virtue of scoring one-half stan-dard deviation above the mean on measures of academic achievement, peer acceptance, and conduct. In contrast, in a study of 213 low-income children of whom 133 were victims of maltreatment, Cicchetti and Rogosch (1997) found only 2 (1.5 percent) highly adaptive maltreated children and only 8 (4.3 percent) highly adaptive non-maltreated chil-dren. Children were defined as "highly adaptive" if they scored in the upper one-third on at least five of seven measures of interpersonal behav-ior, psychopathology, and school achievement.

The lack of agreement on thresholds for defining "high" risk and "suc-cessful" adaptation is a methodological problem of growing import. If adversity is defined by being raised in poverty or, for that matter, by any single but relatively prevalent risk (e.g., living in a high-crime neighbor-hood), a higher percentage of children is likely to be found "resilient."

In the same vein, recent data suggest that if one defines risk as exposure to several risk factors (e.g., the cumulative impact of poverty, poor prenatal care, parental substance abuse, and child maltreatment) a much smaller percentage of children will be found to be resilient (Pollard, Hawkins, & Arthur, 1999). Thus, resilience can be conceptualized as an adaptive response that varies negatively with the degree of risk. It may be necessary to forge greater consensus on definitions of risk and success (or performing better-than-predicted) so practitioners will have a general understanding relative to their practice outcomes.

Although popular writers have been prone to ascribe resilience to exceptional character or mettle, resilience emerges from the intersection of risk and a variety of protective factors, which function to shield children from the effects of adversity or help them cope once exposed to adversity. As described by contributors throughout this book, these protective factors range from individual characteristics to supportive resources in the environment (for a review, see Kirby & Fraser, 1997). At the individual level, they include problem-solving ability, creativity, tenacity, optimism, social skill, and the ability to develop anticipatory responses to problems (Rosenfeld, Lahad, & Cohen, 2001). At the family level, protective factors include parent-child attachment, support and nurturance, supervision and monitoring of children's activities and friends, and consistent discipline (Patterson, Reid, & Dishion, 1992; Pettit, Bates, Dodge, & Meece, 1999; Wyman et al., 1999). At the school level, they include small classrooms, a variety of opportunities for participation, high support from teachers, high expectations for performance, and low levels of school truancy, disruptive behavior, and violence (Richman & Bowen, 1997). At the community level, they include a communal sense of identity (sometimes based on a common cultural, ethnic, or religious heritage), social cohesion, and a commitment to collective socialization, manifest most directly in the willingness of citizens to act on behalf of others (especially willingness to correct the behavior of others' children) (Sampson, Raudenbush, & Earls, 1997). These factors conspire to form a web of support that empowers some children to recover quickly from crises and traumas and other children to resist the negative effects of exposure to adversity in the first place (Fraser, 1997; Prothrow-Stith, 2001).

Contextual Dependence

Resilience is not simply an additive counterbalancing of the number or influence of risk and protective factors. In many chapters in this book, the contributors point out that the degree to which a child may be resilient is contextually dependent. That is, a child may function well in one setting and not in other settings. A child who is neglected and who struggles in school might, once removed from a hurtful home, succeed academically. Similarly, a youth whose noncompliant behavior in school places him at risk of expulsion might develop prosocial behaviors in the context of greater structure in a therapeutic group home or an alternative school. Research suggests strongly that the context shapes resilient responses by providing opportunities and rewards for adaptive behavior. Thus, a bright and talented girl who never encounters a supportive, yet challenging teacher may flourish under the supervision of a new teacher or coach. So, although resilience can be conceptualized as an individual response, the factors that give rise to it and that sustain it over time appear—at least in part—to be contextual in nature (see, e.g., Henggeler & Hoyt, 2001).

Sensitivity to Risk

Research described here (and elsewhere) suggests that children do not respond equally to the same risks, and this has given rise to the concept of "sensitivity to risk" or the degree to which a child reacts to a particular risk factor. A child's response to risk appears to be influenced by a range of psychobiological and social factors. For example, a child's response to a disruptive peer may have genetic roots in neurologically based high impulsivity and tonic arousal (Rutter, 2001; Vance, 2001). It is not clear whether neuro-behavioral sensitivity to risk is the result of prior exposure to risk or whether it precedes risk and moderates adaptive responses. However, as Vance suggests, it is clear that biological factors are underestimated in conceptualizing susceptibility and responses to risk.

Sensitivity to risk also appears to be rooted in cognitive and social development. As children grow, their capacity to understand the events surrounding them changes (Rosenfeld et al., 2001). A seven-year-old child who has lost a parent usually does not grasp the long-term consequences of death nor develop a sense of understanding for other children who have lost a parent. However, an eleven-year-old child is likely both to understand the consequences of the loss of a parent and have empathy for others who have had a similar experience. The loss of a parent is a keystone risk factor whenever it happens to a child; however, the degree of risk—how a child interprets and attaches meaning to a risk event—is mediated by social and cognitive developmental factors.

Risk factors appear to vary in influence at different stages of development. Because sensitivity to risk is developmentally related, resilience at one stage of development seems only moderately associated with resilience at later stages of development. For example, a child who has poor social information processing skills may be able to maintain social relationships in the first and second grades. However, by the third and fourth grades, when expectations regarding the resolution of disputes change, children with poor social skills may be rejected by peers (Crick & Dodge, 1994). Having poor skills in the first and second grades is not a significant risk factor, but by the third and fourth grades, it may be initiate a potentially damaging risk chain (Sandstrom & Coie, 1999). In sum, one of the central themes of this book is sensitivity to risk. A child's sensitivity to a risk factor appears based on a variety of biological, developmental, cultural, and psychological factors.

Steeling Effects: Therapeutically Induced Challenge?

While sensitivity to risk seems biologically, developmentally, and contextually influenced, it may also be related to exposure to prior adversity. In the same way that exposure to a pathogen has the potential to create antibodies, exposure to prior adversity may "steel" children against risk. That is, it may strengthen their capacity to endure adversities (Rutter, 2001). Throughout development, a child's self-efficacy—the sense of personal control associated with the capacity to produce positive outcomes in school or sports or other settings—expands with experience. Moreover, be it caring for a sick relative or completing a ropes course at a wilderness experience camp, prevailing over challenges is widely thought to contribute to desirable developmental outcomes (Baldwin et al., 1993). On the other hand (and as many practitioners and parents have observed), it is clear that insurmounted challenges and strings of defeats or failures can negatively affect a child's self-efficacy and hold potential to damage developmental outcomes. Whether modest, controlled exposure to risk is "therapeutic" remains as an important question for practitioners interested in resilience. In the same vein, whether uncontrolled, naturally occurring exposure to risk has steeling effects on children remains an important question for researchers interested in the etiology of resilience.

RESILIENCE: IMPLICATIONS FOR PRACTICE

A resilience orientation leads to two foundational practice strategies. Based on the best available evidence, intervention must:

- Lower the overall risk level
- Strengthen protective factors and mechanisms.

Perhaps the most successful risk-based intervention to date is the thirty-year-old public health campaign to reduce smoking. As scholars analyze this initiative, important lessons are emerging, and we can use these lessons in distilling broader implications for practice. First, *intervention must be based upon a clear specification of "keystone" risk factors and processes*. These are the principal risk factors and processes affecting the prevalence and incidence of a social or health problem, and they often have both common and specific features. That is, some risk factors affect all children. They are "common" or crosscutting risk factors (Fraser, 1997). Poverty, for example, plays a significant role in the etiology of and is related to many social and health problems. In this sense, it is a common risk that both directly and indirectly affects children (Fraser, 1997). In contrast, some risk factors differentially affect particular populations, or they may be associated with particular problems. For example, failure to use contraception is a risk factor for HIV disease but is a relatively minor risk factor for youth violence. It is a specific risk factor, which has a keystone impact on some social and health problems. In addressing social and health problems, the risk structure must be understood prior to intervention, for intervention must target the principal risks.

Second, *intervention should reduce individual sensitivity to keystone risks*. The developmental, multisystemic nature of risk often necessitates a continuous, multi-element intervention plan, where different services focus on different risk factors at different points in a child's development (Henggeler & Hoyt, 2001). If we wish to reduce violence, for example, services must reduce a range of individual, family, school, peer, and community risk factors associated with aggressive, antisocial behavior. No single intervention is likely to be successful. A menu of interventions that target risk factors as they emerge developmentally is necessary. Moreover, because sensitivity to risk varies developmentally and culturally, intervention should be rooted in both the best available information about risk factors—usually based on research—and qualitative information about sensitivity to risk that can only be unearthed by a rich knowledge of individual children and their families. Resilience-based practice, then, is founded on a combination of understanding keystone risks from the perspective of research and understanding the unique ways a child may respond to risk exposure (Fraser & Galinsky, 1997).

Third, *intervention must interrupt risk chains and mechanisms*. In the smoking cessation campaign, risk chains were identified and targeted. For example, one risk chain involved advertising. Tobacco companies used advertising to portray tobacco products as attractive. Teens who smoked were shown to be grown up and independent. Women who smoked were shown to be slim, attractive, and assertive. Men who smoked were shown to be manly and rugged. Advertising was used to increase experimentation with tobacco products and once experimentation began, the addictive nature of nicotine was known to accelerate regular tobacco use. To break this risk chain, public policies were developed to halt advertising of cigarettes to children and young people. Eventually billboard and television advertising were banned altogether. To identify this particular risk chain and mount a strategy to break it took time. It involved years of research and lobbying. If we expect to reduce significant social problems for youth, families, and communities, risk chains must be identified and broken. One corollary of this lesson from the campaign against smoking is that changing complicated social or health problems such as youth violence takes time.

Fourth, and finally, *intervention must create new opportunities and build on strengths.* It is probably not enough to reduce risk. In fact, the ineffectiveness of many social programs may be related to a focus on risk alone. To increase protection, children must develop new skills, new opportunities to use skills, and a reward structure—reinforcements for behavior—that both sustains skill acquisition and provides support. A skills training group for aggressive, rejected children may be successful in helping children learn new social skills. However, if the training program is comprised largely of aggressive children, the social validity and clinical significance of the program may be questioned because children will have little opportunity to develop prosocial friends. Further, if a keystone risk factor for aggression is rejection by prosocial peers, then intervention must not only help children develop skills, but it must provide opportunities for children to cultivate new friendships. To do this one might ask children to invite a friend ("who does not get into trouble") to join the group on an outing or to become a group member per se. Such a strategy builds upon the strengths in a child's social network—drawing on what may be weaker social ties—and provides opportunities to refine skills in vivo.

CONCLUSION

We do not offer simple solutions to the difficult problems and issues facing at-risk youth, their families, and communities. Quick-fix interventions, that have a reasonable potential to positively impact at-risk youth, do not exist. What is provided is a risk, protection, and resilience framework that is useful across disciplines for understanding and assessing the context of violence and developing and implementing interventions. Each chapter presents a practice perspective that allows the reader to consider intervention strategies that target the full complexity of the bio-psycho-social environment and the variety of ecological influences on children. While this multifaceted approach may seem daunting to researchers and practitioners, it is likely the only perspective that has the complexity necessary to impact the context of violence and the problems facing at-risk youth.

A practitioner may choose to focus his or her attention on risk and protective factors related to some combination of individual functioning, school-based interventions, family and/or peer group support programs, or community level interventions in attempting to build and foster resilience. However, the research presented in this book suggests that successful interventions must be multisystemic in approach, target the reduction of specific risk factors, increase protection at many levels, and be based on the best available practice knowledge—evidence-based practice. Only when we strengthen the web of public and private resources supporting children and their families can we significantly affect the context of youth violence.

REFERENCES

Baldwin, A. L., Baldwin, C. P., Kasser, T., Zax, M., Sameroff, A., & Seifer, R. (1993). Contextual risk and resiliency during late adolescence. *Development and Psychopathology, 5,* 741–761.

Cicchetti, D., & Rogosch, F. A. (1997). The role of self-organization in the promotion of resilience in maltreated children. *Development and Psychopathology, 9,* 797–815.

Coie, J. D., Watt, N. F., West, S. G., Hawkins, J. D., Asarnow, J. R., Markman, H. J., Ramey, S. L., Shure, M. B., & Long, B. (1993). The science of prevention: A conceptual framework and some directions for a National Research Program. *American Psychologist, 48*(10), 1013–1022.

Crick, N. R., & Dodge, K. A. (1994). A review and reformulation of social information-processing mechanisms in children's social adjustment. *Psychological Bulletin, 115*(1), 74–101.

Fraser, M. W. (Ed.). (1997). *Risk and resilience in childhood: An ecological perspective.* Washington, D.C.: NASW Press.

Fraser, M. W., & Galinsky, M. J. (1997). Toward a resilience-based model of practice. In M. W. Fraser (Ed.), *Risk and resilience in childhood: An ecological perspective* (pp. 265–275). Washington, D.C.: NASW Press.

Gambrill, E. (1999). *The role of critical thinking in evidence-based social work.* Berkeley, CA: University of California, School of Social Welfare.

Garmezy, N. (1974). The study of competence in children at risk for severe psychopathology. In E. J. Anthony & C. Koupernik (Eds.), *The child in his family: Children at psychiatric risk* (vol. 3, pp. 77–98). New York: Wiley.

Henggeler, S. W., & Hoyt, S. W. (2001). Multisystemic therapy with serious juvenile offenders and their families. In J. M. Richman & M. W. Fraser (Eds.), *The context of youth violence: Resilience, risk, and protection*. Westport, CT: Praeger.

Kirby, L. D., & Fraser, M. W. (1997). Risk and resilience in childhood. In M. W. Fraser (Ed.), *Risk and resilience in childhood: An ecological perspective* (pp. 10–33). Washington, D.C.: NASW Press.

Masten, A. S., Hubbard, J. J., Gest, S. D., Tellegen, A., Garmezy, N., & Ramirez, M. (1999). Competence in the context of adversity: Pathways to resilience and maladaptation from childhood to late adolescence. *Development and Psychopathology, 11,* 143–169.

Patterson, G. R., Reid, J. B., & Dishion, T. J. (1992). *Antisocial boys.* Eugene, OR: Castalia Press.

Pettit, G. S., Bates, J. E., Dodge, K. A., & Meece, D. W. (1999). The impact of after-school peer contact on early adolescent externalizing problems is moderated by parent monitoring, perceived neighborhood safety, and prior adjustment. *Child Development, 70*(3), 768–778.

Pollard, J. A., Hawkins, J. D., & Arthur, M. W. (1999). Risk and protection: Are both necessary to understand diverse behavioral outcomes in adolescence? *Social Work Research, 23*(3), 145–158.

Prothrow-Stith, D. (2001). Youth risk and resilience: Community approaches to violence prevention. In J. M. Richman & M. W. Fraser (Eds.), *The context of youth violence: Resilience, risk, and protection*. Westport, CT: Praeger.

Richman, J. M., & Bowen, G. L. (1997). School success. In M. W. Fraser (Ed.), *Risk and resilience in childhood: An ecological perspective* (pp. 95–116). Washington, D.C.: NASW Press.

Rosenfeld, L. B., Lahad, M., & Cohen, A. (2001). Disaster, trauma, and children's resilience: A community response perspective. In J. M. Richman & M. W. Fraser (Eds.), *The context of youth violence: Resilience, risk, and protection*. Westport, CT: Praeger.

Rutter, M. (1979). Protective factors in children's responses to stress and disadvantage. In J. S. Bruner & A. Garten (Eds.), *Primary prevention of psychopathology* (vol. 3, pp. 49–74). Hanover, NH: University Press of New England.

Rutter, M. (2001). Psychosocial adversity: Risk, resilience, and recovery. In J. M. Richman & M. W. Fraser (Eds.), *The context of youth violence: Resilience, risk, and protection*. Westport, CT: Praeger.

Sackett, D. L., Richardson, W. S., Rosenberg, W., & Haynes, R. B. (1998). *Evidence-based medicine.* New York: Harcourt Brace and Company.

Sampson, R. J., Raudenbush, S. W., & Earls, F. (1997). Neighborhoods and violent crime: A multilevel study of collective efficacy. *Science, 277,* 918–924.

Sandstrom, M. J., & Coie, J. D. (1999). A developmental perspective on peer rejection: Mechanisms of stability and change. *Child Development, 70*(4), 955–966.

Vance, J. E. (2001). Neurobiological mechanisms of psychosocial resiliency. In
    J. M. Richman & M. W. Fraser (Eds.), *The context of youth violence: Resilience,
    risk, and protection.* Westport, CT: Praeger.
Wyman, P. A., Cowen, E. L., Work, W. C., Hoyt-Meyers, L., Magnus, K. B., &
    Fagen, D. B. (1999). Caregiving and developmental factors differentiating
    young at-risk urban children showing resilient versus stress-affected out-
    comes: A replication and extension. *Child Development, 70*(3), 645–659.

Index

About the Editors
and Contributors

Alan Cohen is the Research Coordinator at the International Stress Prevention Center at Tel Hai College, Upper Galilee, Israel. He has collaborated with Dr. Mooli Lahad in editing four volumes of the journal *Community Stress Prevention* and has published articles on this topic. He is an EMDR (Eye-movement desensitization and reprocessing) facilitator and is interested in various aspects of short-term intervention and treatment of psychological trauma. He has lectured on this topic in Bangladesh, Turkey, Britain, and the Far East.

Mark W. Fraser holds the John A. Tate Distinguished Professorship for Children in Need at the School of Social Work, University of North Carolina at Chapel Hill. He directs the Carolina Children's Initiative, an early intervention research project for children with aggressive, antisocial behavior. He has written numerous chapters and articles on risk and resilience, child and family services, delinquency, and research methods. With colleagues, he is the author of *Families in Crisis* and *Evaluating Family-Based Services*. His book, *Risk and Resilience in Childhood,* explores ways children prevail over adversity. In this book, he and his colleagues describe resilience-based perspectives for child maltreatment, school dropout, substance abuse, violence, unwanted pregnancy, and other social problems. Dr. Fraser's forthcoming book, *Making Choices: Social Problem Solving Skills for Children*—describes a program to help children build strong and enduring social relationships with peers and adults.

James Garbarino is Professor of Human Development and Co-Director of the Family Life Development Center at Cornell University in Ithaca, New York. From 1985–1994, he served as president of the Erikson Institute for Advanced Study in Child Development. He is the author or editor of seventeen books, among them *Raising Children in a Socially Toxic Environment* and most recently *Lost Boys: Why Our Sons Turn Violent and How We Can Save Them.* He was the first recipient of the C. Henry Kempe Award in the United States from the National Conference on Child Abuse and Neglect in 1985. Currently, he is focusing on the developmental pathways that lead to lethal youth. Of special interest in his current work is the role of spiritual development and human rights education in the rehabilitation of violent youthful offenders, a project entitled "From Boot Camp to Monastery."

Scott W. Henggeler is Professor of Psychiatry and Behavioral Sciences and Director of the Family Services Research Center at the Medical University of South Carolina. The author of more than 170 journal articles, book chapters, and books, Dr. Henggeler is on the editorial boards of eight journals. Recent publications include *Innovative Approaches for Difficult to Treat Populations* (with A. B. Santos) and *Multisystemic Treatment of Antisocial Behavior in Children and Adolescents* (with several colleagues). Dr. Henggeler has helped develop the theory and intervention procedures for multisystemic therapy (MST), a family- and home-based treatment that has demonstrated long-term reductions in recidivism and out-of-home placements. Currently, Dr. Henggeler is conducting a NIDA-funded evaluation of the long-term effectiveness of MST with substance-abusing delinquents; a NIMH-funded evaluation of MST as a family-based alternative to psychiatric hospitalization of youth in crisis; and several other studies that examine the viability of MST-based continuums of care.

Stephanie W. Hoyt is a Clinical Psychologist at Maria Parham Hospital in Henderson, North Carolina, where she delivers inpatient and outpatient treatment to a wide variety of clients. Dr. Hoyt previously worked at the Medical University of South Carolina providing MST training and consultation to providers of Intensive Home-Based Therapy, Therapeutic Child Care, and Clinical Day Programming.

Mooli Lahad is Professor and Head of the Dramatherapy Department at Tel Hai College, Upper Galilee, Israel, and Director of the International Stress Prevention Center. His most recent books include *Creative Supervision*, written for therapists, and *On Life and Death*, which focuses on consulting with parents, teachers, and children on death and bereavement. He will soon publish an anthology of the projects implemented under ISPC training in the former Yugoslavia. A consultant for UNICEF, Dr. Lahad currently is studying how prevention training affects the efficiency of coping in real emergencies and stressful situations.

Deborah Prothrow-Stith, Director of the Division of Public Health Practice at Harvard School of Public Health, began her work in violence prevention as a resident at Boston City Hospital. She developed and wrote *Violence Prevention Curriculum for Adolescents,* the first violence prevention curriculum for schools and communities, and co-wrote *Deadly Consequences,* the first book to present the public health perspective on violence to a mass audience. She has authored or co-authored over eighty publications on medical and public health issues. Her work has centered around projects with Harvard School of Public Health, The Community Violence Prevention Project, Neighborhood Health Centers Violence Prevention, and the Hands Without Guns media campaign. Recognition of Dr. Prothrow-Stith's work includes eight honorary doctorate awards, the World Health Day Award (1993), and the Secretary of Health and Human Service Award (1989).

Jack M. Richman is Professor at the School of Social Work at the University of North Carolina at Chapel Hill. His teaching areas for Ph.D. and MSW students are in social work theory and practice with individuals, couples, and families, as well as teaching courses that prepare doctoral students for university teaching roles. His research is focused in the areas of at-risk students, social support, and violence and trauma in childhood. He is co-principle investigator and co-developer of *The School Success Profile,* an evaluation and practice monitoring instrument for practitioners, youth at-risk of school failure and their families. Dr. Richman is a frequent contributor to the professional literature, is on the editorial board and is a consulting editor for *Social Work in Education* and *The American Journal of Hospice and Palliative Care.* He is a recipient of the University of North Carolina School of Social Work Award for Teaching Excellence.

Lawrence B. Rosenfeld is Professor of Communication Studies at the University of North Carolina at Chapel Hill. He is the author or co-author of sixteen books on small group, interpersonal, and nonverbal communication, and two on conducting research in communication. He is also the author or co-author of over seventy articles and chapters in the fields of communication, education, social work, sports psychology, and psychology. He is the 1995 recipient of the University of North Carolina's Johnston Award for Teaching Excellence. From 1979–1981, he served as editor for *Western Journal of Speech Communication,* and from 1991–1993, he served as editor for *Communication Education.* His primary research areas focus on the effects of disasters on children and families, the role of social support in education, and marital and family communication.

Michael Rutter is Professor of Developmental Psychopathology in the Social, Genetic and Developmental Psychiatry Research Centre at the Institute of Psychiatry in London, England. For many years, he has used short- and long-term longitudinal studies to investigate the effects of psychosocial adversities on young people. Currently, he is conducting a follow-up study of children adopted into UK families from Romanian orphanages. The children were seen at age four and at age six and are currently being seen again as they come up on their eleventh birthday. He undertook landmark epidemiological studies in the Isle of Wight in the 1960s and is currently following up this sample of children, who are now in their forties. His most recent books include *Developing Minds: Challenge and Continuity across the Lifespan; Antisocial Behavior by Young People;* and *Psychosocial Disorders in Young People: Time Trends and Their Causes.*

J. Eric Vance is Child and Adolescent Psychiatrist with Seacoast Mental Health Center in Portsmouth, New Hampshire, and formerly the Chief Clinical Consultant to the State of North Carolina's Willie M. program for children with aggression and emotional disorders. His research and academic interests center on the effectiveness of applying resiliency-building interventions to high-risk youth and studying functional and clinical outcomes in such programs. He is currently the principal investigator on a study of the relation between changes in autonomic nervous system functioning and clinical status in youth with aggression. Recently, he wrote a chapter on the effectiveness of community mentoring as a treatment intervention with high-risk and aggressive youth.

DATE DUE

APR 0 5 2012			
APR 17 2008			
			Printed in USA